I0083971

William Osborn Stoddard

The Heart of it

A Romance of East and West

William Osborn Stoddard

The Heart of it
A Romance of East and West

ISBN/EAN: 9783744661720

Printed in Europe, USA, Canada, Australia, Japan

Cover: Foto ©Thomas Meinert / pixelio.de

More available books at **www.hansebooks.com**

THE

HEART OF IT

A ROMANCE OF EAST AND WEST

BY

WILLIAM OSBORN STODDARD

———————

CONTENTS.

CHAPTER XI.   PAGE

THE HEART OF IT.

CHAPTER I.

A MAN, A MINE AND A MULE.

ONLY one man, clad in somewhat tattered buckskins, and near him there sprawled upon the ground, equally solitary, a long-legged, rough-coated, ill-conditioned mule.

The eyes of the mule were tightly shut, but those of the human being were open, and were gazing mournfully into a hole in the ledge of glittering quartz before which he was standing, and which flashed back upon him the hot rays of the morning sun.

Behind these two, in a grandly irregular oval, swept a vast natural amphitheatre, formed by the rugged cliffs that reached down from the Sierras to the endless levels of the South-western plains.

The rocks were mostly granitic, and here and there the broken ledges and terraces gleamed snowy white with quartz.

Westward and above were peaks on peaks. Eastward and below, through a mere cleft in the rocky wall of the amphitheatre, a ravine widened rapidly into a valley, and led out upon a grassy table-land, through mighty fringes of primeval forest.

The opening in the face of that ledge was not a wide one, and it had evidently been made by the well-worn pick which had now been thrown upon the heap of brownish fragments in front of it.

These latter manifestly claimed kindred with a seam or discolored streak some two or three feet in width, which extended on either side of the opening and bore the appearance of being partly decomposed.

They were of a very peculiar and unusual structure, those fragments of brownish quartz, calculated to suggest more than one problem to the miner or the mineralogist. They seemed, however, to have solved one for this man, and he was both.

He was of more than middle height, with a thin, black beard and moustaches concealing the lower third of his bronzed face, and a pair of bright, red lips, of firm but sensuous mould, showed through them as he spoke. Between these latter, moreover, gleamed teeth of dazzling whiteness.

A hawk nose, piercing black eyes, a well formed

but somewhat narrow forehead, and long hair of
Indian blackness, crowned by a broad *sombrero,*
completed the remarkable visage of the solitary
miner.

A seemingly heavy pack was strapped upon his
shoulders but the manner in which his meagre,
sinewy frame moved under it, gave token, to a
practised eye, of a rare degree of physical vigor and
endurance. Near him lay a handsomely mounted
repeating rifle, and his belt was well supplied with
other weapons. Small doubt but what such a man
would know how to use them well.

He was not indulging in merely silent reverie.
The broken remarks and expletives which burst
from him, at intervals, were fairly divided among a
sufficient number of tongues to have started a new
Babel. English, Spanish, French, German, dialects
of the red men, garnished with even a Latin quota-
tion or two. A "polyglot," indeed, but would not
one language have answered the purposes of his
angry discontent?

Or did he bring the others in to keep himself
some sort of company in his loneliness?

If so they were all equally inclined to strong expressions relating to the mine and the mule.

"I give it up," he said, at last. "I can't do it
any kind of justice. I knew there was such a place
as this. I've searched the Sierras for it, year after
year. I followed the lines of the system, when I

learned there was one, from the Dalles of the Columbia to this, on that one mule, and now, here it is, and he has gone under. Oliver, do you hear that? This is what we've been looking for. We've found it!"

Oliver responded by a feeble shake of his ropy tail, and an apparently futile effort to open one eye.

There was no sign of exultation in the expression of his countenance, and he was plainly in no frame of mind to become excited about mining matters. Oliver was a very much used-up mule.

But what was it for which the miner had made so long a search, and what had he now found?

So intelligent and capable a man could hardly have been deliberately throwing away his time, yet there was nothing now before him but a heap of broken stone, and a hole in a quartz ledge.

"There it is," he said, again, "the heart of the gold system. It's in there. Just the out-crop is nearly half metal. There isn't any other vein like that, and it 'll work richer the deeper it's followed. But what can I do, all alone? No mill; no tools; no provisions; no nothing. Not even a mule to carry out a load of specimens. I must pack what I can, myself. Won't stop this side of the eastern cities, either. I can get capital enough there. Money, men, machinery, that's what I must have. The sooner I go for it the better. Oliver, I'll have to leave you for the coyotes and buzzards. I can't stay here. I'd wait and nurse you up, but you're too far gone for that. The Apaches raced you a bit too hard. The sooner I'm out of this the better, for I don't know when they may show again. Wonder if they bagged the boys?"

His preparations for departure, simple as they were of necessity, had evidently been already completed.

He did but pause for another look at his mule and a half affectionate, "Good-by, Oliver, old fellow. You were the best mule I ever had."

And then he strode away towards the valley which seemed the only feasible entrance to the rocky amphitheatre.

Was there no danger that others might come, in his absence, and find and claim the hole in the rock to which he seemed to attach so great a value?

Possibly, but not probably, for that was widely beyond the range of all ordinary mining exploration, and there were excellent reasons, apart from the frail security of mining law, why no other foot of white man was likely to come up that ravine for some time thereafter.

Nearly a hundred such reasons were even then riding slowly across the grassy plain, less than a score of miles away, and several carried at their belts sad answers to the miner's question concerning "the boys," or some of them, for the scalps were freshly taken.

It was many long minutes after his master's departure before Oliver exhibited any noteworthy signs of life. His rough coat rose and fell with his slow breathing, and his hind legs quivered once or twice, as if with a dreamy memory of their departed power to kick, but that was all. A more completely used-up mule, to all outward appearance, never surrendered his right to carry his burdens. Even the richest ores of the richest of all mines would not have tempted Oliver to stand up and be laden for a journey.

By-and-by, however, the sleepy, heavy head was lifted a little from the rock, and one eye came slowly open. Then the other, and Oliver took a swift survey of his surroundings.

There was not a living thing to be seen.

As if gathering inspiration from that discovery, the legs kicked aside their limpness, and in a moment more Oliver was on his feet.

The pick and the shovel? He knew them very well, for he had carried them many a long mile and day, but they were all that was left him of his human guide and guardian. There was the heap of ore, too, and not a pound of it would be packed, now, for his carrying.

Fluttering in the crevice, there by the heap, was something more which momentarily attracted the mule's attention.

No, not good to eat. Only an old letter envelope

which Oliver did not so much as pause to read.
It was adressed to

> " DR. GEORGE MILYNG,
>> · " St. Louis, Mo."

and had been afterwards written all over with pen-
cilled memoranda, before it was lost or thrown away.

Oliver had no pocket for such things, but he had
an aching void within him which called for something more nutritious than he could hope to
find among the barren rocks where Dr. Milyng
had abandoned him. Nor had his lassitude been
altogether sham, else it would hardly have imposed
upon such a keen-eyed master. If Oliver were not
indeed half-dead there was good enough reason why
he might have been, as the doctor was well aware.
Even at the best, he was no mule now to carry ores
to the settlements.

He could carry himself out of that mysterious
amphitheatre, however, and he proceeded to do so,
marching slowly and circumspectly, lest by any
chance he should again intrude upon the solitude of
the discontented miner.

At the head of the ravine there was a little spring,
and Oliver halted by it long enough to drink its tiny
basin nearly dry, and nibble all there was of the few
green tufts on its arid, stony margin, but there was
a wide world beyond, with plenty of grass in it, and
the hand of hunger beckoned him down the valley.

With a more rapid and vigorous stride than his

mule would have been capable of, Dr. Milyng had made his way along that same trail, only pausing for a shot at an antelope as he reached the lower level.

No missing, of course, and the next duty on hand was very like Oliver's, for it carried his master, with his game on his shoulder, deep in among the forest trees.

"I wish I could eat him all, now.   Lay in enough for a week and walk right ahead.   If I knew where those Apaches were camped I'd try for a mount of some kind.   Reckon they've broke up the boys, entirely.   Well, if any of 'em got away, they don't know my secret, and so they can't tell it.   I'll make for the ruins, first.   Sorry to lose Oliver, but a mule's a mule."

Doubtless, but he might have learned a lesson in mule wisdom if his vision had not then been confined by so many tree trunks.

At that very moment the sagacious Oliver was trotting out into the grassy level below and hunting for a hollow where he might eat his fill unseen and undisturbed.

He had voted himself a vacation, and he was, beyond all doubt, fully entitled to it.

If Dr. Milyng was unable to eat a whole antelope, he was clearly competent to provision himself effectually.   All men who have seen much service under uncertainties as to when and where they are to eat their next dinner, acquire a faculty of this kind.   It is truly wonderful how the power of condensing three meals into one can be developed, even in a thin and wiry frame like that of the solitary miner.

The only thing which seemed to trouble him was the fact that he had kindled a fire in the day-time, and that the smoke of it must show above the tops of the trees.

"It'll be spread a good deal, to be sure, but Indian eyes'd take it. They may not be near enough, and then again they may. I mustn't lose my scalp now. It's worth more'n it ever was before. I believe I'm even getting a little excited over it. Haven't talked so much in a long time."

Curious talk it was, too, in a not unmusical voice, and with a sort of drawling, nasal cadence, such as is common among the Indians and Mexicans. The tones grew deep and strong, at times, and the broad, powerful chest from which they came swelled and heaved, while the black eyes flashed and the dark cheeks reddened, and once something very like a laugh of triumph rang out among the long colonnades of the gigantic pines. A strange man was this; one not to be easily disheartened by circumstances, and if it were possible to find a way of escape from his present perils he was the very man of men to do it.

Toil, privation, danger, suffering, desperate enterprise—these had been his daily companions, till they had become half a necessity of life, and their endurance a second nature.

No mule was ever foaled that could out-work or out-travel a veteran explorer of Dr. Milyng's frame of body and mind. Oliver had sustained himself wonderfully well, for as the doctor remarked, he was the very best kind of mule, but even he had been compelled to succumb at last.

There he was now, in his grassy hollow, feeding as energetically as his master himself, but preparing less for a long march than for all the sleep his future circumstances might permit him to take.

"The heart, the golden heart," muttered the doctor to himself, as he again set forward, heavily burdened with supplies as well as specimens. "I must get the right sort of men. It'll take all the rest of this season to put our outfit in shape and get away from the settlements, but we can be at the mine early next spring. It's nearly September, now, and I can't tell how long I may be making my way in. Afoot and alone make a long road of it. I must try and get me some kind of a mount, as sure's you're born. Even a pony'd be better'n nothing."

CHAPTER II.

DANIEL BROWN'S DAY-DREAM.

A NOBLE residence it was, in the outskirts of a great city on the Atlantic seaboard. Within the city limits, yet with enough of shrubbery and greensward around it to give it almost the air of a country-seat. One of those abodes of wealth and refinement which are such an eye-sore to the ascetic on the one hand and the communist on the other.

It is not always easy to see why there should be palaces for some men and huts for others, but so it is, and so it always has been, and the size of the hut has never been increased by pulling down the palace, whatever the man in the hut may choose to think about it.

In one wing of this house the lights were blazing brightly, that evening in August, the wire gauze at the windows baffling the mosquitoes, as the unseen laws of political economy baffle financial theorists.

Only a buzz and a bite thrown away, in either case.

11

That was the "library wing," and the crowded shelves of its ample space bore witness to the breadth and liberality of their owner's wishes. Of course he could not actually have read a very large percentage of the books, being but one man, and a pretty hard working man of business. No doubt he would have liked to read them. It is that sort of feeling and its shadow, " I'd like people to think I've read them," which are the main support of the booksellers.

The tall, strongly-built, square-visaged man, now sitting well back in his easy chair of woven cane, there by the library table, was plainly a man of thought and action, rather than a reader. Few men possess the faculty of being both. All others do well to discover, early in life, how few are the books which cannot be swallowed at a gulp, or squeezed dry at a gripe.

There he sat, now, the strong, iron-gray man, with the thick, prominent nose and the massive chin, while opposite to him, across the library table, there was perched on the edge of the high-backed, richly carved imitation of a mediæval throne, a middle-aged gentleman, whom nobody would have mistaken for anything less than a doctor of divinity.

The consciousness of his ecclesiastical dignity shone from the bald spot on his crown and through all the blandly expressive muscles of his face. His very tailor had expressed it in the fashion of his garments, although the body to which he belonged has neither canons nor customs relating to fashion-plates.

A very good face was his, and it had been beaming wonderfully upon his rich and liberal host, across the library table.

How a man with a good income does get beamed upon in the course of his earthly pilgrimage!

But just at this particular moment a sort of cloud was slowly rising on the benignant countenance of the good man, and his white hands were working uncertainly with a mass of papers before him, and which he seemed to be on the point of folding up.

"My dear brother Brown, do I really get your meaning? These plans of yours, will they interfere with your customary contributions?"

"Can't say, just now, Dr. Derrick. Everything will have to wait till I get my mind clear."

"You have not explained the nature of them."

"No, indeed. I wish I could. When I can, I shall take the greatest pleasure in so doing."

"But are you not assuming a fearful responsibility? Men of money are answerable, Mr. Brown."

"Just what I've been thinking, my dear doctor, and I've told you some of my experiences. It's a great responsibility to take, to put money in other men's hands, instead of using it one's self."

The conversation had evidently not been a short

one, and this was about the end of it, for the clean-shaven lower jaw of Mr. Brown was putting on a firmer look with every minute, while that of disappointment deepened in the dignified face of his guest.

It was too bad that so good a man should present a subscription paper in vain, but there was no help for it, and Dr. Derrick folded up his documents and took his leave.

There had been nothing but the kindliest courtesy in the manner of his reception, and even when the door closed behind him and he marched slowly down towards the front gate, where his cab was waiting for him, he muttered, " Plans? Plans? What has a man like Daniel Brown to do with plans? At his age, too, to be muddling his brains and crippling his charities with visionary schemes. Never heard of such a thing. He'll get over it before long, and then I'll come and see him again."

But the thoughts of Mr. Brown were not following his reverend friend down the lamp-lit avenue. He had resumed his easy chair at the library table, and was leaning back with a dreamy look on his features which hardly seemed at home there. The door through which he had entered was still open, and now there swept gracefully through it the form of a young lady. Very young, and very graceful, and she bore in her hands a tray, of Japanese lacquer work, on which were strewn a number of fragments of mineral.

"Dr. Derrick has gone, Mabel. I'm half sorry, but I fear he's disappointed."

"In not making a gold mine of you?"

"In finding me a good deal like others, I fancy. More mine than gold."

"He can't expect that you will always sub-scribe."

"Can't say. Maybe I've spoiled him. But what do you think of your specimens?"

"Very pretty, Uncle Daniel. Some of them are very interesting. But some of the others seem to have very little gold in them."

"Not that you can see, my dear. Sometimes those are the best, but it takes money to get the money out.

"Yes, for men, and for machinery, and all that. But the others will look better in a cabinet. The gold shows."

"Precisely. It costs enough to get it out, even then."

"I should think you could just melt it out of a piece like that. It's pretty enough for jewelry."

"So it is. If the mines were made up of that sort of thing gold wouldn't be worth a great deal."

"It would come so easily, it would be too cheap. I see—"

"Precisely. Worth very little, but for the labor and cost of getting it. Do you know, Mabel, there's something wonderfully fascinating to me about a gold mine."

"There must be. Why, it's like a story of the Arabian Nights. Digging into the ground and finding treasure."

"What could not a man do, Mabel, if he had access to some of the gold that lies hidden away in the dark among our western mountains."

"Don't speak of it, Uncle Daniel. It's enough to give one a headache."

"He could pay the national debt."

"I thought you said that would be a national calamity, the other day? He could feed and clothe the poor people."

"And that would be a worse thing than the other. But he could set at work a host of men who are idle."

"He could send out missionaries—"

"Mabel, my dear, he could do anything. I'm half afraid it isn't safe for me to think or talk about it."

"Then I wouldn't look at those specimens any longer. You don't own any mines, do you?"

"No, but I easily could. The market is full of them."

"Why, I should want to keep one, seems to me, if I owned it."

" Didn't I tell you it took a great deal of money to work one, after you found it ?"

" Yes, but I'd like to find one."

" I knew a man, once, that knew the way to more mines !"

" Do you know where he is ?"

" I almost wish I did."

" Couldn't you find him ?"

" Hardly. He used to turn up, every now and then, with the most remarkable specimens and the most thrilling stories of where he found them."

" Did they make him rich ?"

" I believe they did, several times. But all he made in one mine he'd spend in finding another. He was a born explorer."

" Look at that piece of quartz, Uncle Daniel. Such a lump of gold."

" Nothing at all, my dear, to what I've seen Dr. Milyng bring in. He was the most complete enthusiast you ever saw. Well educated, too, and the strangest person. Extravagant, reckless, sometimes dissipated, at others abstemious as an anchorite. I'd give a good deal to meet him again. I'd help him work some of his mining claims."

" What for, Uncle Daniel? You are rich enough ?"

" For some things, Mabel, but not for others. I've a plan in my head."

" A plan, Uncle Daniel? What for?"

"That is more than I can tell you, just now. It is educational, denominational, evangelical, and all but universal, and it needs a gold mine to carry it out."

The strong, grim, practical face grew brighter and warmer as he spoke, and his niece herself responded with a glow of girlish enthusiasm which well became the sunny beauty of her rosy but somewhat aristocratic face.

"Would any of these ores do, uncle?"

"If the vein were as rich throughout. But there's the difficulty. A vein is like a man—it always wishes to be judged by the best specimens it can send."

"These are the good deeds, then?"

"And we are not always sure where they come from, any more than if we heard golden things about one of our neighbors. The further off the greater the uncertainty.

"How would you ever know, then?"

"Cultivate a closer acquaintance, my dear. Look him or it in the face, and judge for myself."

"Do you mean you would go on a mining expedition?"

"I mean, I would never pour my money into a hole in the ground till I had at least seen the hole. The contrary course has led to most of the waste in mining interprises."

"But where is your friend?"

"Doctor Milyng?"

"Yes, the wonderful miner."

"I mean to try and hunt him up, between this and winter. I believe I'm getting the gold fever."

"Seems to me I can feel it in these specimens, uncle. It is so strange to think of digging for gold."

"I was sorry to disappoint the good doctor, to-night. But then, all I could do now would be nothing at all in comparison!"

Mabel put herself in mind, just then, of some household duty, and tripped away, leaving her uncle sitting there with a great thought in his strong, comprehensive mind, and a great fever slowly growing hotter and hotter within him. He found himself before long, fingering and gazing at the bits of rock on the tray, prying into their crannies and crevices, and peering curiously around every smallest freckle of dingy yellow.

It is not true that weak men are the easiest victims of enthusiasms and chimeras. Oysters, human or otherwise, never go crazy. It is reserved for them to sit in their shells and wonder why those other foolish fish go darting through the sea with such a useless expenditure of energy, when there is such a world of easy and unexciting loafing to be done. Daniel Brown was no oyster, and he was by no means a fool at any time.

CHAPTER III.

ON THE OTHER SIDE OF THE GREAT GULF OF RESPECTABILITY.

IT is difficult to guess correctly the age of a man, nowadays. The difficulty always existed with reference to women. A man's age has so little to do with time, after all, that the wonder of it need not be great, when the same person may be hardly out of his first childhood on one side of his character, and drooling into his second on another.

The gentleman who was promenading a thoroughfare of that same great city, several hours before the call of Dr. Derrick upon Mr. Daniel Brown, may have been thirty years of age by the almanac, but he was a remarkably old-looking young man, that day. He had neither gray hairs nor wrinkles, and his well proportioned frame was erect enough, but, from his boots to his hat, there was no single thing about him new or fresh. Not that he was ragged or dirty, nor did his dark, steady eyes fall before those of any passer-by, as if he recognized any reason for shunning the faces of his fellow-men.

20

Not a "dead beat," decidedly, but a gentleman whose boots had not been recently brushed, and whose linen was not what he could have desired.

A strongly marked face, and by no means handsome; colorless without pallor, and with lines of weakness crossed and underlaid by others which promised more than usual strength of character. Decidedly, a man with a past, and who might yet have a future, but who seemed to have little or no present to speak of.

Nor did he seem disposed to speak of it to anybody, but sauntered along with the throng of pedestrians for square after square, until he was suddenly halted by a hail, and a man of nearly twice his size stood in his way.

"Fred Heron, is this you?"

"Since you recognize me, I suppose it is, but I was beginning to doubt it."

"Doubt it? Why?"

"I meet so many who seem to deny it. Men of good judgment, too."

"Well, you've only yourself to blame."

"Very likely. But I've not been blaming anybody. Not even myself."

"I mean, you've no business to go about looking this way. A man who has been what you have!"

"I have not asked anybody's permission, Bob Fettridge."

"You've got to ask mine."

The speaker was a big man, well, and even showily dressed, and he had drawn Fred Heron out by the curbstone while he was talking. His face, a singularly hard and worldly face, with a marked tinge of sensuality, had put on a curious expression, which now became almost resentful.

"Your permission? I'd like to know why?"

"Why? Well, because I knew you in old times. Because you have done me favors. Because I owe you for them. It's an insult to me to have you going around this way. I won't submit to it."

"Don't see how you'll help it."

"I do, then. How much do you want? I'll lend it to you."

"I'm not borrowing money. I might never be able to pay."

"No nonsense, now. How much? Say the word."

"No, I won't."

"Yes, you will. Take that, or I'll never look you in the face again. Pay me when you can. I want to keep some self-respect, I do."

There was a weak spot in Fred Heron, somewhere, for his hand closed over the crisp notes held out to him by the big man, and the latter added:

"Come and see me. I'm in a hurry."

A moment more and he was gone, and Fred had not so much as said "thank you."

"Two hundred dollars? From him? Where won't the lightning strike next. But I ought not to have taken it. Yes, but I have, and here it is. Bessie? Yes, I can give her a lift, now. She, at least, has managed to keep her friends."

There was not the slightest external change in his demeanor, but he walked faster than before. Steadily on, for street after street, only stopping a few minutes at a little stationer's shop to write a note, until he stood before a mansion of somewhat more than average respectability.

"Is Miss Heron in?" he asked of the servant who answered the bell.

"No, sir."

"Then hand her that little parcel as soon as she comes in."

"Parcel, indeed! Why, it's only a letter."

"Hand it to her."

The door was closed in his face a trifle briskly, for his appearance was hardly in keeping with the tone of that front entrance, and Fred marched rapidly away.

Long walks, he was taking, and his next pause was before one of those dingy edifices which, in the older neighborhoods of every great city, have no need of a sign. It was an unmistakable "boarding-house."

"Jenny, is Mrs. Gibbs in?"

"Yes, Mr. Heron, but it's no use. Her orders

are that you can't have your things. Even Mr.
Augustus—"

"Tell her I want to see her."

"Yes, sir—O here she is."

"Mrs. Gibbs, I've come to pay my bill. It's an
even fifty, I think."

"Fifty for you, Mr. Heron, and it's a shame, the
way I've been treated. Your brother went off owing
me ten, and he's got a good situation, and I've never
seen or heard—"

"That makes sixty. Please give me a receipt."

"For you and him? I always said you was a
gentleman. Sit down. I'll bring it in a minute."

But Fred did not sit down, although he had
walked into the dismal parlor quite unceremoniously.
A sort of pallor was creeping into his face, but the
lines about his mouth were hardening rather than
softening.

She was as good as her word, for the bills were
ready, and only needed receipting. A minute was
enough.

"Your things are ready any time. The fourth
floor front, the hall room, is vacant just now, but—"

"Keep them till I send for them. Good afternoon, Mrs. Gibbs."

Again the door closed behind him, but not so
unkindly, and he did not hear her say:

"That's queer, Jenny. He isn't even dressed
up, but he's paid his bill."

"Some doesn't need so much dressin' as some does, Mrs. Gibbs. He doesn't seem so sick as he used to be, and I'm glad of that."

"So am I, Jenny. I wouldn't mind lettin' him have the hall room—"

But Fred Heron was walking as fast as ever, and kept it up until he was arrested by a half-sarcastical, "Shine 'em up? Only five cents," from an urchin who seemed to think his street-cry a tolerable joke when thrown at the ears of such a wayfarer.

"Don't care if I do, boy. Give 'em a good one."

"Needs two, sir," responded the irrepressible youth, as he whacked his box down on the sidewalk and went vigorously to work.

That was a very decent looking pair of boots when the job was done.

"A hat, now. A cheap one. They're selling summer styles at cost. Then a coat and pants. No, this coat must do. But trousers, now, and a vest and some socks and shirts, and some under rigging. Then for a Turkish bath and a change."

He carried out his programme, but when he came out of the bath house, an hour later, small as had been his expenditures on personal account, even Bob Fettridge would not have felt his appearance an insult to his friends. Jenny was right about the effect of dress on "some people."

He had, however, two bundles in his hands and they seemed to trouble him.

"I can have the pants cleaned and pressed," he muttered, "but I'd never disgrace myself by letting a washerwoman see those things. I know what I'll do."

It was but a few blocks to the nearest ferry, crossing an arm of the sea, and a half-brick, picked up on the way, was quietly bound in the smaller bundle.

It was but a slight splash in the water, as he leaned over the rail, and when he returned, on the same boat, he carried but one bundle. This too was speedily deposited, in accordance with his muttered intention, at a small "tailoring and repairing" shop, and then he seemed disposed to walk slowly and take an account of stock, financial and otherwise.

"About ten dollars left, eh? Wonder if I've dealt fair with Fettridge. Hardly. He meant me to use it all. But then Bessie couldn't have gone to her western friends. Mrs. Gibbs, too. Let me see. I had a dinner day before yesterday, and a breakfast yesterday morning. It's time I had something to eat."

He entered a restaurant, accordingly, but a prolonged study of the bill of fare seemed to offer him only moderate temptation. Even when his selection was made and the waiter brought it, he ate like a man to whom such things were an effort, a matter of duty, rather than as if he had an appetite. Perhaps his stomach was out of practice, and hardly knew how to begin again.

He ate, however, and paid the reckoning afterwards, adding a dime for the waiter, which was
quite enough under the circumstances.

It was now getting late in the day and Fred
Heron's walk must come to an end, somewhere.

An apothecary's shop?

Was he ill, a man who could walk like that without eating?

"Only three grains," he said to the smug assistant.

"Three? Is it regular?"

"No. I'm cutting down, now. Got it almost
run out. You may give me as many for to-morrow. Only I'm going to try it with two. Perhaps
one."

"No you won't, then. I've seen it tried, lots of
times. Wish you could, but it don't work, somehow.
Opium don't let go."

"Won't it? Well, then, I can let go. But not
this time. Three for now, and three for experi-
ments."

The young druggist silently put up the pills, but
the look of incredulity on his face saddened as he
handed them over the counter, in a way which did
him credit.

An opium eater?

At all events he put those three pills in his
mouth, and the little box with the other three in
his vest pocket.

The shadows were deepening as he resumed his

walk, and the lights in the shops were streaming out brilliantly, one after another.

There are more poisons than opium, and very brilliant places they are sold in, occasionally, but a man of Fred Heron's present appearance, in spite of the elderly character of his outer garment, was welcome to walk in under the utmost glitter of glass and gas and all the splendor of the most pretentious gilding.

Welcome, no doubt, but he seemed in no hurry. In fact, he stood before one gorgeous entrance for more than a quarter of an hour, and then he walked slowly up and down.

More than one passer-by had jostled him. He had even been spoken to, but the voice had not been a man's voice, neither had he answered it.

"This once," he murmured, at last. "It seems as if it would have to be, just this once. I think I've stood it wonderfully well, as it is."

He went in, he drank something, and he came out, and there was no pallor in his face now. Even the weakness was gone from it, but the lines which were hardening instead were not all pleasant to look upon. They were the face marks of the gladiator whose weapon has broken in his hand, but who closes with his enemy nevertheless.

Almost a handsome man was Fred Heron, in the glare of the street lamp near him, as he turned and strode away. Would he never end his walking?

Where could he now be bound, after such an afternoon?

Whether he had any special errand on hand or not, he strode vigorously away, nor did he so much as cast a glance at any other brilliant and tempting entrance. Neither did he speak to any human being as he went.

At that very hour a trim and prim looking young lady, the embodiment of neat respectability, sat by a desk in the house which he had first visited that day—the very respectable house—and she was writing a letter which began with,

"Dear brother Fred."

Of course, it would never do to quote a young lady's letter entire, but there were passages worth quoting:—

"I am truly thankful for the hundred dollars. Not only it will carry me West, but I take it as a sign that you are really reforming, and are disposed to do your duty again. Of course I do not feel like asking you to come and see me here. They are exceedingly particular, you know. But you can bid me good-by at the cars, and I will write to you. What a pity you would not always be guided by me.

" I am so glad about Augustus. His salary is a hundred dollars a month. He is such a dear boy. I am finishing some shirts and things for him, and to-morrow I shall get him a new necktie. It is a long time since I have been able to do for him·

as I would have liked, but now, if you will redeem yourself, I hope for better things. I wish you were more like Augustus, but you will not listen to me. I shall pray for you. I feel sure I have had a good influence here, and Mrs. Baird tells me so; but I doubt if she really understands me. She is a good woman and means to be kind, but she is sadly lacking in some things. I have told her all about you, and she sympathises with me. Don't forget that a hundred dollars will not last forever."

An excellent letter, from a good young woman, but it was a long time before it reached the eyes of Fred Heron.

CHAPTER IV.

HOW OLIVER ADJOURNED A CONVENTION—A HINT AT THE ORIGIN OF METAPHYSICS.

OLIVER was a mule of more than common experience, as well as natural abilities, and he had thoroughly mastered the features of his own case.

Rest and grass were what he wanted, the same to be taken in a state of as complete concealment as possible. The hollow he had chosen promised well for his requirements, and he did his full duty by the grass.

Not that he ate steadily. No mule was ever known to do that. At the end of an hour or so he slowly and solemnly marched up the nearest slope and took a position in a dense thicket of prairie-willows. It was just the place where a practised herdsman would have gone to look for a lost mule, but Oliver was in no dread that anybody would be looking for him. On the contrary, it almost seemed as if he were looking for somebody.

Not that he walked around, or made any vain excursions upon the open plain, for he maintained his position among the willows as obstinately as the Turks did theirs at Plevna.

The difference was that nobody tried to drive him out of it.

Nobody even looked at him, but it was not long before he himself had a view of a solitary man, evidently heavily laden, plodding steadily along through the short grass at a distance of nearly a quarter of a mile, without any kind of quadruped to help him.

Ought Oliver to have hailed the doctor? Or was he justified in harboring feelings of resentment at the heartless manner in which he had that morning been left to shift for himself?

At all events he sent no hail, not even a "good-by," across the intervening silence. He did but stretch his ungainly neck and head in that most ridiculous of all pantomimes, a noiseless bray. There was just a perceptible wheeze and whimper at the end of it, for Dr. Milyng was at that moment disappearing over a distant roll of the plain, and it might well be that Oliver would never look upon his like again.

He could bear that, perhaps, better than a load of ore, gold or otherwise. There was more grass to be eaten, and then a *siesta* to be had for purposes of digestion, but Oliver was no longer so weak and feeble a patient as he had seemed when he lay down in front of the mining claim.

Shade there was none, in that immediate vicinity, and Oliver decided against an expedition to the forest. The short grass would answer his temporary purposes.

Still, it would have been wise to have first assured himself of solitude. Even young ladies at boarding schools know enough to look under the bed for burglars before they turn the light out, and Congressional conventions inquire whether their candidate has ever been convicted of anything before they set him up.

There were burglars on that level, and they held a convention around Oliver before he had been asleep half an hour.

Undersized, gray-headed, hungry-looking fellows, with the faces of politicians and the tails of foxes, but with slanderously sharp teeth and an inborn disposition to use them on anything helpless.

Anything like a dying deer or a dead mule, for instance.

That was the question before the convention.

Was Oliver dead? Or was he dead enough for the purposes of such a band of coyotes as were now gathered around him?

Had he been a statesman with a flaw in his record, he could not have been smelt of with more respectful care before venturing an open assault.

More than a dozen of them, and they were working their way closer and closer, for Oliver did not exhibit the slightest appreciation of their presence. He could not be very dead, they were beginning to be sure of that, and one elderly coyote who had advanced from the rear, like the cautious and self-preserving brute that he was, suddenly dropped on his haunches, threw up his head, uttered a sharp bark, and was about to follow it with a howl of grief over the fear he felt that their prey might not yet be quite ready for them.

Little he knew about mules, or the Creedmoor accuracy with which a mule's hoof can extend itself south-westerly.

Right in the middle of his howl and his head, the hoof of Oliver struck him, and nothing more was needed to prepare a small lunch for his indignant comrades. They began at once to explain why nobody has ever seen a dead coyote.

As for Oliver, he had slept enough for the time, and was now on his feet, lazily gazing at the snarling group around the carcass of the wolf who had begun to wail for him. No such thing as disturbing them seemed to enter his mind, nor was there, to him, any novelty about them. Had he not been familiar with their tribe and their ways from his very cradle?

He did not so much as call for help, but he walked leisurely along, picking at a bunch or so of grass, in a direction which would carry him close past them. Under other and less exciting circumstances they would have increased their distance, but as it was, they fought and tore just the same, even when he turned his head contemptuously away from them. He must have had the range to perfection, for, in another instant, that villainous pack was scattered right and left as if something had burst among them, and Oliver sprang away at a pace which would have astonished Dr. Milyng if he had witnessed it.

There was very little doubt but what they would follow him, but not so many would come, for the coyote which had been in the way of Oliver's heels had all the travel knocked out of him before he knocked over his companions. No wonder they at once took out their spite on all that was left of him. He ought not to have been where the mule could hit him.

There was something very human about it all, on both sides, and Oliver could not hope to be forgiven.

As for Dr. Milyng, a couple of hours of resolute marching sufficed to bring from his iron lips:

"I can do it. No doubt of that. But I must try and do better. The ruins are ten miles yet. I can reach them by noon, and then I must look about me. What a pity Oliver broke down. He was the best mule I ever saw, and the knowingest. He'd have made the fortune of a circus, he would. I'd never have left him, if it wasn't a matter of life and death. There's that mine, too. The heart of it. The golden heart of the continent. As if there could be a system without a heart. All the veins and arteries lead to it. There's as sure to be a heart as a backbone, and ain't the Rocky Mountains a backbone, I'd like to know?"

Not many men could have sustained that steady, unvarying stride, under such a weight as he was carrying. Fewer still would have made the attempt, but there is no enthusiasm, except that of an apostle or a missionary, which will nerve a human being like the gold fever. Witness the deeds and endurances of the early Spanish explorers and their English buccaneer assailants.

Pity that humanity develops a Pizarro or a Drake so much more frequently than a Paul or a Marquette or a Judson.

On plodded the doctor, as if he knew the path where there was no sign of a path, and his eagle eyes were continually scanning the horizon, right and left, in swift, keen glances, as if he half-expected, at any moment, to detect some sign of coming peril.

"It'll come," he said to himself. "Of course it'll come. No man ever found a gold mine yet but what he was followed by it. Don't I know? But I'll beat it this time. It can't follow me very strong, with just these specimens. No, I ain't so sure of that. Maybe a nugget's enough."

He had turned a little southerly, now, and before long struck into the slowly increasing channel of what seemed to have been, in some old time, a water course.

There were traces of it further west, towards the highlands, and here and there the nature of its too regular banks and borders was strangely suggestive of skill and purpose in their construction. As, for instance, the skill and purpose of forgotten men.

The signs of human operation increased as he plodded onward, and even in the deepest hollows crossed by the channel, the sloping, grass-grown banks went with it.

It was now quite deep enough to protect a foot passenger at the bottom of it from being seen by any one at a short distance on either side, and Dr. Milyng's moccasined feet made no sound on the yielding sod.

"Gone, all of 'em. Gone," soliloquized the doctor, as he now and then looked around him. "They knew how to build an *accquia*, but they didn't understand gold mining. "That's one reason they didn't stay. To think of their living so near the golden heart and never knowing it. It's a dangerous thing for one man to know, however. I must divide my luck as soon as I can. Even lightning doesn't hurt if it has plenty of conductors to run through."

Many and diverse and contradictory are the superstitions of the mining community. In all climes

and ages they have nourished an ample demon-
ology of their own, and have deemed themselves in
peculiar relations with those occult and eccentric
agencies and intelligences of which the rest of the
world has no knowledge.

Even a man of Dr. Milyng's education and force
of character could afford to admit, talking to himself, there in the dry bed of the old *accquia*, ideas
which his pride of intellect would have studiously
concealed had he been in the society of men. He
might even have scoffed at them on the lips of another miner.

Now, however, as mile after mile was patiently
overcome, the path on which the doctor was walking changed its character.   Dry enough, to be sure,
but gravelly instead of grassy, and strewn at intervals with fragments of stone.

Could those be fragments of earthenware, also?

They looked like it, but they must have been familiar objects to the miner, for he paid them no
manner of attention, strong as was their testimony
to some by-gone human workmanship.

They meant something, even to him, nevertheless,
for pretty soon he clambered cautiously up the
steep bank of the *accquia*, now more than thirty
feet high, and peered over through the fringe of
tall grass.

There was a good deal worth looking at, but the
only remark drawn from Dr. Milyng was :

" Not here, I should say, but it's a good place to watch for 'em. I'll have to run the risk of being cornered in one of those traps."

They had never been set for traps, at all events, those grim, solid, mysterious ruins of the ancient city.

Up and down, at broken intervals, and with little apparent regularity, as far as he could see, were scattered tumbling walls and fragments of walls, many of them still retaining the form of houses. A few were of more than one story in height. Some had been of three and even four, if an opinion could be formed from the successive apertures which may have served for windows. There is no certainty in indications of that sort, apt as men are to accept them.

As soon as he had completed his precautionary survey, the doctor directed his rapid footsteps to the entrance of the largest ruin near him.

Temple or palace, or both, it were hard to say, and mattered little, just then, for all that was now asked of it was a hiding-place.

It was easy to find that, among the heaps of rubbish and fallen masonry which cumbered the ample space of the interior, and the pile behind which the miner threw himself may have covered an altar or a coronation stone equally well.

To rest, but not to sleep, for his keen black eyes were not closed an instant, and his every sense seemed to be on guard as he lay and munched a fragment of cold roast-antelope.

It was a good place to be watchful in, for an hour had hardly passed before there came a sound of horse's hoofs outside, that drew nearer and clearer until it ceased before the entrance of that very ruin.

"Trapped," he whispered, "Let's see how it 'll turn out."

A good horse, with a highly ornamented Mexican saddle and bridle, and the rider who dismounted from him was worth crossing the street to see.

A tall and somewhat corpulent Indian, with a face in which pompous self-conceit strove with coarse animal cunning for supremacy.

Such a face as comes to the front, inevitably, in the councils of red savages, the caucusses of political parties, and the conferences of ecclesiastical functionaries, as a "medicine man" of some kind or name.

Safe to win, in either case, great influence in the synagogue, and great power over ignorance, greed, prejudice and superstition.

The first act of the new-comer, after tethering his horse, was to take off his moccasins, and lay them together in the doorway with the toes pointing outward, as if to suggest to other men a similar direction for their own.

A good enough idea, probably, among barbarians, but in any highly civilized christian community, it would but have cost him that elegantly embroidered pair of moccasins.

This done, he went back among the cool shadows, near the heap which sheltered Dr. Milyng, and lay down, spreading under him the broad folds of an immense robe of skins which he had taken from behind his saddle. Many and marvellous were the hieroglyphics painted on the velvety inside finish of that robe, and some of them seemed to correspond with the tattooing now exposed on the dark skin of its owner.

Not a man in his tribe would have stolen that robe, for his life, much less wrapped its mystery around him.

A pipe, tobacco, a tedious struggle with flint and steel for a light, and then the comfort of a smoke. All Indians are fond of smoking, when they can get the wherewithal.

But there was something curious in the odor of that tobacco.

Well, could a great medicine man be expected to produce the same odor with ordinary mortals?

Certainly not, and the odor left by some of them has indeed been extraordinary.

There was more than tobacco in the bowl of that fantastically carven pipe, and more was expected from it by the man who smoked.

It was "big medicine," but who shall say from what unknown plant of the far West he had obtained the strong narcotic which speedily put an end to even the gentle exercise of sucking the pipe-stem?

These, doubtless, were a part of the devotions which obtained him the reverence of his fellows. Not another man of them could put himself in such a state of absolute oblivion, without the aid of whiskey, and he was to be respected accordingly.

For now there came the sound of the feet of other horses, many of them, and, as they passed, their riders paused briefly for a stare at the pair of moccasins. One or two of the bolder ones threw themselves off and peered in for a moment, but it was only to make sure of the presence and condition of the "Big Medicine." If they envied him, or if they feared him, they said nothing about it, but remounted and rode on. A mile or so further down, the whole band halted near a spring, and went into camp as if they meant to stay for a day or so. They may have numbered a hundred braves, with squaws and pappooses to match, and could not, therefore, have been on any war-path. It was a capital place for an Indian camp, with plenty of grass and water, game in the neighborhood, and a big medicine man smoke-drunk in the immediate vicinity. They were not likely to trouble him, however, but would patiently wait till he should wake up and come to tell them all he had learned during his slumber. If he should happen to tell them anything over and above, he would not be the first of his kind to exhibit that species of liberality.

But then he was not altogether alone in the old ruin, just now.

CHAPTER V.

WHEN good Dr. Derrick transferred his just
chagrin and disappointment from Daniel
Brown's library to the cab which was to bear him
home, the form of a man stood by the gate as he
hastened through it.

It may have been a gentleman, for all he knew,
but his glance at it was too brief for certainty, and
the word which escaped him by way of comment
or recognition, was only—

"Tramp."

It could not have been an order, for it was not
uttered as such, and the man on whose ears it fell
had been tramping all day, through the hot streets
of the wearisome city. The cab rolled away at once,
and the man stood there by the gate, but he was now

44

repeating in a low voice, the remark of Dr. Derrick.

"Tramp. That's it. Whoever he is, he's right. I'm a tramp, and I have been one for a month. I, Frederick Heron. Homeless, houseless, penniless, friendless, hungry, dirty,—a tramp. No, Bob Fettridge taught me a lesson, to-day, and I mean to hunt up my friends to-morrow. I feel more like it, somehow. Won't borrow any money, though. Glad Gus is provided for, but he might have paid his board bill. Bessie, too,—all her piety's going west. No, I guess I won't see her off. A tramp has no business among so much respectability. I'm clean, now, though; I can feel that, all over. Got a clean shirt on and some stamps in my pocket. Mustn't waste them on a lodging, such a fine warm night as this. I reckon I can get a place on some newspaper. I understand that sort of thing. Hallo, what's that? More tramps?"

He stood in the shadow of the great stone gate post, while he talked to himself, and all the street and neighborhood seemed utterly deserted. Not even a policeman in sight, though that by no means implied solitude.

Perhaps it invited the company of the two persons who were now walking so rapidly around the corner.

"I saw them throw something over, I'm sure I did. It lit on the gravel walk, inside. I've heard of an empty pocketbook disposed of in that way. Can't help it. I must investigate."

Noiselessly the gate was opened, and in a moment Fred Heron was hidden among the shrubbery.

He had but a few rods to go, and then he once more came out into the dim light.

"Not a pocketbook, this time. But how came they to throw away a good piece of meat like that? Cooked. Let me see. Dogs eat meat. Some meat doesn't agree with some dogs. I must try an experiment. There are plenty of poor dogs with no meat. I must find one."

The spikes of the iron fence compelled a return by way of the gate, but Fred was quickly in the street.

"O for a dog. My kingdom for a dog. There comes one. Yellow as the hair of Sigurd, and as hungry as a boarding house. He shall try my experiment. It's the way the patent medicine men test their new pills. If it doesn't kill him I'll make him give me a certificate."

Gently and kindly, like a fly at the wary head of a trout, the savory half-pound of beef was launched in the path of the wandering quadruped.

A sniff, a yelp of joy, a gulp, and the dog went on.

"He is carrying off my experiment. I must follow him."

More than one square, but not many, and then a

sudden change made itself manifest. A pause, a shudder, a growl, a yelp, a spasm, and then a mass of yellow hair and legs lay kicking for a minute in the gutter.

"A most convincing certificate," remarked Fred. "The city is thoroughly cured of that dog at one dose. But I think the wrong patient got it. I must continue my investigations. Verily, this is gay. But I care not to make too close an acquaintance of the other dog."

Strange spirits for a tramp to be in, and strange recklessness on his part to venture again among the shadows and shrubbery of Daniel Brown's princely residence.

There was a sort of fascination in the adventure, and he drew nearer the house, till he stood under the dense foliage of a lilac bush, near one of the library windows, looking up. The wire mosquito-gauze protected the privacy of the interior, but just then a shadow fell upon it. A clearly out-lined shadow, growing clearer, until a robe of white and then a face was pressed against the dim and misty barrier. A sweet, sunny face, as pure as a new moon, but with a trace of hauteur in it.

Fred looked and looked, and then, as it disappeared, his own face went down upon his hands.

"They are not all dead, those women. That was one of them. I used to know such. Would any of them know me now? I guess not. Only such men as Bob Fettridge. The more a man or a woman thinks he or she is imitating Christ, nowadays, the more careful they are not to speak to publicans and sinners. It's 'most two thousand years since He died, and He has not yet come again. The publicans and sinners are here yet, though. I'm one of 'em. Hey, there's that dog!"

Not the same animal, indeed, but a most lordly compound of mastiff and St. Bernard. The kind of dog whose acquaintance is better to be cultivated by day than by night, and in other grounds than those of his own master.

It was too late to try for the gate, for the stately promenade of the rich man's guardian was carrying him down the gravel walk in that precise direction.

"Glad there are trees in the world," remarked Fred. "I'm a bigger man than Zaccheus, but I need some kind of a sycamore as badly as he did. Nobody could sic a more disagreeable brute than that on a fellow."

The big dog was evidently on a scouting expedition, after being released from his day's confinement, and meant to make sure of the safety of his beat, like a policeman, before he lay down anywhere. The first incident to disturb his mind was the spot on the gravel where the meat had fallen. His detective nose at once informed him that something was wrong. Meat there had been, and meat there was not now, and he rapidly ranged to

and fro in all directions, with a plain desire to meet
the solution of his problem.

Foot-prints!—and his nose again suggested that
these were not the accustomed prints of the place.

"A very good tree," remarked Fred, as he swung
himself into the lower branches of a fine horse-
chestnut.

"I'm glad the dog is not a climbing animal. He
has not yet reached that stage of his development.
The squirrel and the tree-toad are between him and
humanity. He owes at least that much to Mr.
Darwin. Here he is, now, right under me. A
lower form of life, and I'm wonderfully glad of it,
just now. But what a voice he has. Great native
power, but no cultivation."

He was there, declaring by great bounds and
cavernous growls his disgust for the fact that he
could not climb.

He could summon help, however, and in less than
a minute more he was joined, as Fred expressed it,
by "one of those nobler types of being who can
climb."

"What are you doing up there?"

"Keeping out of the dog's way."

"But how came you up there?"

"Climbed the tree."

"I'll have you arrested. What are you doing on
my grounds?"

"I came in, my dear sir, to steal a piece of meat

which a couple of gentlemen had presented to your
dog. Perhaps it is just as well I succeeded, judg-
ing by its effects upon the other dog."

"What other dog?"

"The one I gave it to. If you'll call off this
one, I'll go and show him to you. It's only a little
way. He is waiting for the coroner."

"Down, Prince. Be quiet. He'll not hurt you,
sir—"

"My name is not Prince, but I'll come down. I
should hardly care to spend the night here. Your
dog might take me for the moon, and I like not his
baying.

"Explain, sir, I beg you. You seem to be a
gentleman—"

"By no means, my dear sir," said Fred, as he
alighted, "I am a tramp, but when a dog is to be poisoned, I have my preferences. Permit me to add
that if I were you I would put up extra mosquito
bars, to-night. You may have visitors before
morning."

"Prince will take care of that."

"Not unless you can cure him of his fatal and
most brutal fondness for animal food. Will you
come with me and view the remains of the other
dog?"

"I will, indeed. It seems I owe you a debt of
thanks. I am Mr. Daniel Brown, of No. 340
Beaver Street, merchant—"

"And I am Mr. Frederick Heron, cosmopolite, which means that my politeness is cosmic in its character. Your dog should reflect upon his past life, Mr. Brown. He has had a very narrow escape."

The dignity of the man of wealth and standing chafed sorely under the easy freedom of the chaff he was undergoing, but his blood was up a little and he had plenty of it.

Fred had apparently paid no manner of attention to three or four servants, male and female, who had by this time made their appearance. He had even ignored the presence, a few paces back among the shadows, of a slight and graceful shape in a white robe, nor did he turn his head when a clear but anxious voice inquired—

"Uncle Daniel, shall you be gone long?"

"Only a moment, Mabel. Our friend here has something to show me."

"Come here, Prince."

The dog looked wistfully at his master, but the question of his duty settled itself at once. He could not climb, but he could march back like a hero and take up the position of a defending champion by the side of that young lady in white. She would be in excellent company during her uncle's absence, and any tramp who should come too near would be likely to get a lesson in the tendency which large dogs have for animal food.

As Mr. Brown and his strange visitor walked onward, the former received a brief and clear account of the suspicious occurrences, and the yet warm carcase of the yellow dog afforded abundant corroboration.

"They'll come again, sir, depend upon it, but then you—"

"Yes, I came again," drily interrupted Fred. "I am fond of sleeping in the open air in such weather as this, and besides, I wanted to see the rest of it."

"The rest of it? O the operations of those two men. Why did you not give the alarm?"

"I did not feel any. Besides, I have not the honor of your acquaintance."

"I told you—"

"So you did, but I should prefer an introduction by some responsible party known to me. No offence, my dear sir, but there are so many impostors, nowadays. You would probably have told me the same if I had rung your door-bell or called upon you at your office."

"But then you did not scruple to trespass on my grounds?"

"Certainly not. They are yours, no doubt, but then, since I became a tramp I have learned to doubt your right to them."

"My right to them?"

"Any man's right to so large a slice of the earth's surface, when there is so little of it in this neighborhood."

"A communist?"

" By no means. Only a tramp. I believe in the rights of property. I only mean there are some other rights, that's all. If I were rich, now, I might not see some things so clearly. I doubt if the rich men ever will see them until it is too late."

" What do you mean by too late?"

" Until the men who are crowded off, over the edge of things, get to be more numerous and powerful than the men who are doing the crowding."

They had arrived again in front of Mr. Brown's gate, and the latter responded :

" You interest me very much, sir; will you not walk in? I would like to talk with you."

" I should be glad to do so, I assure you, but I never accept a courtesy which I cannot return."

" The courtesy is to me, my friend. Besides, you have saved the life of my dog, and warned me of a danger. I think your pride need not be in the way."

" I will, then, but I think I had better not come in as a gentleman. Simply as a tramp."

"As you please."

Fred Heron looked around him admiringly as he shortly took his seat in the library, and his host noticed that he seemed very much at home. It was not the first time he had been in such a place as that, and the vagabondish "chaff" of face and manner disappeared the moment he crossed the threshold.

Did such men ever go unfed, and sleep in the open air? Men with good clothes, polished boots and clean linen? Mr. Brown's keen common sense told him that he had gotten hold of either a very remarkable or a very suspicious case, but he soon found that it was all in vain to ask leading questions of his singular "tramp."

Books, social, political, even religious questions, he was quite ready and willing to discuss, but not himself, from any point of view. Mr. Brown found that he had met his match, and a little more, conversationally, and now, as they warmed up to it, not the rich man himself was more gravely, dignifiedly courteous, than the stranger he had found in his horse chestnut tree.

"Uncle Daniel?"

"What is it, Mabel?"

"There's a policeman at the front door. I think Mike spoke to him."

"A policeman? O yes, I must tell him about the tramps. Sit still, Mr. Heron. My niece, Miss Varick."

And Mabel Varick's bow was not one shade more icily distant than Fred Heron's own.

Had he failed there he would have failed indeed, but when Mr. Brown returned, after an absence of five minutes, his astonished ears informed him that his exclusive niece was defending the bay and sky of Naples against a subtle assault on the part of the vagabond who had poisoned the yellow dog.

"No, Miss Varick, the Italian sky is very well in its way, for Italians, and so forth. It gained its reputation before ours was known. It keeps it because so few good judges have ventured to cross the sea or dared to tell the truth afterwards."

And yet there was nothing at all irritating in the way he said it.

Mr. Brown was compelled to say to himself:

"He may be a tramp, now, but he has been a gentleman. I must and will know more about him."

The evening was slipping away, however, and shortly after Mabel Varick withdrew, Fred arose to excuse himself.

"I hardly know what time it is, Mr. Brown, but I'm sure it is late."

"I have enjoyed your conversation exceedingly, my dear sir. May I not offer you a bed? I think you told me you intended—"

"To sleep in the open air? Certainly, as becomes a tramp. I could not accept your hospitality."

"Not even the wherewithal to purchase a lodging?"

"No, indeed, for I am also a gentleman."

"I am sure of that. You are evidently a man of good family and education."

"The best in the world, sir. I have been taught in the school of adversity. None better. As for

family, I am a lineal descendant of Esau, an Edomite of the purest blood."

" An Edomite ?"

" Yes, indeed, and I have even consumed my
pottage, now my inheritance is gone. Esau could
have done no better. The descendants of Jacob
are even now in possession of all I had left."

" I think I understand you. They are always on
the lookout for Edomites. But shall I not see you
again ? I should be glad to do you a service."

" To-morrow, then. Not to-night. This is my
last day of tramping."

" I hope so. I have never met a man in whom I
took so deep an interest."

" Thank you. Please suggest to Prince that I
have no further designs on his trees. Good-night,
Mr. Brown."

" Good-night, Mr. Heron. Prince, come here,
sir."

CHAPTER VI.

ONE KIND OF GUARDIAN ANGEL.

BESSIE HERON descended into the parlor, after finishing her sisterly letter to Fred. She had done her duty by him, speaking very plainly, as was her wont, and her conscience was therefore as clear as was the gaze with which her comprehensive, blue-gray eyes met those of Mrs. Baird and her lady visitor.

Not above the medium height was Bessie, and although she could hardly be called pretty, there was a good deal about her that was interesting and even attractive. She had, above all things, the rare and valuable gift of concentrating upon herself and her own affairs the attention of any little coterie of her own sex in which she might happen to find herself. She was one of those young ladies who, from childhood up, are invariably in need of a helping hand, and who just as invariably manage to get it. How they escape becoming self-supporting, at some period, is a miracle, but they do it. There are men of the same sort, but unless

they are very "religious," and they sometimes
are, they drift out of sight sooner than the women
do. Defects of early education are sometimes
largely to blame, but the puzzle is, after all, that no
amount of later education, even in hard schools,
seems adequate to correct the difficulty. Never by
any chance, however, does a male or female of this
class admit the possibility of any fault or failing on
their own part. To do so would in a manner forfeit
their best claim to the sympathy of a soft-hearted
and well-meaning, but, in their eyes, a very imperfect
and unappreciative world.

Good Mrs. Baird was already aware that Bessie
had obtained the means for her proposed transfer
of residence, and her strong, kindly, motherly face
was beaming with good will as she said:

"Mrs. Boyce and I have been talking about you
and your prospects, dear. Have you written your
letter to your brother?"

"To Fred? Yes, Mrs. Baird. I have said all I
know how. I am hoping, sincerely, that he is on
the right path, at last."

"Do you know what he is doing?"

"O no. He does not tell me. I have suggested a
great many things, but he never would follow my advice. If he had, things would have been very different."

"Your brother Augustus is doing well, is he not?
Mrs. Baird tells me he has got a place," said Mrs.
Boyce.

"Yes, I'm thankful for that. He went to some old friends of Fred's, and they were glad to take him. I wish Fred would do something for himself."

"Was he not out of health, for a long time?"

"Yes, very much," and a deep sigh conveyed a world of meaning as to the nature of her brother's illness.

"Something he contracted in the army?"

"Yes, it was in the army."

And the second sigh was deeper than the first.

. A polished, admirably well-dressed lady was Mrs. Boyce, with a soft, winning music in her tone, and a subtle caress in every smile, but her smooth handsome face told no tales whatever of what might be going on behind it. The faintest suggestion of grief was in the colors she wore, for she had left her married life behind her for nearly a second year. Such a friend she might have been to a young woman like Bessie Heron, and Bessie had often thought of it, but it was too late now, at least for the present.

"My dear," she said, melodiously, "perhaps I can help your brother. He is very capable, I am sure, from what Mrs. Baird has told me. I will speak about him to my friend Mr. Brown, the great merchant. He is retiring from business, a little, but I'm sure he could find a place for your brother."

"I would be so thankful, Mrs. Boyce, but then he ought not to be misinformed. He should know all

about Fred before he takes him. Mrs. Baird will
bear me witness that I have concealed nothing from
her. She can tell you anything you want to
know."

"Why? Does he drink?"

"Please, Mrs. Boyce, it is so very painful to me.
He is my brother, you know, and I do so want to
help him! I would not prejudice you against him
for the world. He will redeem himself, I feel sure
he will."

Mrs. Boyce smiled very sweetly and sympathiz-
ingly, and Bessie looked for a moment like a nice
little martyr in a picture, but Mrs. Baird's foot was
tapping uneasily on the carpet.

"Does he gamble?" she exclaimed. "Where
did he get the hundred dollars he sent you to-day?"

"Did he send her a hundred dollars?" softly in-
quired Mrs. Boyce. "He is a good brother, then.
He cannot be all bad. I should so like to see him.
Does he not write for the newspapers?"

"O yes," replied Bessie, willing to skip financial
questions, "and I have often urged him to take a
place on some newspaper or magazine, as editor.
He would have a good salary then, and I should no
longer be dependent on friends."

"That would indeed be an excellent thing to do,"
said Mrs. Boyce, "or he might start a newspaper of
his own. Just think how profitable some of them
are."

"But that requires capital?" vaguely suggested Mrs. Baird. "And they all have editors of their own, have they not?"

"Fred himself made some such objection, when I spoke to him," said Bessie, "but I told him that where there was a will there was a way. Other men have done it, and he could. He lacks ambition, I fear."

"Pity he is not married," cooed Mrs. Boyce, "that would tend to steady him."

"O Mrs. Boyce, that would be dreadful. Think of Fred with a wife. He came very near it, once. Quite a fortune, too."

"Was it broken off?"

"Long ago. About the time he began to go down."

"But what was the trouble?"

"It is so hard to say. Of course I cannot give her name, but I went to see her, myself."

"Went to see her? What did she say?"—and there was a curious look on the widow's face when she asked the question.

"O it was no manner of good. I told her all about him, and begged her to try and reform him, but she would not listen to me."

"Ahem! There's nothing a sister will not do for an erring brother. But I must be going, Mrs. Baird. Miss Heron, I really mean to speak to Mr. Brown about Fred. He was a near friend of my husband, and I know he would be glad to oblige me. I hope you will have a. nice time with your western friends."

Parting words, plenty of them, a kiss or two, and Mrs. Baird and Bessie were left alone.

" Such a sweet woman," said the former.

" But I fear she is worldly, Mrs. Baird. She has so large a share of this world's goods. Do you not think she is inclined to be politic ?"

" She is a great fool if she's not, my dear. I notice that she is exceedingly careful as to what she says about other people."

" But one should always tell the truth, Mrs. Baird."

" If they know it. Or else say nothing at all. I wish I knew the truth about your brother."

" So do I, indeed, but he never tells me anything, and he is so proud and independent. If he would only learn a little true humility and be more frank, I should take it as a hopeful sign of his repent-.ance."

Mrs. Baird had something like a doubt written on her face as she listened, and it was not long before Bessie excused herself for returning to her own room to pack up.

It was after she had gone that Mrs. Baird came out of a long fit of musing with—

" No, I shall not ask her to come back here. It is not my duty. I think I've done my share. But I mean to ask Mr. Baird to hunt up her brother

Fred. What can he have done that is so dread-ful. She ought to tell, if she knows. Mr. Baird can find out, anyhow."

And Bessie, in her own room, was arranging a good-sized trunk and soliloquizing—

"No, I sometimes fear Mrs. Baird herself does not understand me. But how can I expect that from strangers, when my own brother will not yield to my influence? I have done all I could for him. I think I will write and tell him I've enlisted Mrs. Boyce for him. So many friends and opportunities I 'have brought him, and he has thrown them all away. If I could only see Mr. Brown, myself, now, and tell him just what Fred is!"

If she could but have done so, what a grand opening Fred Heron would have had, right before him. A grand one!

And yet she was a good young woman, and her intentions were excellent. She would have said as much herself, and believed every word of it. Fire . could not have burned that conviction out of her. Neither as to her own goodness or the goodness of her good intentions. But they would have paved quite a section of—well, of Boston, for instance, nevertheless. And Mrs. Boyce, lazily lying back in her carriage, on her way home, was not thinking of either of the two ladies with whom she had been talking. No, nor of Fred Heron, either.

She was saying to herself—

" Well, it did me good to go out. I'd have gone wild if I'd remained any longer cooped up at home. I must see Mr. Brown to-morrow, indeed. He will know what is best to be done. I could hardly do better than to leave everything in his hands. The clearest head! And then he's got a heart of gold. I wish there were more such men. And what a sweet girl Mabel is. Wonderfully set in her way. If she belonged to our church she'd be a terrible ritualist. But then Mr. Brown's liberal enough. He thinks for himself. So do I, but I think I'm in dreadfully hot water, just at this present time."

CHAPTER VII.

"UGH!"

THE sun had passed the zenith when Dr. Milyng
crept behind the pile of fallen masonry in the
ruin, and the day was well spent before the "big
medicine man" of that band of Apaches surrendered
himself to his log-like slumber. If the trapped miner
intended to get out of his cage it was well to be
moving about the matter, for even such a lethargy
as that could not last forever. There could be no
danger from the sleeper, whatever might come from
his roving clansmen outside.

No danger, indeed, but the doctor's views of the
situation were broader than that, and worthy of the
sagacity and courage which had carried him through
unnumbered perils in adventurous days gone by.

They were broad, courageous and sagacious, but
their morality belonged to that latitude and longi-
tude, for they were aboriginal rather than christian,
at least in theory.

No lawyer in the settlements, not in the largest

65

of them, could have relieved a client of his estate
with greater patience and skill than Dr. Milyng displayed in obtaining possession of that splendid robe
of skins. No unmannerly tugging, but the little
pulls followed one another as gently and as persistently as fees in a long bill, and only once was the
sleeper in the least disturbed. He had to be, a little,
towards the end, but it did not wake him up. Well
for him it did not, for in that event the doctor
would have been compelled to use the long, keen
hunting-knife which he drew and laid beside him
when he began his operations. It would, perhaps, have been easier to have used it at once,
and it would have greatly shortened the job,
but it would have been imprudent, for several
reasons, and, after all, it is a mean thing to cut the
throat of a sleeping man merely to steal the robe
he is lying on. There was no reason, however, why
his well-filled cartridge box should not be examined.

"All right," said the doctor. "Regulation size.
Just what I want. I'll make 'em last me to Santa
Fe. Now for it. It covers me from head to foot.
Couldn't be better."

Not, certainly, if he meant to conceal himself entirely, head and all, with his sombrero under his arm,
and his various valuables stowed around him. He
was simply a moving column, and a fat one, of fur
robe.

At the entrance he avoided disturbing the pair of

moccasins, but he dropped a handful of gravel in each one by way of a joke.

"They'll never dream an enemy did that," he muttered, as he cast loose the lariat of the really noble animal that stood waiting him. "I could hardly have asked for a better horse, but I'll try for a pack-pony. I'll need one, if only to carry meat for me."

Once in the saddle he covered himself as completely as before, and rode slowly away in the direction opposite the Apache encampment. Such simple-minded red horsemen as he met were well acquainted with that peculiar outfit, and never dreamed of asking it any questions, much less of interfering with its freedom. Whatever mummery might be on hand, to induce their Big Medicine to wear furs in summer, was no business of theirs, and they rode by in naked comfort, like sensible savages.

About a mile from the ruins the doctor met a little drove of ponies, under the guidance of a half-grown Indian boy, mounted on the best of them.

A deep growl came from under the robe as a hand reached forth, grasped the hide lariat of that particular pony, and vanished. A few harsh gutturals followed, which might have been interpreted: "Get off, you young wolf," and they were obeyed with an alacrity which spoke well for the religious training of the stripling horse-thief who heard it. He sprang upon another at once, for he would have scorned walking with a horse at hand, but it did not seem to occur to him that anything unusual had happened.

As for Dr. Milyng, he soon began to quicken his pace now, and took a more northerly course. There were mountains in that direction, but it was likely their passes were not unknown to him. At all events he meant to make the best use of his time before the former owner of his sultry garment should awake from his prophetic dreams. Even after the shadows lengthened and the mists began to gather in the lowlands, he steadily pursued his way, and the darkness itself did not halt him. The stars and the moon were light enough for such a flight as his, and he had ridden both fast and far before he deemed it prudent, out of regard for his quadrupeds rather than his own tough and tireless frame, to find a place for a camp.

" No fire," he remarked, " but they must feed. I've a bit of cold meat left. To-morrow I'll do some more cooking. But this has been the biggest kind of a day's work. If I can throw them off the scent I'll make a bee-line for Santa Fe."

Iron nerves, he must have had, to be able to sleep under such circumstances, but sleep he did, and the robe of skins was an excellent addition, by way of comfort, to his own Navajo blanket.

Not an Apache in all the band he had left behind him, but would have awarded the most unstinted

admiration to such a feat as the doctor had performed, if he could have known how it was done.

But that was the precise question which disturbed them, a little after sunset, that evening.

The interior of the ruined quadrangle was growing more than a little dusky when the Big Medicine
awoke. He might have slept longer, but for the
unprotected sharpness with which some of the
stony fragments under him worked their points
and edges into his naked flesh. Changes of position did him no manner of service, and his dreams
were of a character which threatened woe to the
entire nation of the Apaches.

If they were bad, however, so were his sensations
on awaking. At first he imagined that he must
have, so to speak, rolled out of bed, and he looked
gropingly around for his precious robe. Many a
day of toil had his own squaws and those of lesser
men toiled in the tanning of all that peltry, and
many a thoughtful hour had he exhausted upon its
skilful illumination. Its pictured interior had
grown into a sort of panorama of his greatness.
That is, of his own opinion of his mighty deeds
and character. It was dreadful to wake up from
stony visions to find even his autobiography gone
from under him.

But it was gone. And where?

He sprang to his feet with greater agility than
could have been expected of him, and the exclama-

tion he uttered was a cross between a grunt and a yell which testified his barbarism. A civilized man would have sworn at or by something sacred, but that privilege was as yet denied the untutored high-priest of the red men.

There was just about light enough left by which to satisfy himself of his solitude, as well as of his loss, and he rushed for the entrance.

His horse, with its splendid equipment, where was that?

Gone also. But there were his moccasins, pointing their toes outward on the threshold, as if indicating the general direction taken by his other property. He overlooked the vagueness of it, and hurriedly pulled on one of them. It was the left foot first, which is always unlucky, for he instantly pulled it off with a hoarse " ugh !"

Nothing worse than gravel, but that is hardly the correct thing in shoes of any pattern. Even if he had heard of the pious devotee who boiled the peas for his pilgrimage of penance, it would have done him no service. No amount of boiling would have softened that gravel.

The other moccasin was gravely examined before putting it on.

Somebody had been trifling with his dignity and he was too well trained a savage not to look around at once for " sign !"

Foot-prints there were, in abundance, and they

came from the ruin, but they were those of a man.
No mischievous boy had ventured to play this
prank. Curious foot-prints they were. Not precisely those of an Apache, but just as unlike any
white men's feet that he had ever seen. The toes
did not turn out, nor did the manner of putting
down the foot betray an accustomed boot-heel and
a body-lifting stride. Dr. Milyng was too much of
an Indian in his habits of life not to have caught
their walk to a certain degree of perfection.

It was a very interesting study, but it produced
no practical results, and the Big Medicine's temper
was rising too fast and too hotly for calmly scientific
investigation.

It was at this point, too, that he discovered the
lightness of his cartridge-box.

Why had not his carbine also been taken?

Perhaps because of its weight, seeing that the
removal of the hammer-pin of the lock had turned
it into a very useless kind of freight for any man
to carry. One gun was all the doctor had thought
he would need on that trip, but the Big Medicine
would require a new one—or a gunsmith.

It was a long time since that powerful conjurer
had walked so fast as he now did, on his way to
the camp of his brethren. His wrath swelled
within him as he went, and he paid no attention to
the inquiring glances cast upon him by chance
braves of the meaner sort, and by squaws of the

older, as he strode along. He did not even seek
the retirement of the lodge his faithful wives had
set up for him, but plunged at once into the aristocratic circle where a dozen chiefs, distinguished
in field and council, were discussing the morrow's
hunt.

Rich were they in scalps and stolen horses, and
the Big Medicine himself had been second to
none of them, before he began to grow fat and
gather wisdom.

With fierce gesticulations, but half-choked with
passion, he detailed the intolerable practical joke
which had been played upon him.

It is an odd mistake, a musty memory of the
manners of the vanished Pequods and Iroquois, to
suppose that Indian warriors never laugh. When
they are parading their pride in the part assigned
them in that ancient comedy known as "Treaty,"
they are usually as solemn as owls, but it is to be
doubted if even then they fail to see and enjoy the
fun of the thing.

There in their own camp, at all events, they were
quite ready to take up the joke on their man of mystery, and the gravel in the moccasins nearly cost
one grim old scalper his life.

But there was a serious side to it all, and it
quickly turned up, for more than one of the increasing assembly was prepared to say that he had met
the conjurer, that very afternoon, wrapped in his

own great robe, and riding his own horse. The boy, too, from whom the pony had been taken, came incautiously forward with his contribution to the general fund. It cost him, afterward, a pony's worth of lariat end at the hands of his disconsolate father. It would be long before another pony would be taken from under that same boy.

Of course there was an immediate adjournment to the ruin, but it was too dark now to look for signs, or to follow a trail, and all that could be done was to study thoroughly all the points they had in hand, and to make ready a dozen of their best-mounted men for an early start in the morning.

It was remarkable with what unanimous sagacity the dusky investigators came to the conclusion that "a white man has done this." No hostile savage would have been contented with horse and robe, when a scalp also lay ready for the taking. They knew that by their own feelings.

"Want hoss, want robe. No want scalp. No hurt. Good. Like him much. Big chief, anyhow."

Dr. Milyng's conduct was therefore more thoroughly appreciated than he had thought or cared. It is even possible that a friendly feeling mingled with the general admiration. But not in the disgusted soul of the Big Medicine. Even his squaws required beating, that night, for the unseemly levity of their behavior towards their lord and master.

CHAPTER VIII.

BEATEN BY MORE DEVILS THAN ONE.

FRED HERON was not to sleep in the open air, that night.

On coming out of Mr. Brown's gate he felt no desire to sleep at all or anywhere. Not only was all his mind in a tumult of excited wakefulness over the events of the day and evening, but it seemed to him that there were two lives within him, between which a fierce struggle for mastery had been provoked. He had felt that way before, and many a time, and the recurring strife had been of ever-increasing severity, but never had it risen to its present height and bitterness. The influence of his poor "three grains" had been worked off by his severe exercise of mind and body, and had left behind it an augmented hunger of that gnawing pain which does not come to human beings in any other way.

With the narcotic, too, disappeared the side of

74

his character which had been uppermost for the past few hours. Drugs create nothing. They only call out this or that or the other set of faculties in undue relation, or without any relation, to other faculties and developments. These, then, the stimulus abating, sink out of sight fatigued, and leave yet others in undue and unwholesome prominence for the time being. Insanity of any kind has a somewhat similar analysis. And yet Fred Heron was not insane. He had those other three grains in his pocket, but he touched them not. Not even when the tumult and tearing within him grew to a great and exceeding bitter conflict.

There were endless successions, too, on the street corners he was passing, of those places where the other great poison is sold, but he entered them not, although he had in his pocket the wherewithal to buy oblivion.

" Strange," he said to himself, " I began with this thing to save myself from suffering. I did but accumulate pain, putting it safely at usury, to be paid me now, both principal and interest. What an awful dividend it is, to be sure. An honest debtor is pain, and it will surely pay. I wonder if hell is anything like this? We won't have our bodies, there. Not these bodies. But then it is not my body that is suffering. Take the soul out and the body would be quiet enough. Quiet as that yellow dog with his unexpected supper. Things that come to us in that sudden way are very apt to have poison in them. I've tried it. Made a tramp of me. But then about hell. I think I know how it feels, just now. I can reason about it, too. It isn't this gnawing I want to be rid of, but the cause of it, so it won't come again, forever and ever. I want a complete salvation. I wouldn't give a cent to be saved from hell. Somehow I don't appreciate it very highly, after what I've been through."

He had wandered from the street, just then, into an open square, thickly strewn with grand old shade trees. The skies had clouded rapidly, as if for rain, and the gloom was intense, for there were no lamps, away in there. He had stopped under a great elm, and was looking upward.

There came a flash of lightning that played through the branches and over his face. A pale, working, suffering face, full of pain, and of a great longing.

" No," he exclaimed aloud, " I would not give a brass farthing for a salvation that only saves from hell. I want to be saved from sin!"

Was the lightning the outward form of a thought?

Perhaps, but as it passed, and the utter darkness came again, deeper than before, his head sank upon his breast and he muttered:

" Is that it? Emmanuel? I read that once. Does anybody believe it, nowadays? It's true, though. I can feel it. Or else there is no God. And if there were no God there could not be any hell. The one implies the other, so long as a man is able to ask a question about it. It is all getting dim again."

The dimness of suffering. The darkness after the flash. Strange contradiction there is in human nature, for now Fred Heron took out the little box and swallowed the other three pills, and then he went straight to the nearest corner for a half tumbler full of whisky to wash them down and increase their effect.

Was that a breaking off? Or was it a breaking down?

Would it ever be well to shut up such men at such a time, till the last struggle is over? It is a hard question to answer, but Fred had been making a magnificent fight, after all.

He turned now towards the leading thoroughfares, which were already beginning to be somewhat deserted. The gnawing pain was gone, and in its place was coming a strong elation, a combative, heroic energy, such as made him feel sure that he should yet come off victor, and more than victor, over all his evil circumstances.

" Moses himself had a rough time of it, at first, after he smote that Egyptian," he was saying, as he plunged into the greater privacy of a somewhat disreputable cross street, but at that moment his quickened senses were assailed by the sound of blows and curses.

"Get up. Get up, I tell you ; come along with me."

The prostrate form of a man, a not very well-dressed one, was on the sidewalk, and over him bent one of the uniformed guardians of the peace, whose business it is to keep the streets clear of fallen men.

The blows of the locust were heavy, and were rapidly repeated, with small care as to where they fell.

"Stop, there. What are you striking that man for? Don't you see he can't get up?"

The policeman was silent for a moment, with the very wonder of it, but he permitted no such invasion of his rights, and the bitter profanity of his reply to Fred Heron was accompanied by a vicious whack on the head of his victim.

In another instant his arm was seized by what seemed a grasp of steel.

"Don't you strike him again."

The locust changed hands, and an alarm rap was made on the pavement before any attempt to use it on Fred.

That followed, of course, but it was of no manner of effect. The excited young man, naturally athletic, seemed to be endowed with the strength of Antaeus for the moment. The policeman could neither strike nor escape.

Not so the roundsman, who quickly came to his assistance, and the last thing Fred saw, for the next half-hour, was a sudden shower of stars.

A locust club is a terrible weapon in a strong hand, accustomed to its use, and that roundsman had had years and years of practice.

When Fred came to himself he was in darkness, relieved only by a faint glimmer through a grating at about the height of his own head from the ground.

He was in a cell at the station-house, and in the hands of the police.

His head felt badly, and he discovered that it had been washed and bandaged. There was something odd in that, but he was unaware of the fact that a surgeon had been in the office when he and the other man were brought in, on stretchers, and that a good deal of a fuss, a ridiculous fuss, had been made by the man of science. It had been of no use to tell him the first case had been drunk and disorderly, for he had curtly said:

"Epilepsy. Beaten horribly. The man will die. Even if he'd been well and drunk it would have been outrageous. This other man has a bad scalp wound."

"He resisted the policeman."

"Bully for him. Wish he'd shot him. Looks like a respectable party."

"Tremendously powerful."

"Nonsense. A man of very ordinary strength. Could handle him myself, without clubbing. Cowardly outrage. I shall report it to the Board in the morning."

He did what he could, but he had not been long on the force, that surgeon, and he knew very little of the ways in which unpleasant facts will slip out from under impertinent fingers. By the time his complaint was ready, on the morrow, the dying epïleptic had disappeared among the small-pox cases, and was beyond his jurisdiction, while Mr. John Rogers, as poor Fred gave his name, not wishing to sully his real one by appearing in the police returns, had been sent to "the Island," for sixty days, for disorderly conduct. Why he got no more was a problem which the police justice was angrily called upon to explain, and which he solved for his uniformed inquirer with:

"Nonsense. Don't you s'pose I understand it? The clubbing was punishment enough for all he did, anyhow. I only sent him over to oblige you. He isn't the kind of man that fights the police. He wasn't even drunk. You're carrying this thing too far, anyhow, nowadays. The people may go back on you, the first you know. They would, now, if it wasn't for the good they know of some of you, and the bad they don't know of the rest."

A rough man was the justice, and he wanted to be popular with "the boys," but he had some dim notions of right and wrong, and of what was the wise policy to pursue with a club. He knew there was a possibility of overdoing the most humane and necessary public service.

And so Fred Heron did not spend that night in the open air, but the cell he lay in contained no hindrances to thought. Even the burning thirst which consumed him, and for which no relief was to be had, brought with it a copious fund of pertinent suggestion.

"Well," he muttered, "if Abraham wouldn't send Lazarus, it's no use for me to ask favors of one of these fellows. I'll just bear it. Dives had to. But then he got in by a different way from the one I took to-night. Would I do it again? I would. Every time. Now I like that. I'm glad it's in me. It's a good sign. Wonder if that other man was dead. Maybe he'd been eating the wrong kind of meat. Adam and Eve did—that is, apples. If there ever was any Adam, or any Eve, or any apples. Mr. Darwin suggests monkeys and cocoanuts. Well, some of us have got beyond the monkey level, and some haven't. Or if they have they're sorry for it, and are selecting themselves back again. That's a strong argument for Darwin. If I had my way with that policeman for awhile, I think I would reduce him to his original jelly. Think of a protoplasm in a blue uniform."

Perhaps Fred's brain was getting a little flighty, and if it was no one could wonder, seeing what it had undergone that day, and before that day, not to speak of the concussion of its retaining shell against the hard and heavy "locust" to wind up with.

CHAPTER IX.

A PRACTICAL LESSON ON THE VALUE OF INSTITU-
TIONS.

THAT was an uneasy night for Mr. Brown's dog
Prince.

He had fully comprehended that he did not understand the situation, and had thereby surpassed the
intellectual achievements of many a modern statesman.

There had been the smell of meat on the gravel-
walk, where no meat was, or should have been.
There, too, had been the strange man in the horse-
chestnut, where he had never before seen a human
being at that time of night. All the subsequent per-
formances, even to the departure unbitten of the
suspicious stranger, had been of a nature to disturb
the canine mind, and Prince felt himself called upon
for an unusual degree of watchfulness.

For that very reason, perhaps, he stoutly adhered
to the neighborhood of the front gate, when he
would have been in a fairer road to usefulness in the
rear of the house.

82

For it was only a little after one o'clock when the lonely streets of that aristocratic and therefore thinly-peopled neighborhood were favored with another presence than that of the police.

A double presence, of two men, between whom neither the artist nor the moralist could have found much to choose, so perfectly could either one of them have sat for the portrait of a vagabond.

At one corner they paused for a moment.

"Dead dog, Bill."

"Eat somethin' didn't agree with him, most likely."

"Guess he ain't the only one in this 'ere vicinity. It's a bad night for dogs."

"Wust kind. Hain't seen a sign of a cop, not yet."

"Sleep, somewheres, most likely. No need o' givin' them chaps any buttons."

"Not much, thar ain't. Now, Bill, we mustn't hurt anybody, not if we kin help it."

"Of course not. They don't foller it up so close when nobody's hurt, unless the swag's big enough to set the 'tectives at work."

"And then they won't settle the hash at all, if any harm's done. Still, I don't mean to be imposed on."

"Nor I, nuther. All they've got to do is to lie still and let us fellows take what belongs to us."

"That's all. Thar'll be a gineral divide, some day, you see 'f thar ain't."

"I'll be thar, my boy. But I want part of my sheer now. Let's cut for the back street. No dog this time."

"You bet. But he was an all-fired big one, he was."

They passed the front gate, but Prince was at that moment looking up into the chestnut tree, and he was much too dignified a dog to bark at chance passengers who seemed to be minding their own business.

City dogs learn in time that a contrary course involves much useless labor, if not a peril of bronchial difficulties.

A similar course of reasoning may account for the continued silence of some city pulpits concerning the every day current of evil of which they make no mention.

Prince could afford to wait, like other guardians of the sleeping, until his own particular fences were assailed.

He did, at least, and so, a good deal like the others, his fences were scaled for him before he had the slightest notion of coming danger.

Over the fence, with noiseless feet, and swift, crouching, watchful advances, until the two invaders were standing under the bay window on the opposite side of the library wing, right across from the window in which Mabel Varick had appeared to Fred Heron. She was in her own room, now, dreaming wild, fairy-land dreams, of mountains of gold and silver, while her uncle was rolling uneasily from side to side on his solitary couch, in the room adjoining, trying vainly to drive from his heated brain the distorted remnants of his conversation with that remarkable tramp.

"A terribly keen thinker. I never met a man whose talk disturbed me so. Can the lower classes really be moved to any depth by the ideas he presented? If so, it is high time something should be done to counteract it. And yet, mere repression won't do. Might as well pile weights on a safety-valve. Only make a bigger explosion by-and-by. Blow things all to smithereens. Wealth has its duties, and I do not mean to shrink from mine. But has religion no power? Of course not, unless it is put in operation. How much religion filters down among these fellows, and what sort of stuff is it by the time it gets to them? I'd like to know that. I got a glimpse of it, to-night. He thinks our church-work is a species of humbug, and so it is, a good deal of it. Religious clubs, he called them, and so they are. I must carry out my plans, but it will take a perfect mountain of gold to do it. Then I must get my mountain, first. I wish I knew where I could find Dr. Milyng. Hark, was that a noise inside the house? Can't be, or I'd have heard from Prince before this."

The noise was inside the house, nevertheless, for it was made by the breaking of a small brass bolt, a filagree affair, on one of the frames of the mosquito-net at the library window.

The noise was inside, but that was all, as yet, for one man stood braced against the wall of the house, with out-stretched hands, while his companion stood on his shoulders and pried skilfully at the frail barrier before him.

But an unusual sound travels further by night than by day, and that sharp little snap had reached other ears than those of Mr. Brown.

Prince heard it, as he turned away from his horse-chestnut tree, and it seemed to make another dog of him in the twinkling of an eye. If he had seemed, for the time being, over given to contemplation and inclined to study things hopelessly above him, in imitation of ordinary human folly, he was now once more a watch-dog, and in a desperate hurry to get around the house.

The window was open by the time he got there, and the uppermost burglar was withdrawing his stockingless feet from the shoulders of his pedestal.

Not the sound of anything breaking, this time, unless it was the silence, but a sharp, irrepressible yell of pain, such as rises from the lips of a man in whose rear the fangs of a large and pitiless dog are sinking.

"Bill, is that the dog?"

Only another yell, with verbal expressions to match.

"Then the job is busted!"

He alighted on the grass as he spoke, and his duty was to have made an immediate assault on Prince.

There is one difficulty, however, with all organizations whose only cohesive power is the hope of plunder.

Realize the hope, and they are disintegrated by the sure quarrel over the spoils. Take it away, and the moral corpses remove themselves in all directions according to their instincts and interests.

Both the instincts and interests of that burglar forbade his lingering longer in Mr. Brown's backyard, and he sprang away for the fence.

Alas for him!

The fence was there, and so was a stalwart man, in blue uniform, with a locust club in one hand and a revolver in the other, and a perfect willingness of mind to make use of both or either.

The agility of the fugitive was proved by the vaulting spring with which he cleared the fence, and the efficiency of the policeman by the vigor with which the locust was plied the moment the fence was cleared.

"I give in! I give in!"

"You better had. Here, put these on. Hands behind your back, now."

No help for it, and the moment the handcuffs were sprung it was safe to tie them to the fence and rush to the assistance of Prince.

Not that he needed help half so much as Bill did, for that worthy was now flat on the ground, and the

double-barrelled gun of Mr. Brown was bearing on
him from the window.

It was of small consequence that there was no
cartridge in either barrel of the gun, for Prince was
"loaded to the muzzle," and especially well at the
muzzle.

"Call him off, Mr. Brown. I'll take that chap in
charge and rap for assistance. There isn't any fight
in him, I guess."

No, not a bit, but there was a good deal in Prince,
and it required all the authority of his master, most
vigorously exerted, to overcome what Fred Heron
might have called the dog's innate tendency to
animal food.

The rights of property had been fully vindicated,
and communism pure and simple had suffered a
most ignominious defeat. So it always will when it
comes to the front otherwise than under cover of
the forms of law. When it succeeds in doing that,
it will have the dogs and other public servants on
its side, and there is no telling what it may put them
up to.

But the policeman's rap was speedily answered,
for notice had been given of a possible need, and
the two nocturnal adventurers were speedily as safe
from doing any further mischief, that night, as was
poor Fred Heron himself.

Neither one of them would be compelled to sleep
in the open air, but whatever slumber was taken by

the man named Bill did not come to him while he was lying on his back.

And Prince himself passed his time till morning in a stately promenade from the back window to the horse-chestnut tree, as if he in some mysterious manner connected them in his mental analysis of the events which had upset him.

He was not the only member of that household who could be fairly said to be upset. Every closet was looked into and every barrel in cellar and garret was looked behind, and every bed was looked under, before Mr. Brown felt justified in turning to his niece to say, "Well, Mabel, we owe a debt of gratitude to that Mr. Heron. If he had not saved Prince, as he did, those fellows could have walked right in."

"They might have murdered us all!"

"Well, I had my shot-gun"—

"O uncle Daniel, you will not leave it loaded?"

"No, dear, I'll remove the cartridges at once. They can be replaced in a moment if there should be any necessity. I left it on the library table."

All the gas-jets in the house were in a blaze, and it was safe to go anywhere after so thorough an investigation. The deep voice of Prince in the front yard was itself a magnificent guaranty that peace reigned to the very frontiers.

But Mr. Brown examined his weapon somewhat anxiously when he took it in his hand.

An elegant piece, of the best and latest pattern,

and its owner had tested it on snipe the previous season. In capital order, too, not a spring or a screw out of place, and it was really a weapon to charm the eye of an amateur sportsman.

"I declare, if I didn't forget to load it! Why, it wouldn't have gone off if I'd have pulled the trigger all night!"

No more it would, and Mr. Brown had a splendid chance to go to bed and moralize on the uselessness of brilliant institutions with no powder and ball in them. He put the gun away, looked very carefully to the fastenings of all his doors and windows, sent an encouraging whistle to Prince, for which a most loyal wag of the tail was duly returned, and then retired once more to his lonely reveries, not slumbers.

If Mrs. Brown had been alive, what a lesson he might have secured on the comparative usefulness of good dogs and empty guns! But then he thought the subject up, for himself.

CHAPTER X.

THE DANGER OF BELIEVING IN A LIE.

WHAT between eating and sleeping, Oliver passed as comfortable a day as an overworked mule could well have asked for, in that country, but he would have been glad of either more or less company when night began to fall. Less, if he could have had his own way, and more if he could have had his choice, for the coyotes had speedily overcome their annoyance over the events of the morning, and persisted in following his motions, go where he would and do whatever he might.

Their numbers, moreover, had been reinforced, and they were beginning to exhibit a degree of cautious familiarity which worried him, while they avoided taking up any position which offered an opening, or the smallest portion of a wolf, for the exercise of his peculiar talents. They were beginning to understand mule better than they did at first, and they were content to wait for such opportunities as the future might bring them.

There was an increasing unpleasantness about it,
and Oliver hesitated about selecting a night's lodging for himself so long as his couch might be sur-
rounded in such a manner as that. The darkness,
he knew, belonged to his enemies, and they would
have a degree of courage in it which sunlight deprived them of. It was best, therefore, to keep in
motion, and he was better prepared for such exer-
tion than he had been a few hours before.

The night was not a dark one, and, as the beleag-
uered mule marched warily on from one roll of grass
to another, annoyed by an occasional yelp, and even
a castanet-like snap of hungry jaws, he saw, at no
great distance in front of him, a huge, ungainly
shape, looming up in the gloom.

Anything for company and a possibility of help.

A sharp trot, and Oliver was no longer alone, but
he might almost as well have been. If he had been
besieged, the stranger was beset.

A mighty fellow, too, with the strength of a nation
of prairie wolves yet remaining in him, for he was a
buffalo bull of the largest size. Not even enfeebled
by age, and yet—

Yes, that was it, the arrows.

Three of them were sticking in his flanks, and the
life was slowly ebbing from his huge bulk as he tot-
tered over the plain.

He had made his last fight, his last run, and there
was no help for Oliver in him.

It looked so, indeed, for the vicious miscreants had already assailed his hind quarters, from time to time, in efforts to further cripple him, and his foes were more numerous than Oliver's own.

His weapons of defence were all in front, as completely as the mule's were at the opposite extremity of his organization, and the very shape and garniture of his massive shoulders made it difficult to properly watch and guard his rear. A proper combination of two such forces as his and Oliver's might have done well, but generalship would have been required for that, and the world knows how rare a thing is a good general. So rare that it often takes years of war to find him. He is then discovered by the light of other men's defeats, and neither Oliver nor the bull enjoyed any such precious privileges.

The bull had one comfort, just one, as Oliver drew near, and his own followers dashed suddenly forward to ascertain if their neighbors were doing better than themselves. In the rush and confusion of the moment a luckless coyote was jostled within reaching distance of the disabled monarch of the herd.

A sickly lurch, a quick lowering and lifting of the furiously angry head—who would have thought such electric motion was in that massive neck.

But how high that prowling rascal did go!

The horn went through him—there was comfort in that—but it had no barb to detain him, and up he

went, as if the bull had put his last despairing energy into the cast.

He fell in the grass a score of yards behind his
destroyer, but the latter sank forward on his knees
with a low, thunderous, suffocating bellow.

There is no earthly thing from which other earthly
things retire to a safer distance than the deathbed
of fallen greatness, and Oliver did not linger a moment after he saw the bull go down. He trotted
as if for his life, without so much as looking behind
him, cutting a dismayed bray of his own short off
in the middle.

But the coyotes of either pack?

Well, a few of them hesitated and cantered doubtfully after Oliver for a short distance, but the political economy of the case was too plain for even a
congressman to have erred in making it out. A bull
in the hand was worth two mules in the bush, and
so they all stayed to get their share of the coming
feast. What they might do or think of doing, afterwards, was quite another matter, but here was a
great and rich corporation already on its knees, and
they were just the lawyers to foreclose those three
arrowy mortgages. The only drawback was that
they would, after all, be compelled to leave the rails
and roadway—that is, to speak less figuratively, the
skeleton—to whiten on the ground, after the meat
should be picked off. A pity, when there might be
such toothsome marrow in those bones, if it could

but be got at. They would have to leave all that
to the ants.

But Oliver had done very well, considering, and
it was not his fault that he was less attractive than
a dying buffalo. He ccculd now march on, after he
tired of running, until he found another thicket of
willows and could obtain therein both safety, and,
what all travellers call for, "a room to himself."

It is hardly to be supposed that Oliver troubled
himself much about the fortunes of the master who
had so completely deserted and forgotten him, and
Dr. Milyng had quite enough to think of, that
night, without recurring to the mule he left behind
him.

The spot he had chosen for his camp was at the
foot of a long, outlying spur of a chain of mountains which arose to the north and east of him, and
it was so deeply buried in a wooded ravine that an
army might have marched past it, that night, and
never guessed that it contained a camp.

With the earliest light of returning day the doctor was on his feet, but his first attentions were paid
to the wants of his quadruped friends, rather than
his own. They could hardly ever before have
known such thorough grooming. He evidently
knew well the secret of making a horse hold out on
a long journey, and the one before him was likely
to test to the uttermost the capacity of his two
prizes.

Prizes they were, and he remarked concerning the first:

" Wonder where they stole him? He never was foaled in any Indian corral. Not an army horse, either; isn't branded. Must have come from the settlements. Fine fellow. Worth a dozen ponies. And yet that pony's a good one. Don't look as if he'd been overworked. If I'd have had my pick of the camp I could hardly have done better. That's just what he had, I reckon. The old impostor. Wonder what he said when he woke up. They'll be after me, sure, but I'm more afraid of what I may meet than of anything behind me. If I can clear the passes, there won't be so much difficulty, but it's a long road to Santa Fe, and a thirsty one. I must lay in some meat before I strike the alkali plains. Pity I've nothing to tote water in."

He gave his beasts a hearty breakfast, so far as grass would go, for they were not likely to feed again, that day, and then he set out at a singularly steady pace, for a man on whose trail the Apache horsemen might even then be racing. A wary man was he, and could calculate to a fraction how much of speed would be left in Indian ponies after long spurring in a hot sun.

He kept the lowlands for a few miles, keenly studying the changing outlines of the neighboring knobs and ridges, until at last he halted at the side of what looked like a beaten path.

And how could that be, in such a wilderness, where the feet which came and went must be so few and far between?

Feet of men, of horses, yes, but what about other feet? Buffalo, for instance? Did their mighty multitudes never find their way from one slope of the ranges to another?

Assuredly, and their innumerable, endless trampings, year by year, had worn and beaten that narrow, hard, and at some points deeply sunken path, and had, at the same time, pointed .out for all future travellers the place where any other animal, biped or quadruped, could find a pass over the mountains.

Could they not have gone around that long spur, away there to the South?

A long detour, cañons and chasms beyond, a river beyond that, not always fordable and always dangerous, lay in that direction, and so the four-footed engineers had led their followers by a better and surer way. Trust them for that. The doctor knew enough to do so, and he struck into the buffalo path with a feeling of absolute certainty of the result.

No theologian, following the familiar rut of an ancient doctrine, could have been more complacently devoid of doubt as to the security of the road before him, however threateningly the opposing heights might seem to rise on either hand.

" Where they've tramped it we can follow " he

cheerily exclaimed, "and I'll see if I can't find a place where I can set up a stop-thief behind me. There must be more than one narrow track and sharp corner before we get onto the other slope."

No wonder he travelled leisurely, with such an idea in his head. But then he was no novice in mountain ways and warfare, and there was no law compelling him to leave that natural highway as passable as he found it.

It might have been as well, however, if he could have known just how long it had been since the last drove of buffaloes had plodded along that steep and winding ascent, and what had been the then condition of the track, and what the end of their journey.

That was one of the things he was to learn, before the day was over.

There were places as he rode along where distances might have been saved by shorter cuts, but there is no haste in the migration of a herd of bisons, and their trail followed natural curves and easy grades as accurately as a railway survey.

It would not do to risk possible loss of time in uncertain efforts to improve on their guidance, and the doctor steadily plodded on, now and then halting to breathe his horse and take a look behind him.

He could command, from one elevation after another, unobstructed views of a good deal of the ground he had passed over, and, for a couple of hours all his observations seemed to be encouraging.

"They may have struck it, but they can't be very close," he said to himself, after one long and careful scrutiny. "If they'll give me two or three hours more I won't care whether they follow or not. Hullo! What's that? The Apaches? And that close to me? They've done it. Well, it's as hard climbing for them as for me, and the pass is getting narrower, every reach we make. But I must push along."

The pass was indeed growing narrower, winding along the side of a treeless mass of granite, which rose for a thousand feet above him, in rugged grandeur, with a broken declivity below of almost equal depth, except where here and there some natural rift of the ledges led the trail between walls of rock on either hand.

In more than one of these latter the doctor paused a moment, as if studying its capacity for purposes of obstruction, but each time he hurried on again, to seek a gap of better promise.

It was not likely that he would have to climb much higher, but he had no doubt that his pursuers had been gaining on him. If so, to be sure, it must be at the expense of their ponies' wind, while his own animals showed as yet scarcely any tokens of fatigue.

A man of iron nerve and imperturbable coolness, was the doctor, and he needed all his steadiness of head and hand for the frightful path upon which he was now entering. So nearly perpendicular fell the sheer descent at his right, so narrow was the foothold between that sure destruction and the beetling cliff at his left. The Alps, the Appenines, our own Sierras, have many such giddy tracks to show, and the wonder is that human hearts can find the will to go over them with any less powerful incentive than death to drive.

The buffalo herds had made the passage, however, time out of mind, and therefore it must be safe.

But what about that last herd?

The doctor had just turned the corner of a projecting rock when he drew his rein with almost dangerous quickness, and his good horse stood still, shivering, and with the cold sweat streaming from his flanks.

The path was gone!

Some mighty mass, set free by frost and sun, had fallen from above and broken away at a blow not less than thirty feet in length of the narrow ledge.

The doctor looked dizzily down, and there, among the shattered fragments at the bottom of the precipice at his right, he could discern, heaped in white and bleaching confusion, uncounted bones and horns, as if all the bisons of the plains had come thither to die.

Not all of them, indeed, but vast must have been the numbers of the last drove which had tried that pass. And they had marched on in single file, each pressing closely on the heels of the brute before him, till they reached that fatal gap.

There could then be neither pause nor retreat, with the blind instinct of their nature urging them slowly on, and so the foremost bulls, the patriarchs of the plains, had gone bellowing down, and after them had been crowded their stupid followers, like human beings believing in a lie, till the last bison of the drove found himself unable to turn around on the narrow ledge. And he had stood and bellowed and pawed and trembled over the failure of his faith, till the faintness of starvation came upon him, and he too toppled helplessly over the remorseless edge.

There was not even room to dismount, apparently, and the doctor could already hear the whoops and yells of the foremost Apache warriors, as they urged their wearied and dripping ponies forward up the pass behind him.

In a few minutes, now, they would be upon him.

But what of that, when there could be as little return for them as for him from the awful trap whose jaws had received the horned multitude before them?

"The golden heart," he said, mournfully. "The golden heart of the continent."

CHAPTER XI.

A NEW DEPARTURE.

THERE was a great deal of good in Bessie Heron.

There always is in young women of that cast of mind, although it may seem to develop itself abnormally.

She had, among other excellent traits, that reverence for the " correct" which is sure to work out in a sense of order, a rigid orthodoxy, and a commendable degree of personal neatness.

She would have made a methodical and scrupulous housekeeper, it may be, but an unkind fate had denied her that field, and so she kept the narrow domain of her own wardrobe in a state of organized precision which admitted of almost an instantaneous change of base.

If Fred could have had his own way, the collection would have possessed more bulk and variety, and with it less celerity of mobilization. As it was, no default of her preparations prevented her being ready in ample time for the train which was to take her west, on the day following the receipt of her supplies.

She was a good sister, too, as all good women are, and she labored hard to find excuses, to Mrs. Baird and her husband, for Fred's non-appearance, at the house or the railway depot, to see her off.

Her apologies were necessarily conjectural, and were received as such, but it was impossible that they should all be complimentary to Fred, and for that very reason Bessie was fully entitled to the flood of tears with which she said good-bye to her kindly host and hostess.

It was too bad that they should have any reason for unpleasant surmises concerning her brother, but it was all his fault and not hers.

What would either of them have thought had they known that the scapegrace was even then on his way to "the Island," with a broken head, after a collision with the police?

As it was, when the conductor shouted "all aboard," the train moved on with its precious freight, and the wonder concerning Fred was fairly divided.

"A very excellent young woman," remarked Mr. Baird, as he gave his arm to his wife, and turned away. "But she is a good deal tried."

"So she is," said Mrs. Baird, a trifle sharply, "but what do you know about it?"

" Why, her brother—"

"Mr. Baird, I wish you would hunt him up. He sent her some money. I'd like to know what there is against him."

"Why, of course you could not expect her to tell."

"No, indeed I couldn't, that's a fact. I don't know as it's the hardest thing in the world to confess the sins of other people, though. Will you try and find him?"

"Find a needle in a haystack, my dear. Where am I to look for him?"

"She might have given me some address or other. I'll hunt up all I know and put it together. You might get the police to help you."

"He'd hardly thank me for that. If I knew some of his friends—"

"There's his brother. He must know something. Only I don't believe he knows much. He never sent his sister any money, that I know of. Too good, I suppose."

"Now, my dear, I must say you are making remarks."

"So I am. What do men know about women? Not but what I admire Miss Heron, but then I'd like to know what to think. It's too bad to be left in the dark, imagining all sorts of awful things, when they may not be just."

"Well, my dear, I'll hunt him up, or try to. It ought not to be impossible. By the way, there's one of the Tiloogoo missionaries—"

"Coming to board with us for awhile? Well, I'm almost glad of it. I'd like to see somebody that has done something, or tried to do it."

"O he's never been there, but he's going in a few weeks."

"That's all the same. He means to try and do something. I'll give him the room Miss Heron had. It's as neat as wax, I'll say that for her. She hasn't a fault in the world. I almost wish she had."

And so it was settled that Fred Heron was to be hunted for, but the chances of success were even poorer than good Mr. Baird himself imagined, and his faith would not have balanced the tiniest dwarf of a young mustard-seed.

And all the while Bessie, poor girl, was carried further and further from her brothers, and from one great army of her friends, and her crying-spell lasted her a long time.

She was exceedingly lonely, and she could but wonder why she had been singled out from the great world of human beings for a fate so hard and uncongenial.

So many good things came to others, on the right hand and on the left; homes, husbands, incomes, influence, friends, good brothers, wealth; while to her, without a single fault or error on her part, had been drifted only the dry and tasteless sand of an unsupported existence.

Such a text that was which came to comfort her, and when she came to the clause: "Of whom the world was not worthy," she said it aloud, and the smile on her face was one which would have done Mrs. Baird good—if not Mrs. Boyce.

The latter lady, at that moment, was not thinking of anybody's goodness, no, nor badness, but of how provoking it was that Mr. Brown should have been compelled to go down town so much earlier than usual, that morning.

Mabel Varick had been exceedingly glad to see Mrs. Boyce, and to tell her all about the burglars. The library window had been exhibited, with the broken bolt, and so had Mr. Brown's double-barrelled gun.

Prince himself had been called in for commendation, and when he yawned, probably from the effects of a sleepless night, he displayed such a sharklike range of teeth that Mrs. Boyce found her sympathies rapidly going over to the side of the man he had used them on.

"How he must have suffered!" she exclaimed.

"Not a bit," replied Mabel. "He isn't hurt at all. But they tried to poison him, and they'd have succeeded, but for a gentleman who saw them. Such a strange man."

"I didn't mean Prince—"

"Nor did I. He said he was a tramp, but Uncle Daniel says he is a gentleman of unusually good mind and education. His name is Heron. At least he said so."

"What, the burglar?"

"No, there were two of them, and we did not get their names. Uncle Daniel went down to the police court to appear against them. He will go from there to his office. He is almost excited about it, and that, you know, is a rare thing for him."

"Dear man! He is so cool and collected, always. Such admirable judgment. I value his advice above that of any other friend I have. I need it, to-day, too, my dear."

"He will be glad to give it, I know. But, Mrs. Boyce, how dare you live alone, the way you do, in that great house. Think of such men as came here last night. You have not even a dog."

"I've never thought of such things, my dear. Burglars are not the worst misfortunes that can come. But I must go, now. By the way, what did you say his name was?"

"Whose name?"

"The man that poisoned Prince."

"O you mean the gentleman tramp who took the meat away from him. Heron, Mrs. Boyce, and Prince drove him up a tree, and uncle found him there, and asked him in. It's a funny story, but I mustn't keep you now. I'm afraid it 'll be days and days before I feel like myself again."

Mrs. Boyce could have sympathized more completely than she cared to tell, before seeing Mr.
Brown himself, and she cut short her call with the
kindly haste which is allowable in an older person
and an intimate friend of the family. She had always been especially sweet on Mabel Varick, and
Mabel in turn had learned to consider her a very
lovable woman.

"So little understood by those who call her
worldly."

Mr. Brown himself had passed a morning of more
than a little annoyance. If there was one thing he
disliked more than another, it was newspaper noto-
riety, and here he was, now, with a dead certainty of
being published in connection with a "criminal
sensation."

He did his duty by the two prisoners, however,
and they were both bound over for trial, being
locked up in default of bail, and their coming sentence was likely to be a good deal of a matter of
form. Even the man who entered the window
could be so easily identified. He had upon him no
marks of having been arrested by Prince.

It was on his way down town that the thoughts
of the worthy merchant returned to the man to
whom he deemed himself in great measure indebted
for the safety of his household, and he grew decidedly anxious, as he turned the matter over, for another meeting with his eccentric benefactor.

"I wonder if he will call to-day? I hope he will. There's something worth saving in that man. I'm sure there is."

A remark which implied that, in the respect indicated, Mr. Frederick Heron was a species of exception. A piece of heathenism very prevalent among the most orthodox, and it is mainly caused by exceeding vagueness of idea as to what "saving" consists in. A pity, too, when one's cursory judgment may so readily err in an estimate of the relative value of souls. Precious stones will at times deceive experts, let alone the common run of dealers, and a soul—

Well, no man can tell how a soul will turn out, until it has been cut and ground and mounted, and even then it has to be shown in a good light. That of heaven, for instance, or a time of trial.

But whether or not Fred was one of the exceptional cases "worth saving," he did not make his appearance at Daniel Brown's office that day.

There were plenty of others who did, however, and among them was a very brisk and smiling gentleman, with a diamond pin and a confidentially husky voice. He did not interrupt anybody else, for he blandly waited some minutes in the main office, until his opportunity arrived for a solitary approach.

He did not see, therefore, the slight shade of annoyance on the merchant's face when his card was

laid on the desk in the little private business parlor.
If he had seen it, it is likely he would have opened
his budget in precisely the same tone of confident
expectation.

"Your usual contribution, of course?" he said,
after a brief exchange of preliminaries. "We must
begin early. Our foes are already in the field. A
sharp campaign before us, I assure you. We must
do our best, or the state and the nation will fall into
the hands of those—"

"But, Mr. Magrath, what are we to divide on, this
time? What's to be the platform?"

"Platform, Mr. Brown?" exclaimed the distinguished political manager, with astonishment rising
in his rosy face. "Platform? Why, sir, we shall
adhere to our time-honored and fundamental princi-
ples, without wavering or quavering. Every plank—"

"But, Mr. Magrath, what's the difference between
the two platforms? Ours and the other? I've read
them both, and I can't see."

"Difference, sir? The difference? Why, sir, it's
the difference between the two parties, sir. Between
fraud, treachery, corruption, false doctrine, on the
one side, and, on the other—"

"I know what's on the other, Mr. Magrath. At
least, before election. But how is it that we divide
up differently after election, say in Congress, from
what we do at the polls? I'm beginning to feel as
if I wanted to think matters over a little."

"You would not have us abandon our magnificent historic organization? You would not withdraw your support?"

"By no means, Mr. Magrath, a good body is a splendid thing, but how about the soul of it? I've a new idea at work in my head, and I hardly feel like paying out much money till I get it clear."

"Your contribution will be delayed, for the present, Mr. Brown?"

"I think it will—"

At that moment a card was laid before him and he remarked:

"Ah—indeed!—a lady, Mr. Magrath. You will have to excuse me. Not many lady visitors, you know, and even politics must give them precedence."

"O by all means. Certainly, I'd never,—of course, Mr. Brown. But then I must call again and explain matters. We really have the salvation of the country—"

"Yes, yes, Mr. Magrath, it needs a terrific amount of saving, just now. Never needed more. Good-morning."

And, as the discomfitted "wheel horse" of a great party bowed himself out of the merchant's parlor-office, another door opened, and an attentive clerk bowed in the exquisitely lady-like presence of the widow Boyce, with a smile on her face which grew more and more sad and confiding as she stepped forward.

CHAPTER XII.

A PRIME necessity of the case which the meddlesome police-surgeon had threatened to report was that the two offenders should be gotten out of the way.

The battered epileptic, consigned to the security of Potter's Field by way of the small-pox hospital, would make no audible complaint sooner than the Day of Judgment. His treatment had been based upon the prevailing official notion that either no such day is coming, or that the leading witnesses will not then put in an appearance. False teaching and superstition have put so indefinitely far away among doctrinal uncertainties an ordeal which is really so close at hand for every one of us. It is so hard for a man with a free club in his hand, and cruelty in his heart, to understand that the domain of time does not at all lap over into that of eternity, and that the narrow rules of the less do not control the operations of the greater. What awful sur-

112

prises must come, occasionally, to men who pound epileptics, and to some other kinds of men!

As for the man Rogers, he was well satisfied not to be known as "Fred Heron," when he was marched out of the police court, that morning. He shuddered as he entered the Black Maria, as the prison-van is called by those who know its name, but his emotion was misunderstood by the policeman who had just been saying something to him. It was not so much fear as disgust, and, after he had taken his place among the horrible collection of human wrecks within, he muttered to himself:

"Worse will come to me, eh, if I make any more noise after I get out? Then I'm afraid worse will have to come. That is, if I live through it. My head must be a pretty hard one, but it feels as if there was a mill in it, just now."

The receiving authorities of the "Island" were by no means neglectful of their duties, and Fred went, therefore, to a cot in the hospital, on his arrival. It was quite the customary thing with fresh consignments of disturbers of the peace, but it was the best that could have come to Fred, under the circumstances. It relieved him of a part, at least, of the unpleasant rigors of the place.

Sunlight, fresh air, silence, and a decent place to lie down and go crazy.

That was about all the prisoner could have asked for, that morning, and before long his delirium, aided

by the remaining effects of those last three grains, and
the blow on his head, sent him into a deep, troubled,
dreamy lethargy, in which there was hidden enough
of the healing medicine called sleep to do him a
world of good.

There must have been an unusual degree of re-
cuperative toughness in that much-abused organization of his.

The hospital surgeon, going his rounds among his
over-numerous patients, looked down on him, felt
his pulse, examined his heart, and said to the nurse :

"Let him sleep. It's the best he can do. I'll see
him again, to-morrow or next day."

A deal is necessarily left to nature in a great hospital, but she is a better physician in some disorders
than she is in others. She would do all the better
for a little help, sometimes. But Fred slept on, undisturbed, for hour after hour, and when at last he
awoke, there was a strange looking man, of middle
stature, standing beside him.

Long haired, with a pinched, pale face, and a seedy
coat of an old-fashioned, semi-clerical cut, there was
an expression in his watery blue eyes which partook
oddly of both benevolence and anxiety.

"Poor fellow. They'll do you good. Take them.
Here, I'll cut one in two. Eat it right away."

A withered little pair of hands had been fumbling
in his coat-tail pockets till they came out with three
lemons.

The sunlight from the window fell on the yellow fruit, and seemed to invest it with a kind of halo in the half-dazed eyes of Fred Heron, *alias* Rogers.

The cutting was quickly done, at the cost of dropping one lemon on the bed, and another on the floor, and while the stranger scrambled for the latter, Fred squeezed the sharp, delicious juice into his burning, foul-tasting mouth.

O how good it was, and how evident the purpose for which lemons had been created!

But Fred was not indulging in that kind of speculation just then.

"Thank you," he said. "Do you belong here?"

"Yes, I belong anywhere. Don't I know how you feel? I've been there. You was pretty bad? I'm almost glad of that. Tasted good, eh?"

"Wonderful. But what brings you here, with your lemons, if you don't regularly belong here?"

"Hunting, my dear fellow. Hunting—that's all. I do it for pay, and I may not get it, after all."

"Guess I can pay for three lemons, unless they've picked my pockets," remarked the puzzled patient.

"Not from you, my dear fellow, not from you. I run my own risk. I'd like to give a cup of cold water, or a lemon, or something, to one of Christ's little ones. There must be some of 'em left, somewhere, and I hunt for 'em in the hospitals and all over."

"You've missed it, this time," said Fred, half-mournfully. "I'm not a little one, and I don't belong to Him. You'd better take back these other lemons. Try some of the rest."

"I have. I begged a box of 'em yesterday, and these are the last. No, you keep 'em. His little ones are born so very small they don't always know it. I wouldn't say about you. I run my risk. Keep those and eat 'em by-and-by. He made 'em. Did you ever see Him?"

"See whom?"

"I mean Christ. Did you ever see Him? I did, once."

"And he told you to carry some lemons to folks in hospitals? It sounds like what I've heard about Him. I can think of Him, just now, with all His pockets full of lemons."

"Can you? Then I may have hit it, this time. If ever you meet Him, tell him I did it in His name, will you? There, I must go now, or I may lose my reward. I'm getting self-righteous every minute. Good-morning."

And the strange man hurried away, just as Fred was trying to gather his wits and ask:

"But where shall I find Him?"

Perhaps the stranger could not have given very intelligent directions. but it looked as if he were on or near the right track, himself.

Fred ate the other half of the lemon, put the two that were left under his pillow, and then arose with more of strength than he had expected, and

sat on the side of his bed, looking around on the
great room and its occupants.

Plenty of them, all males, and in every stage of
physical disability, but what struck Fred, was the
very good order and general neatness, while there
was such a seeming dearth of attendance. It almost looked as if the hospital was running itself.
Perhaps he did not dwell with sufficient force on
the fact that people who cannot get up are rarely
disposed to create any disturbance. and that this
was about the quietest ward of all.

He did not know that, but in a few minutes he
arose, with no man to hinder, and walked to one of
the windows. He could see other buildings, and
he knew enough of the locality to bring to his
mind's eye a picture of all he could not see.

" Prisons, hospitals, almshouses, insane asylums,
workhouses, a great piece of property like this, and
cords of others. Police, soldiers, courts, lawyers,
detectives, charities, Black Marias, a gallows, now
and then. What an enormous tax it all is. A
perfect mountain of gold thrown away, every year.
Why couldn't Congress pass a law, abolishing sin?
If there wasn't any sin, now! But then that would
never do. There wouldn't be any more, Congress.
The kind we have. Nor any lawyers, or police, or,—
no, it would never do. Too many people would be
thrown out of employment, and there'd be the worst
kind of a riot unless the law was repealed."

Fred's brain was not yet in the best of working order, and he felt now, in spite of the lemon, the growing pain of an awful craving within him.

He turned deadly pale as he felt it, for the thought came upon him that in this place he would be compelled to face it, once for all, without any possible palliation or escape.

The thought was maddening.

Could he live through it?

"That's just what I will do," he exclaimed aloud. "I can't get any here. Now's my best chance for a victory."

"O is that so? Can't you get any?"

A soft, clear, but tremulous and deeply-agitated voice, close to him, and it made him spin around on his feet in utter astonishment.

A lady, a young one, and well dressed, with a refined, intellectual face that many would have called handsome, if it had not been so pale. She seemed to be shaking from head to foot with a nervous tremor, and Fred could hardly help saying half-aloud:

"Delirium tremens!"

"No, sir, not quite that, but I could not stay in the woman's ward. It's right across the passage, yonder. It was easy to slip out. Did you say it was impossible to get any here?"

"Any what?"

"O anything. Seems to me I could drink whiskey, though brandy is what I always want when the fit comes on."

"Try a lemon, and then tell me about it."

"Are you one of the physicians? I haven't seen one yet. Not till I saw you."

Fred was cutting the lemon, and did not make any answer, but the young lady grasped the half he handed her with a feverish, thirsty eagerness.

"It is good for me. I know that by experience," she said. "How nice it is. But, O that I should come to this. I, Carrie Dillaye! I'm glad my mother is dead. What would Uncle Daniel say, now, and Mabel? I wouldn't dare to die, though. And yet I don't believe there is any, over there."

"A little flighty,' thought Fred, but he had not missed a word of her incoherent soliloquy.

"Try the other half, Miss Dillaye," he said, gently. "How did all this happen? When did you get here?"

"Yesterday morning, sir. I must have drank myself crazy, and then I don't know what happened. All I know is that I'm here. I haven't even told them what my name is. How do you know it? Did I ever see you before?"

"No, but what do you mean to do? Shall you write to Mr. Brown or Miss Varick?"

It had been a somewhat daring guess and venture, and Fred was taken all aback by the consequences.

Such a frightened, appealing, earnest gaze from those deep, sorrowful gray eyes, and then a lady kneeling at his feet in a storm of passionate weeping.

"No! no! A thousand times no! O sir, do not tell them of this disgrace. That I am on the Island. Indeed, sir, I have done nothing wrong. Not a single thing. Seems to me I did not even sin in taking the brandy. It was in me before I knew. I can't tell how it was. Don't let them know. It's only for twenty days. I can bear it."

Fred took her folded hands to raise her up, and just then one of those rare birds, a hospital assistant, came hurrying up to ascertain the meaning of it.

A female prisoner in that ward!

How could such a thing have happened?

As if it had never happened before!

"Silence, Miss Dillaye," whispered Fred. "I will keep your secret, and I will see you again. Take this lemon. You must go back, now. On no account take any stimulus."

And then he turned to the rapid questions of the nurse, not answering any of them, with:

"She had better have a soothing draught of some kind. There's been a mistake. Can't you see it? Be as respectful as you know how, or it will be the worse for you."

Something of authority in his voice and manner

had its effect on the natural born subordinate before him. Men who were made with a cringe in them quickly understand who is and who is not a proper object of their temporary tyranny, and the nurse obeyed with alacrity. A female assistant was called from the adjoining ward, and Caroline Dillaye was led back to her own quarters with a show of gentleness which owed something, even then, to the additional injunctions and imperative words of Fred Heron.

" If you're a doctor, sir," said the assistant, on his return, " I wish you'd lend us a hand. There's so many on leave, workin' up the primaries in their own wards, that we hain't men enough to feed 'em, let alone bandages and medicines. The surgeon, he's wild about it, but then he dasn't peep, you know."

"Guess I know enough to help you a little," replied Fred. " Fix this bandage of mine, will you, and give me an egg and a cup of coffee, and I'll see what I can do."

There are those who would have called it "cheek," but a better phrase would be, "Readiness to take advantage of circumstances."

When his own hurt was dressed, he quietly remarked:

"Thank you, but if I can't beat you at that I'll give up. Where'd you get your training?"

" Never had much. I was an iron-moulder before

I went into politics, and I most wish I was back at my trade, sometimes. On'y this 'ere's lighter work."

There were sufferers in that hospital whose needs called for defter and more delicate fingers than those of the ex-iron-moulder, and the latter openly expressed his admiration of the rapidity and skill with which his new helper did his work for him. He conformed to Fred's requirement about the coffee and eggs, and when the surgeon came around he made a fair report of the matter.

"Glad of it," replied the man of science, "but he must go to bed himself, now. He's worked up a fever with all you've put on him. How long's he in for?"

"Sixty days. Case of assault."

"I'll keep him here, then. He's no primaries to attend to. I wish the police would pick up a few more like him and send 'em over."

And yet all the skill Fred had displayed had been " picked up," for he was as devoid of regular professional training as if he had been appointed to that hospital for political services instead of resisting a policeman.

As the surgeon said, however:

" He's a gentleman, and well educated. He couldn't know less than the rest of 'em, if he should try. Seems to have a touch of humanity, too."

CHAPTER XIII.

SAVED BY A SACRIFICE—OLIVER ACCEPTS A CALL AS ASSISTANT.

OVER such a path as that had been, Dr. Milyng had led his pack pony by a precautionary length of lariat, and it had not yet brought his head around the corner of the cliff.

The horse, of course, bore no burden except his own trappings and the doctor.

Had the path behind been straight, or nearly so, a perfect horseman might have ventured to rein back, for a few yards, at least, but, as it was, the length of a man would bring him over the edge, at the curve.

Louder and clearer rang the yells and whoopings, up the pass from the rear, and the end was evidently drawing very near.

But the doctor's iron face took on no pallor, nor did his hand tremble as he lowered his repeating rifle and leaned it against the rock at his left.

His long knife was out next, and he cut the throat-latch of his bridle and the strap around the robe of skins behind him, on the crupper.

"Can't save the saddle," he said, "but I can do without that if I can keep the pony. Good-by, old horse; it isn't my fault. I never hated anything worse than this in all my life."

As he spoke, he lightly removed his feet from the stirrups, and in an instant he was down, wedged between his horse's side and the wall. The trembling beast braced himself as if he understood it all, but he had no foothold sufficient to bring his strength to bear.

Off came the bridle, and then, as if to add yet another triumph of nerve and pluck, the doctor seized the horn of the saddle and severed the surcingle at a blow.

"I'd give a ton of gold rather than do it, but I've no other chance," he muttered, hoarsely.

And then, with a sharp, despairing neigh of sudden agony and fear, the noble animal before him reared and went over into the abyss, while the conjurer's great robe of skins floated after him like the out-spread wings of a condor hovering over his prey.

There were drops of cold perspiration on the doctor's face, but he was lying flat on the narrow ledge, creeping along with his rifle in his hand.

The savage warriors had been but a short quarter of a mile away at that moment of terrible decision, and they saw enough of what had happened to bring them to a sudden halt.

A moment of silence, and then a shrill yell of exultation.

But after that there came to them an occasion for careful thinking, for their keen, practised eyes were searching the ravine, and the presence of those whitened bones explained the mystery to them in a moment.

Warned in time, but no more, for any further following would have brought them upon that track from which there was no return.

There was nothing there, now, to tempt them on, and even their curiosity gave way to a feeling of dread which had something closely akin to panic in it.

Weary as were their panting ponies, they wheeled in their tracks and fled along the pass as if they feared that at any moment it might give way beneath their feet.

It was Bad Medicine, the whole of it, and they felt assured that only a suitable fate had befallen the sacrilegious thief who had dared to carry away the sacred robe during the mystic slumbers of its owner.

The authority of the conjurer had received a tremendous lift, but he had not recovered his property.

Dr. Milyng lay and watched the retreating horsemen until the last one was out of sight, and then slowly arose to his feet. He had saved his arms and equipments, and the pony still carried his other valuables. But what was to be done about them and him?

The path was a trifle wider where the pony stood, and his own size, between fourteen and fifteen hands, was in favor of the doctor's next undertaking.

Carefully, slowly, with pats and caresses and reassuring words, the frightened animal was relieved of his burdens, and these were drawn forward out of his way.

Could any horse be backed for such a distance, over such a mere gangway?

Patience and strength and skill are great things, and the doctor had them all.

Foot by foot, rod after rod, until a spot was reached where the path widened into a little table of flat rock.

No room to spare, but if the pony would do his part it was a possibility, and the doctor slipped quickly past him.

Gentle pulls, plenty of time given for him to gather his feet under him, and then the doctor wanted to shout, for the pony's head was safely pointed down the pass.

For a little distance he led him on, till he reached a place where he could tether him, and then he returned again and again after his baggage. He did not leave a pound of it on the ledge, and he even sat down and repaired the saddle and bridle. He knew

that his enemies were using that time to get further
and further away from him.

The pony was laden but not mounted, and the
descent began. His master was not sure enough of
his training to risk his neck on him there and then.
Besides, it is even possible the doctor's nerves had
endured all they were capable of, that day.

"If I only had Oliver, now," he said to himself.
"He was the best animal for mountain work that
ever stood on four legs. I'll never get hold of such
another mule as long as I live."

Probably not, for Oliver was as much of an exceptional character among his kind as the mining
explorer was among his, and he was having his own
peculiar experiences, that day.

His sleep had been refreshing, and his breakfast
of dewy grass had been every way to his liking, but
he could not easily forget all he had learned concerning coyotes and their manner of life. He knew,
too, that in any further wanderings on that plain he
would be sure to fall in again with its various aboriginal inhabitants.

In short, he found himself longing for company,
and yet in dread of the sort he was most likely to
obtain.

Noon came and went, and Oliver moved forward
uneasily, sheering away as best he might from even
a group of buffaloes and an occasional deer.

None of them attempted to molest him, but at

last Oliver suddenly halted and shook his ears. There could be no mistaking the character of that short, yelping, vicious bark. He had felt sure they would come again, or others like them, and here they were. He had no heart for eating any more, just then, but trotted nervously forward, and it may be he thought of the buffalo bull, and wondered if he could already have been entirely eaten up.

It was a moment of great anxiety, but Oliver was travelling in the right direction, so far as his immediate safety was concerned, albeit he was running from one trouble into another.

The world is full of troubles, and here were more than a dozen of them, cantering across the prairie on their wiry mustangs, and ready to bring affliction to any created thing which might cross their path.

Oliver recognized them at a glance, and he was too much of a white man's mule to regard Apache warriors with unmixed complacency. He paused and hesitated for a moment, but a chorus of whoops informed him that the recognition had been mutual, and that it was now too late for him to take counsel with himself as to the policy he should pursue.

Similar information, if hearkened to in season, not unfrequently leads individuals with shorter ears than Oliver's to their wisest strokes of genius. That is, the world looks on and calls it genius, when the actor himself is growling: "Couldn't help it, you know."

It was of no use to run away, and therefore Oliver uttered a long, sonorous bray of peace, threw up his heels, and trotted straight towards the half-surprised line of yelling horsemen. He had no fear for his scalp, there being no treaty, nor any chance for one, between the mules and the Apaches.

He was hardly prepared for the immediate consequences, calmly as he submitted to them, for the tallest, fattest, heaviest of the tattooed and painted riders, dismounted from the undersized brute he had been killing, transferred his bridle to Oliver, and sprang on his back in token of asserted ownership.

It must be said that the Big Medicine looked better on an animal of Oliver's size and general dignity of appearance than on the wheezing dwarf he had abandoned. His pride returned to him as he urged his new servant to his paces, and his comrades looked on in glum doubt as to whether they should quietly surrender their claim to a share in such a prize. They knew that, although a mule may not have the speed of a mustang, such a specimen as that, with a little fattening, would trade for a dozen of their mottled quadrupeds. There seemed to be no help for it, however, so suddenly had the Big Medicine made his pre-emption. Besides, the fact of his recent loss was in his favor, and he was the "biggest Indian" of that squad.

And so, for the day was well spent and their hunt had been fairly successful, they wheeled in the direction of their camp, and Oliver's mind was relieved of any further anxiety on the wolf question. But he was in the hands of the aborigines, for all that.

That is, unless the cities whose ruins are to be found in that region were actually built by the hands of men, and if the race that built them found no other race there before them.

Perhaps the coyotes were the real and only aborigines, after all.

It was not a long march to the camp, and it led through the scattered remnants of the ancient town, many of which could have been turned into very fair stables for valuable live stock, now they were no longer needed for men.

There was no special occasion for glorification over the capture of one solitary stray mule, but the Big Medicine seemed to feel that the plaster for his wounded vanity ought to be exhibited in the village, and he rode right onward to where, in default of a tavern or a barber shop, the influential gossips of the dusky community were accustomed to gather. It was the inevitable parliament of those who are able or anxious to live on the labor of others, and to whom, therefore, the disposition of affairs is committed by those who do the work—stupid braves, squaws, and the like.

They were gathered in good force, for the expedition in search of the daring horse-thief had not returned, and it was necessary to guess when it would,

and if it would or would not be successful. Not
even the conjurer himself surmised, however, how
rare a feather for his own cap the absent warriors
would bring with them.

Still, he rode his new mule gallantly in before
the circle of admiring eyes, and it looked to them
a good deal as if their mystery man must have
dreamed to some purpose, after all.

A whoop, a sharp jerk at the reins, much sharper
than Oliver's mouth had been accustomed to, and
he halted with a promptness of obedience which did
him no end of credit.

In fact, he not only stopped as if he had been
shot, just as he reached the centre of the circle, but
he sat down, in polite imitation of the other chiefs
among whom he found himself.

It was admirably well done, but the Big Medicine
was not Dr. Milyng, and his horsemanship had
taught him no preparation for manœuvres of that
description. The whoop had hardly died away on
his lips, therefore, before he found himself rolling
on the ground behind the highly intelligent beast he
had come there to boast of.

For the second time within twenty-four hours the
conjurer had provided that gathering with occasion
for unlimited mirth, and he arose with a feeling that
if this was to go on his influence with his con-
gregation would be gone forever. At the same
time he discerned that any severity towards Oliver

would do him no good, and that there might be more in that mule than appeared on the surface. He therefore, when he regained his feet, advanced and reached out his hand as if to stroke the long ears. Instantly, for the sign had a meaning he had learned well in days by-gone, Oliver lay down at full length, as if dead.

A loud shout greeted the discovery that, at last, the Big Medicine had secured the services of a " medicine mule," and Oliver's reputation was made. He was free of the camp from that day forward, and neither coyotes nor mischievous little Indian boys would be permitted to molest him.

Whether his exalted character would exempt him from the duties of a burden bearer on long marches was yet a problem of the future, but it was glory enough for him, when he arose, not to be immediately remounted. On the contrary, he was conducted away from the assembly of the magnates with the degree of respect belonging to a stranger whose powers and qualities were as yet only guessed at by those who led him.

CHAPTER XIV.

WISE AS A SERPENT AND HARMLESS AS A DOVE.

WHEN Mr. Daniel Brown returned to his luxurious home, that afternoon, he carried across the threshold a face so clouded with anxiety that Mabel Varick exclaimed, on meeting him:

"O Uncle Daniel, what has happened? What is the matter?"

"Come with me into the library, my dear. I don't think I could eat any dinner till I've talked it over."

Mabel's face assumed at once that look of loving sympathy which is the best help in the world for a man who has troubles to talk about, for her good, kind uncle was the one being on whom her girlish affections as well as her reverence had centered themselves. He was worthy of it, every bit, and yet, if the particular trouble in hand had been strictly his own, it is quite possible he would have kept it to himself, much as he confided in his fair and right-minded niece.

The library table was the very thing to hold a council over, although it was more than usually cluttered that day. Books and maps were scattered over its surface, and the presence of the tray of quartz specimen-ores might have told a tale concerning one of Mabel's idle hours, if any one had been in a mood for studying such indications.

Mr. Brown was a very direct and simple sort of man, which may have been one secret of his success in business, and he was at once in the middle of his first subject.

"There's a good deal to tell, my dear. To begin with, your cousin Caroline has disappeared."

"Disappeared! Uncle?"

"Gone for two days, and no one seems to have a trace of her. You know the physicians declared her entirely cured of her mania for stimulus, and they had almost ceased to watch her movements. Still, I'm inclined to connect it with that."

"She's as good as good can be, Uncle Daniel. O poor Carrie! What can have become of her."

"Every means is being taken to find her. It can hardly be a question of suicide, however it may be of insanity. You know she has sometimes been quite violent in her fits of excitement."

"So gentle, too. To think of her inheriting a disease like that. And yet her father is a good man."

"And so was his father, except that he was pretty

wild when he was young. We can't go back of that with any certainty. I don't believe we understand these matters very well. We call things inherited for want of a better explanation."

"Do you think there is one?"

"I do not know. I've been thinking a great deal lately, and a good many things are less clear to me than they once seemed to be."

"Carrie's case has always been a mystery. It is now. I wish I could stop thinking about it."

"I can't. Besides, if I've been on the wrong track, all these years, I would like to know it. Do you know, I'd give something to ask that odd fellow— I don't like to call him a tramp—that Mr. Heron, what he thinks of such a case."

"What could he tell you?"

"Something from his own experience, it may be. Something better than guess-work. But I'll talk to you more about Carrie, by-and-by. It's too sad for anything, and I hardly know which way to turn."

"Why, uncle, are there any more misfortunes coming upon us?"

"Not on us, my dear, but on our friends. Mrs Boyce—"

"O Uncle Daniel, she was here this morning, to see you, and she hardly seemed like herself. She said she meant to go to your office."

"Well, she came, and she was there a long time.

I knew the firm of Boyce, Millington & Co. were in doubtful credit, but I'd no idea things were so bad."

" Have they failed?"

" They will to-morrow. And that is not the worst of it. They've been running on in a bankrupt condition for several years—even before Mr. Boyce died. They have tried to regain their lost foothold by speculation, and have only made matters worse. There is absolutely nothing left, and poor Mrs. Boyce will be stripped of all she has in the world. There has never been any settlement with her. Indeed, none could have been made, as I understand it."

" Will she lose her home?"

" Everything. The money she has been living on ought never to have been paid her, but the firm were afraid to curtail her expenses, for fear of injuring their credit. It is a very sad affair."

" But what can you do, Uncle Daniel?"

" Can not you do something, my dear?"

The idea in the benevolent mind of the merchant was a vague one, and he would hardly have wished to be the first to express it in words, but Mabel caught it and put it in shape at once, like the enthusiastic, warm-hearted girl that she was.

" May I ask her to come and visit with me, Uncle Daniel? I'm lonely sometimes, and I'm so young, to be all by myself."

"Take your carriage, after dinner, and go over
and see her. If she will come, she is welcome. Joe
Boyce and I were schoolmates, and I'd hardly like .
to see his widow without a house over her head, or
wherewithal to procure a meal of victuals."

"She's a very independent woman."

"I know she is, but then—"

"I know she has an immense respect for you, and
if I tell her it's your invitation as well as mine, I
feel sure she'll come."

"You may tell her anything you please, Mabel.
Come, now, let us go in to dinner."

"Did that Mr. Heron make his appearance to-
day, uncle?"

"No, my dear, and I half-hoped he would."

"He's another independent person, if I am any
judge of faces."

"He would not come to ask a favor of me, I am
sure of that. And yet I'd like to do him one, if
only for keeping old Prince from poisoning himself."

"So would I. Dear old Prince. He has been
the proudest dog you ever saw, all day."

And so they went into dinner, and Mr. Brown
found his appetite returning, now he had in a manner discharged his mind of its load. It was a brief
meal, however, for some things could not be dis-
cussed before the servants, and both uncle and
niece were anxious to be back in the library.

A lonelier meal than theirs had been that of

Mrs. Boyce, for she had taken it in her own room.

Already she had given warning to her servants, and all but two or three had been paid and dismissed.

"I don't know what the law is," she said to herself, "but they are poor, and the creditors of the firm are mostly rich. I shall be poor to-morrow, and I wouldn't like to be disappointed about my wages—if I ever earn any."

A sound spot in the mind and will of the charming widow, but for all that she had been planning a "situation" for herself.

Truth to tell, she had not been so ignorant as her husband's business partners imagined, of the true state of affairs, and if, when they objected to her drafts on them, she had insisted so strenuously and urged the necessities of her household as a ground for them, she had had her own notions as to how long those drafts would continue to be honored. That was the reason, too, why all the money so drawn had not slipped through her fingers, and why she was even now so much in the habit of recalling to mind the parable of the unjust steward.

Mrs. Boyce was not the sort of person to go into voluntary starvation, but she was all the better prepared to meet the impending crash because it did not come upon her as a surprise.

She had thought, planned, studied, and no part of her plans had been more carefully elaborated than her interview with Mr. Brown, that morning. She would have preferred the house, with Mabel within call, but she had made up her mind, afterwards, that the down-town office was just as well, if not better.

So dignified she had been, so carefully self-controlled, so business-like, in short, so wise as a serpent and so harmless as a dove, that Mr. Brown had heard her story in utter forgetfulness that the world contained serpents, and with an increasing pity for the undeserved misfortunes of its widowed doves.

"I think he will," she said to herself, as she poured out a second cup of tea. "I think Mabel will come into it at once. They'll never be willing to let me go after I am once settled in the family. But I must not let Mr. Brown know I've any money left. That would spoil it all. It isn't much, to be sure, but after the failure is all arranged I can make some disposition of it, so it will grow. I'm sure Millington and the rest have taken care of themselves, but not one of them will think of caring for me."

It was a time of peculiar anxiety, nevertheless, in spite of her confidence in the skill with which she had managed her campaign. The greatest generals must have their moments of doubt as to the battle's issue when they hear the rattle of the first firing along the skirmish line.

Patiently, over her tea, and not expecting any immediate tokens of success, the widow sat and studied the plans she had matured for her future, and the unflinching courage she was displaying was worthy of any man's admiration. She was no ordinary woman, and her wisdom merited success as much as any purely worldly wisdom ever can.

Faint and far away, from the lower part of the great house, came the tinkle of the front-door bell.

"Who can it be? O I will not receive any callers to-night, and I forgot to say so. Well, I don't care who it is, I'll send word that I am engaged. Martha—"

The door of her room was pushed gently open as she spoke, and she turned her head expecting to add her message, but the door-bell had been rung by a hand that did not intend to be pushed away.

"Mabel Varick! My dear girl, what does this mean? I'm glad to see you, but has anything happened? Your uncle?"

"He has told me all about it, Mrs. Boyce. I've just come to cry and to ask you to visit with me. Uncle Daniel said so, and he means every word of it."

"My dear, do you mean he has made up his mind to cry? Now, Mabel, sweet."

And the widow's arms were around her guest, for there were genuine tears in Mabel's eyes, and the widow had a heart of her own in spite of her worldly wisdom.

"Oh, no, he won't cry. I must do all of that. Don't you do any, please. But he wants you to come and take care of me for awhile. You'll come, won't you?"

"Why, Mabel, dear, not now. I could not come to-night."

"Can't you? I shall be so disappointed. I thought from what he said you had lost everything."

"So I have, dear, except the golden hearts of some of my friends. The house does not belong to me any more, nor the furniture, nor anything. Except, I suppose, my own wardrobe, and my jewelry. Mr. Brown tells me I've a right to keep all of that. I mean to be guided by him in everything."

"But you can see him better at our house. I've brought the carriage. Come, now. In the morning you can drive around and attend to matters. It's dreadful to leave you here, all alone, at such a time."

Mrs. Boyce had been thinking rapidly, and she saw that the iron was hot. It was therefore the time to strike, and she allowed herself to be over-persuaded. There might have been a mistake or a risk in not doing so, and Mabel had her own sweet, kind-hearted way.

CHAPTER XV.

BEARING ONE ANOTHER'S BURDENS.

THERE had been that in the previous experience of Fred Heron which gave him a trained capacity for adapting himself to circumstances, but for all that his feverish slumbers, during the succeeding twelve or fourteen hours, were disturbed by all sorts of mental phenomena. He awoke in the morning, a good deal refreshed, though still weak, and it required half an hour or so of thinking before he had quite mastered his peculiar surroundings.

It all came to him, at last, and by no means the least important of his new interests was his curiosity concerning his lady acquaintance of the previous afternoon. He arose and dressed himself with little difficulty, his control of his limbs improving with every use he made of them, and, by that time, Miller, the hospital assistant, made his appearance.

The surgeon's remarks were duly reported, and Miller added: "He'll fix it all for you. It'll be a

heap better, every way. You won't be turned in
with the rest of the crowd. You'll have better quarters and better rations. Plenty to do, perhaps—"

"O I won't mind that," interrupted Fred. "Any,
thing but idleness for me. I'm glad of a chance.
How about breakfast? I'll be ready to go to work,
after that."

The rules of the place were briefly explained to
him, and they were simple enough for any man's
comprehension. Breakfast was an affair for which
he would have to wait his turn. He felt no appetite, but he had an idea growing within him, and
it was very necessary to its carrying out that he
should eat and recover strength as fast as might be.

Food, too, was likely to be his best help against
that gnawing enemy within him, and constant occupation another nearly as good.

After awhile he ventured to ask a question or two
concerning the female ward, and Miller replied with
a grin:

"O you want to learn somethin' 'bout her, do ye?
Well, I'll make out to send ye in there on an errand
of some kind, by-and-by. She's a lady. There's
no mistaking that. Do you know 'bout her?"

"Ought not to be here at all. It's a stupid blunder of the police. They'd never have done it for
anything, if they'd known. She probably got away
from her friends, and was violent, that's all."

That was not all, nor did Fred so much as guess

what a providence had carried Miss Dillaye to the station-house and the Island, instead of leaving her in the hands of the demons who were surrounding her when her own excesses attracted the attention of the blind ministers of a blind justice.

Miller was as good as his word, and it was all the better for Fred's purpose that his " errand" was to the matron of the female ward.

A word in the private ear of that experienced individual. A suggestion concerning influential friends, wealth, position, good things to come, and he could afford to say with emphasis:

"She must be kept here, you know. Not turned in with the rest. It's an exceedingly delicate matter."

"I understand. Guess you can't teach me much. Do you want to see her?"

"Of course I do. And you must be careful she doesn't get hold of stimulus of any kind."

" Dipsomania. That's what they call it for rich people. Gin fever for common folks. Well, she's up and dressed. There she is, over yonder. Guess she sees you."

Fred approached in a straightforward, business manner, as became a hospital assistant, but the first word he heard was:

"O sir, you have not let them know? And yet I shall die if I cannot get away from here. Such things as I have heard and seen!"

"I am powerless to help you, except in one way. I am as much of a prisoner as you are."

"You? A prisoner? Why, you are a gentleman. Your head is hurt, I know, but then—"

"I haven't anything in the world I'm so proud of as I am of that bandage," said Fred, "but we won't talk about that, now. I must send word to your friends."

"Not to my father. O not to my father. I can never look him in the face again."

"To Mr. Brown, then, or Miss Varick. I think I shall do so, even without your permission."

"O sir, what shall I do?"

"Get out of this. Do you feel any return of your thirst?"

"Not so much, but it was dreadful last night. I don't know what I'd have done, but for that lemon."

"Then I guess it did come from Him, after all," muttered Fred, "and maybe He knew beforehand where it was going. I thought it could hardly have been meant for me."

"I don't quite understand you?"

"No more do I. The matron is waiting to speak to me. Keep as quiet as you can. I must go now."

And to the robust and all but masculine official, he said:

"I shall write to her friends, to-day. You won't be forgotten."

There was little more to be said but, somehow, it was three days before Mr. Brown received the letter Fred wrote on going back to his own ward.

There was enough for him to do there, for the exigencies of a great political party had rendered the corps of helpers exceptionally thin, at that juncture, but he had a trial in store for him that day.

The hospital dispensary, with its store of drugs of every description, was under the especial and very competent charge of the regular surgical and medical authorities of the institution and their more or less educated pupils and assistants. Fred soon found out that a line was drawn, after all, between the former and men of Miller's class, but he also discovered that if anything once got out of the dispensary, its chances for getting back again were small, indeed.

Somehow or other, too, a great many things did get out, and they were not always the precise articles covered by the written prescriptions, in every case.

There was a mystery in it, and one not to be solved by a "sixty-day man," on duty as a temporary nurse. Fred readily understood that there was no purpose of making things clear to him, but he was none the less startled when, that second afternoon, in the cot of a patient who had been unexpectedly removed, he found a small paper box labelled " P. Ophii. 2 gr.," and which contained a full

dozen of little round pellets. He felt morally sure
that no one of the hospital magnates had ordered
the issue of such a prescription, although it was not
impossible. At all events, he stuck the box in his
pocket, until he finished making up the cot.

When he mentioned it to Miller, the ex-iron-
moulder looked at him vaguely, and said:

"Well?"

"What am I to do with it?"

"I dunno. Eat it. We never minds them things.
If it's wuth anythin' it's your luck, and if it isn't,
why, tain't hard to get rid of a box o' pills."

"Then I can keep it?"

"Make a breastpin of it, if ye want to. We don't
watch no sweepin's here."

Little did Miller imagine the importance of what
he was saying, or how every nerve in Fred Heron's
body was quivering with eager appreciation of the
untold wealth contained in that little paper box.

Even the gnawing within him released its busy
teeth for a moment, as if in anticipation of better
things to come, and Fred felt a warm glow arising
in his pallid cheeks and forehead.

It was his, to do with as he chose.

His by the rules and customs of the hospital.

But what would he choose to do with it?

That was the question, and a tremendous question it was.

He was glad he had written concerning Caroline

Dillaye before this other matter came up. He could not have held a pen or spelled a word after that.

Even Miller wondered what was the matter with him, for it seemed as if the whole hospital did not contain work enough for him to do.

"Guess he must have a mighty big practice when he's out," muttered Miller, "and he's kind o' makin' up for it. He's the smartest feller we've had sent over since I've been here. Wonder what he'll do with them pills. He can't eat 'em. They'd kill him, sure."

There is no natural power in a box of pills to generate heat. No locomotive was ever run by means of a box of pills under the boiler. But, for all that, it seemed to Fred Heron as if the hottest thing he had ever heard of were burning and burning in his left vest-pocket.

Would he be able to stand it after sunset, and all through the night?

He could throw them away.

No, he could not. He felt that he could not, and that there would be no good in it, if he did. He had taken the pledge too often not to know how slender a thing is any sort of "dodge" in a struggle between a man and his appetites.

There was no definite shape or form, however, in the thoughts and purposes which came to him and went from him, and he was all in a mist, when, a little before sunset, he stood by the window near his own bed and looked dreamily out towards the great city.

"There it is," he muttered. "The city. And I cannot get there. I've no place there, if I could. I wonder if I'll ever have. There's another city somewhere. Even the old Norse heathens had heard of it, and they called it Asgard, and said that the good fighters would go there. Especially if they fell in battle. I'm not a good fighter. I'm being whipped, now, by a paper box of muddy-looking pills."

"Please, sir, if you'd only take it away from me."

The same soft, silvery, tremulous voice he had heard in that spot the previous afternoon, and, when he turned around, there was Miss Dillaye, with a strange flush in her face and a brightness in her eyes, holding out to him a small, flat flask of glass.

"I gave one of the nurses five dollars to bring it to me, but now I've had it in my hands I feel stronger. I can't give it up, but if you would take it away from me!"

"I'll do that, Miss Dillaye, but you must do something for me at the same time."

"If I can. Only don't wait too long. I can't wait."

"Feel in my vest-pocket, there. No, I'll hand it to you. I'm not so far gone as that. I'd rather hand it to you, of my own free will. I'll keep the flask."

"You won't drink it?"

"No, and you'll not eat the pills?"

"The nasty things. No, indeed, I feel so much better. All I ever need is a little help at the right time. I'm so glad you were here. Have you sent the word?"

"Yes, Miss Dillaye. I've written to Mr. Brown. But you must promise me one thing."

"What is that?"

"Never to tell Mr. Brown, or anybody else, that you saw me here."

"Certainly. But I'm glad I did see you here. I don't believe you are bad."

"Yes, I am, but I'll tell you how I came to be sent here."

And he did so, briefly and simply, not concealing anything, and Miss Dillaye's pale, refined face, took on a tinge of the most respectful admiration, by the time he finished his story. It did not go an an hour back of his interference with the policeman. She exclaimed:

"O sir, you are a kind of martyr."

"Only a sixty-day martyr. After that I shall be something else."

"I'm not even that. I can't tell you anything, except that I think something was born in me."

"To be thirsty?"

"Once in awhile. It had not come for a year, till the other day. It came so suddenly. Then I don't know what happened, after that. O here's the matron. You'll keep the flask?"

"Of course, and glad to. You won't have them bring you any more?"

"Not for the world. But O what shall I say when I see my father!"

The matron was inclined to be surly in her protest against so reckless a violation of rules, even by a privileged character, and Carrie was led back within her proper meets and bounds in a state of something like humiliation, but Fred Heron felt as if he had made a long march towards the City— the City of Asgard, where the gods live.

CHAPTER XVI.

THE SITUATION CHEERFULLY ACCEPTED BY MAN AND BEAST.

DR. MILYNG felt very positive that he would find no hostile presence in his way, as he retraced his steps down that winding and perilous pass, but he kept up the keenest and most cautious outlook. He did not intend to stumble into another trap, after his narrow escape from the one set for him by the buffalo drove.

"So much," he said, "for blindly following too old a trail. It was made too long ago. Led over the mountains well enough in those days. Everything gets played out in the course of time. Even a buffalo-path. But the mountains don't play out, and I've got to find my way across 'em, somehow. Sorry I had to throw away that horse, but there was no help for it. Glad the pony's a good one. I can manage with him after a fashion, but I'll have to foot it a good deal. Don't mind that. I can outwalk anything that ever went on four legs, except Oliver. What a mule he was. Wish I had

him now. He'd be worth a whole corral of mustangs."

No doubt of that, but the pony was plodding
along very patiently, and really looked well in the
trappings which he had fallen heir to. He even
seemed to take a kind of pride in them, as if he
had been promoted and felt the dignity of his new
shoulder-straps.

Still, they did not make a full-sized horse of him,
any more than an extra allowance of stars will
make a general out of a successful demagogue.

It was by no means pleasant to come out again on
the same side of the range, after all that toil and danger, but the doctor was compelled to content himself. And, after all, it was something to have
brought whole bones and his breath back from
such an adventure.

"The luck of the mine ought to be pretty well
used up, for awhile," he said to himself. "I'm
kind o' glad it came all in a heap and got beaten.
Now, if I make good time, it may not catch up with
me again before I get across the alkali plains. It
wouldn't, if it was any ordinary mine, but then,
that one—I must make the best kind of time."

Precisely what he meant, he might not have been
able to put in words, but it was a real and practical thing to him, nevertheless. As real as Napo-
leon's "star" was to him, or Cæsar's "fortune," or
any gambler's "run of luck."

Intangible, chimerical, fanciful, the creations of diseased or overheated imaginations, unworthy the serious consideration of scientific investigation, are all these puerile superstitions, but sometimes one turns from the positive chemist in his little shop, so sure of his "laws" and their operation, and thinks of Attila, Timour, Hannibal, and the rest, and wonders if the party in the shop has got it all.

If one has ever heard of Moses, Abraham, Paul, Daniel, and a few others of that sort, still another field is open to him, unless he is in fear of the derisive smile of the little man among the crucibles.

And he?—Well, he is ever as ready as an inch-worm to raise his derisive back and measure his infinite length of worm over anything and everything which he has decided is "immaterial."

But the doctor kept steadily on till he came to the place where he had turned into the ancient highway of the bisons.

Not a redskin was in sight, nor any other sign of danger, as he wheeled southward, but he turned and looked along the path which had cost him his day's work and his best horse, with the remark:

"There's just one thing I'd like to have some-body explain to me. All the droves took that trail, up to the one that was lost on it, and it's safe to bet that not another hoof has tried it from that day to this. Now, how did the rest of 'em get the secret? It beats me. I've known such things come

out in a good many ways. A fellow told me, once,
it was a good deal the same way with fish. I tell
you what, there's something talks to the animals
that don't and can't talk to men. Wish it would,
talk to my pony and tell him where we'd best try
and circumvent this spur."

He pushed onward, however, until the sun went
down, and he found a spring of water, as if he had
a good deal of confidence in the means of finding
his own way which were his birthright as a human
being.

Alone, with enemies behind him, if not before;
with a great and terrible wilderness to cross;
mountains, deserts, heat, hunger, thirst, fatigue, all
possible perils to be overcome. And yet the veteran
explorer did not lie awake an hour thinking about
them. They were to be met in their turn, as they
should come, not sooner, and the present demand
upon his resources was met as accurately as a bank
teller would have paid a recognized check. Not a
fraction more or less, and not a thought given to
the possible face of the next draft to come. Sufficient unto the day had been the evil thereof, and
the night was meant for rest, even to a man whom
the Apaches had so nearly driven over a precipice.

If he could but have known, for his comfort, that
his old friend Oliver had also overcome the difficulties of his situation!

And Oliver had certainly done so, and he availed

himself to the uttermost of a night of safety.

Not a coyote barked in his hearing, during all the slumberous hours, and when the sun again looked in upon him he was the first animal in that corral to mention the matter.

Any mule can bray, but there's as much odds in mules as in the traditional Connecticut deacons.

Oliver was not one of the smaller representatives of his kind, for his father had come from Spain and his mother had pulled a dray in her time.

From the latter he had inherited his bone and muscle, and, perhaps, his capacity for straight kicking, but from the former all the sonorous echoes of the Andalusian hills had come down to him.

At least, that camp of Apaches had never listened to such a reverberating *reveille* as rang among their scattered lodges within five minutes of the time when Oliver decided that he did not care to have another nap before breakfast.

The effect was electric, so to speak, and one too-ready brave found himself mounted on his pony, with a whoop half-way up his larynx, before he discovered the meaning of the strange alarm.

Then he also discovered that his pony was yet tethered, and that the bow in his hand would be of no manner of use until he should fit a string to it. So he dismounted and proceeded to give one of his squaws the beating required to keep her in good condition.

A grand bray was that, and a proud Indian was
the Big Medicine when he listened to it, but some
of the sager counsellors of the band shook their
heads doubtfully.

What if that clarion should ever be sounded at
the wrong time?

There was danger in it.

Still, a question of the sort could well be left to
that indefinite future which contains the solution
of so many other important problems.

What would the world do if it were compelled to
settle all its mules the first time it heard them
bray?

There is nothing more peaceful than an Indian
hunting camp, with braves enough to kill the game,
and squaws enough to do all the hard work afterwards. The natural relations of the sexes are nowhere else presented in so striking and picturesque
a light. What is called the "Chivalry of the Middle
Ages," the barbaric era of our own tribes, can nowhere else receive so complete an illustration.

The Big Medicine was not disposed to do much
hunting, and when he did go forth he preferred
some other bearer than Oliver. It would hardly
have answered to be sat down with in the middle of
a drove of bisons.

Besides, before the next sunset, the band of young
braves which had followed the trail of Dr. Milyng
returned with a full report of their doings and ob-

servations, and the Big Medicine was, thereupon, restored to all, and more than all he had lost in the reverence of his fellows.

He on his part was prepared to take the entire credit of what had happened, as fully as if he had himself driven the hapless drove of bisons through that pass and over the precipice, and had now induced Dr. Milyng to follow their example. He was not the man to hinder the faith of the wavering by any false modesty, and he was altogether ready to smoke himself into another dream, while the men he smoked for galloped around the grass and killed his meat for him.

What could civilization have done for such a man? Nothing, now all the sheepskins are used up.

CHAPTER XVII.

DISCOVERY OF A HOUSEHOLD TREASURE—CON-
FLICTING VIEWS CONCERNING A LOST SHEEP.

THE failure of the old firm of Boyce, Millington
& Co. surprised some people more than it did
others, but there were a good many to whom it was
a severe as well as a sudden blow. The business
had been a large one, and time had been when few
houses stood higher or had better connections, at
home and abroad.

The downfall was every way as complete as Mr.
Brown had intimated to Mabel Varick, but he did
not figure in the long list of creditors. His own
private counsel, however, speedily made his appearance as the especial representative of the widow
Boyce, and all concerned were free to admit that
her interests needed looking after.

There were even a good many expressions of
sympathy, as of right there should have been, for
a lady of her social standing and accustomed surroundings, so hopelessly reduced to penury.

Of course she was an innocent party, and nothing

159

could have been more satisfactory than the manner
in which she surrendered every atom of property in
her possession to the assignee. She even offered
to submit her neatly kept housekeeping books of
account, but an examination of these was gallantly
and considerately waived by the gentlemen creditors
of the ruined firm.

She was also permitted, by an unanimous vote,
to keep and reserve from her household effects—
the property of her late husband—a good many
articles which would not have brought any considerable sum at auction, but which, it was surmised,
might afterwards be of use to her, or might have
some special value from association.

Mr. Brown's attorney took care of all that, and
Mrs. Boyce herself attended to the selection and
removal of the list of articles specified.

You can always squeeze one more paper under
an india-rubber band, particularly when you have
only one band and there are a good many papers
lying around loose.

Nevertheless, Mrs. Boyce was a lady of the highest moral character and the strictest integrity. The
auctioneer testified to that when he came, afterwards, to make the sale, and found not a single article missing which was called for by his schedule,
and all things in excellent condition and order.

The schedule was copied from a list furnished
the assignee by Mrs. Boyce herself, and must there-

fore have been absolutely correct, but the auctioneer did not know all that.

The bankrupt widow went home with Mabel
Varick, that first night, and not only Mabel but
her uncle were compelled to admiration of the even-
tempered fortitude displayed by their unfortunate
guest.

Mabel began to speak of it, but was interrupted
with:

" Now, my dear, I did not come here to bring a
cloud with me. I certainly have not lost everything when such a home as this opens its doors to
receive me. I do not propose that my own life
shall be soured and spoiled, and I won't be mean
and selfish enough to make my friends uncomfortable."

The look Mr. Brown shot at his niece, across the
breakfast-table, at the end of Mrs. Boyce's remarks,
was as much as to say:

" There, my dear, there's a lesson for you. If
ever you lose your husband and your property, remember that."

And he might have added, if he had known
everything:

" There's nothing will help you do it well, like
about two years of getting ready. You won't mind
it more than an old tombstone, after two years'
daily contemplation."

Wise people do not show how much they really

mind their tribulations, and Mrs. Boyce dropped
into her niche in the household organism as perfectly as if it had been fitted to her by her own
dressmaker.   In less than a week it began to seem
as if there must have been something lacking in
that establishment before the widow came, and
surely would be if she should take it into her head
to go away.   This, too, in the very heat and worry
of her own affairs, and when she was by no means
neglecting them.   She had studied the campaign
she was now fighting, and the ground on which her
forces were moving was tolerably well known to
her.

That she was an accomplished woman, well educated and well read, was an understood thing, although she was not in the habit of forcing her
strong points on the attention of other people, but
who would have expected her to possess so intimate
an acquaintance with technical geology and miner-
alogy?

Not Mr. Daniel Brown, surely, and all the greater
was his astonishment at the critical examination
she gave, a few evenings after her arrival, to his
tray full of specimens.

"I've a bag of them at the office," he remarked,
after asking a good many questions which he himself could not have answered.   "I'll have them
sent up to-morrow.   Perhaps you can tell me something about them."

"Indeed, I may not. But I've paid pretty dearly for what little I know. Or others have for me. I cannot help thinking that if my advice had been taken, long ago, there would be fewer worthless mining shares among the assets of the firm."

"You disapprove of mining speculation, then?"

"Decidedly, Mr. Brown. I am opposed to all gambling. But even gold mining need not be speculation."

"I understand you, I think. Well, I've no notion of speculating, or of getting up bubble companies, but then a really good mine—"

"If you can find one?"

"I could never find one for myself, but I know a man who can."

"Where is he?"

"That's what I'm hoping to learn before long. He will turn up, one of these days, with a whole pocket full of mines."

"Better than these, I hope, then. And yet some of them are quite promising."

"You shall see the rest. I am in no manner of hurry about it. You have already earned a fee as an expert."

"Have I? That is splendid. Please let me earn as many as you can."

And Mr. Brown's keen senses recognized the laudable feeling of independence, and the desire to return a compensation for favors, which underlay the widow's request.

"She is a good deal more than earning her board," he thought. "She will be invaluable company for Mabel. Stir her mind up. I'm half glad the firm failed, for our sakes."

But Mrs. Boyce and her troubles and accomplishments were not the only matters of importance which pressed upon the mind of the merchant during those next few days.

He was alone in his office, about noon of the second, when a gentleman entered who had not taken the pains to send a card of announcement before him.

"Brother Dillaye? I had been both hoping and fearing to see you. Have you any news of poor Carrie?"

The visitor was a man of medium height, slender, well-proportioned, admirably well dressed, and did not seem to be above fifty years of age. His clean shaven face was almost cadaverous in its thinness, and its hard, resolute, haughty lines, revealed themselves with singular distinctness as he replied, in a steady, modulated voice:

"Nothing, Brother Brown. I doubt if we ever shall. To you, as a near connection, I am willing to say, I hope we never may."

"Mr. Dillaye?"

"I mean it. This is the last drop in the cup of

our disgrace. If I should find her, I could not take her back again."

"But what would you do?"

"I cannot say, just now. An asylum might answer, if far enough away, or if I could make it perpetual. My own house, never."

"What, not if you found her? Would you steel your heart against her misfortune? It is not her fault."

"How do you know that? Who made you a judge between me and my daughter?"

"Who made you a judge between her and God?"

"She is my daughter."

"And He is her Father, a good deal more certainly than He is yours, just now."

"I did not come here to be dictated to, Brother Brown."

"I'm very much in the habit of saying what I think, Mr. Dillaye. I wonder how much real search you've had made for her."

"Good-morning, Brother Brown. I think I may as well go. I can manage my family affairs without your help, I think."

"Good-morning, then, but I may as well say that the daughter of my wife's sister will not be sent to an asylum, if I find her, you to the contrary notwithstanding."

Curiously stiff and dignified had been the brief, formal exchange of views, as became men of their age and standing, who were family connections and officers of the same church, but it needed no special acumen to discern that there was small love lost between them, and that no very tender ties were severed when Mr. Dillaye so politely marched through the office doorway.

"The old flint," exclaimed the merchant, a moment later. "I hope I do him no injustice, but I'd like to know in what shape her mother's property is. I'll see, before many days. It's my turn to hunt for Carrie, now. I ought to have seen him before. But then I've been so busy, and he and I never did hitch teams. I'm glad it happened in my office rather than his. He can't say I interfered without a reason. I wouldn't like to stand in his shoes when God asks him what has become of his daughter. No, nor some other questions, either. Cain's case was nothing to it."

Mr. Brown's color had been improving, from the moment of Mr. Dillaye's entrance, and there was a good deal of red in it when he came to the mention of Cain.

It was not the first time, by many, that he had found himself called upon to criticise the exceedingly correct and respectable gentleman who had been his wife's sister's husband, and the blood may have been all ready to rise at the word.

Nothing was said about that interview in the home circle, not even to Mabel Varick, for it might well be that no news of Carrie would come, but there was as little sleep on the merchant's pillow, that night, as if he had been listening for the voice of Prince to announce another pair of burglars.

The third day passed without any special excitement, except a conference or two with sharp-eyed gentlemen whom nobody knew, but who, nevertheless, knew a great many other people. The detectives were set at work with a vision of good pay before them, and there was no telling what they might do.

On the following morning, before Mr. Brown left his house, the postman deposited at the door, among other things, a small, yellow envelope, which looked as if it might have been constructed for the purpose of containing " powders" of some sort.

It was addressed to the merchant himself, and he carelessly opened it, as a man will to whom many envelopes come, from day to day.

" Mabel! Mrs. Boyce!"

The exclamation was so sharply sudden that even the widow came very near upsetting her coffee, and Mabel arose from her seat.

" After breakfast, please," he added, in a calmer tone, "I will see you in the library."

" Mabel, your uncle means you."

" Both of you. I may need your advice, Mrs. Boyce."

It was well the postman did not reach that distant part of his route too early, or that breakfast would not have amounted to much.   As it was, so little of it remained to be eaten that its neglect was of small consequence.   They were all the sooner in the library.

"It's all in a word," said Mr. Brown.   "Carrie Dillaye is in the hospital on the Island, and we must get her out."

"On the Island, uncle?"

"Why, Mr. Brown!"

"I'll see my lawyer, at once.   Get ready, both of you.   I'll order the carriage.   Here's a matter, indeed.   We must observe the most utter secresy. Not even her father must know a word of it till she's safe under our own roof."

"Not even her father, uncle?"

"No, and I'll tell you why, as we drive along. Mrs. Boyce, your aid and counsel will be invaluable.   I'm not afraid to trust you with a family secret."

"My dear Mr. Brown—"

"Haste, now—it seems as if every minute were a week.   Her own sister's child.   Poor Carrie.   And yet, there's no name signed to the letter.   I can't understand it.   There's something under it all."

No doubt.   There always is.   But Mr. Brown's legal adviser was just the man to prevent that something from being made in any manner unpleasantly public.   What wires there were, he knew.

CHAPTER XVIII.

A THROUGH TRAIN AND ALL THROUGH A NIGHT.

BESSIE HERON reached the end of her journey in perfect safety. There had been, from the word "all aboard," something almost orthodox, whatever that may be, in the behavior of that train of cars, and Bessie felt that they were all doing their duty by her. Not a connection was missed, not a violation of the time-table occurred. If the latter had been a creed, settled by a majority in a "council," it could not have been more conscientiously adhered to.

And yet, not one of the benighted servants of the several railways the train passed over had a glimmer of an idea that all this was by reason of having for a passenger a young lady of such a high moral character and such exceptional deserts.

Bessie knew it, however. She had often noted similar things before, concerning cars and steamers and such things, when she was on board, and it was a great comfort, especially when members of her

169

own family, not to speak of short-sighted members of the same church, failed to appreciate her.

Nor is there any call for a laugh at Bessie's expense, just there.

The prevailing notion among too large a section of that part of humanity which assumes to be " good" is that God's providence, though generally correct, within limits, in its management of other people, is decidedly out, so far as they are concerned. Whether wilfully so or ignorantly, they are not always careful to state, but of their convictions in the premises there can be no manner of doubt. One of these days there will be a reckoning, they plainly intimate, and even if they shall then refuse to accept an apology they will get their back pay with interest.

Not so much as an adventure came to relieve the monotony of the long ride, until the afternoon of the second day, and Bessie had an ample opportunity for an historical review of her career as well as a prophetic summary of her future.

The past and the present could be summed up in one word.

They were in every respect and altogether " inadequate," and they had been made so by the lamentable short-comings of those who, if they had no regard for themselves, might at least have remembered, having been born under the same roof, what a treasure had been committed to their guardianship.

Where would she have laid the blame if Fred Heron and a few others had been drowned, or something, when she was yet in her teens?

Some people's relatives do get drowned early— but then the question of relative "goodness" remains to be settled, after all, and the argument amounts to nothing.

But that second afternoon was fruitful of one break to the prolonged dulness, and it came in the shape of a young man in spectacles and a white necktie.

He could hardly have told, without help from Bessie, just how it was he came to be seated opposite her, carrying on so delightful and improving a conversation. The names of mutual friends and acquaintances had fluttered to the surface, one after another, till he found his soul divided between a wonder as to who his fellow-traveller could be, and whether or no his collar were too disgracefully wilted.

He would have given a new pair of gloves to have known if there were any cinders on his face.

And yet he need not, for Bessie Heron would unquestionably have told him, if there had been.

Duties of that kind, whether of a spiritual or material nature, she never under any circumstances neglected.

But then he did not know Bessie Heron.

"May I ask if you are settled over a church?" she inquired, at last.

"Settled? Church?" he stammered, with a perceptible wilt now in his shirt-collar. "I'm not in the ministry, I'm in the grain trade. The one thing that troubles me about it is that our house sometimes takes a turn in whiskey. I don't mind pork, though I once had quite a prejudice about that—"

"Not in the ministry?" exclaimed Bessie. "Well, now! I felt sure of it. Have you not mistaken your vocation?"

"Perhaps I have, but it isn't always easy to tell, you know. I was unfortunate at college—"

"Tickets, please," interjected the conductor, and Bessie was doomed to hear no more, just then, of the course of events which had perverted the career of her railway acquaintance. She said to herself, however:

"Well, if he is not a minister he looks like one. What business has he to dress in that way, white tie and all? It's an imposition."

So it was. All that sort of thing is.

There were reasons for doubting, however, if Bessie would have received a correct account of the college misfortunes so vaguely referred to. They probably amounted, at the uttermost, to some stupid blunder or gross injustice on the part of a narrow-minded and misguided "faculty." Our institutions of learning rarely know what they are

about, but now and then they do a good thing for
the grain trade, and other lines of commerce and
industry.

Bessie Heron reached her journey's end in safety,
and was most hospitably received, in accordance
with the invitation she had applied for, but all that
while, Fred had been devoting himself to his duties
as hospital assistant's assistant, over there on the
Island.

A very unsatisfactory way for a man to spend
his precious time, no doubt, but it was not at all a
bad thing for the crowded and half-cared for in-
valids, for Fred continued to take hold with a singular and most unselfish energy.

It did not seem to matter to him whether he
were sick or well, although the effects of his interference with the roundsman's club had not by any
means departed.

"Let her ache," he muttered to himself, as he
passed from one cot to another. "There don't
seem to be any chance here for the little ones that
fellow spoke of, unless they're too small to be seen,
but I may as well take my chances for these sixty
days. They won't be so long, anyhow."

Dreadfully long they were, nevertheless, and
Fred had that within him which made them longer.
It was not so hard, nearly, when he was on duty,
and as busy as a lobby member in the last week of
a "long session," but the tug came during the in-

terminable hours when he was supposed to be asleep.

It was never entirely dark in the great room, but, at times, there was just light enough left to see all the shapes that were not there.

A strange population is that, in any room. For instance, in a church while funeral services are going on, and the handkerchiefs pressed hard against aching eyes prevent the use of any but interior sight.

Fred Heron knew all about that, and some such experiences came back to him, while he lay there. Particularly one, where the sweetfaced woman in the coffin, before the pulpit, yonder, wore a smile on her dead lips. They had always worn a smile for him, so long as the soul was in them, from the earliest day he could remember. He hoped nobody would tell her where he was now, or, if they did, they would explain how he came there.

He could remember once, when he was a little fellow, coming home with blackened eyes and a bloody nose from a fight he had in defending a cripple, and his mother hugged him instead of scolding him.

"I'd as lief as not tell her all about it," he said to himself. "She was an angel, then, and she must feel a good deal the same way now, about some things. I'd tell her, anyhow. But how queer all the cots look, with the sick folk in them. And

every body of them has a soul in it, they say, only
no one seems able to explain what they mean by
a soul. Suppose, now, some of these fellows
haven't any? I've got one, I know that. I can
feel it, now, as I lie here. That isn't correct,
either. I don't mean I have one. I mean I am
one."

And as that thought took possession of him, he
seemed to become a little more the master of his
vulture-like internal craving, but the shadowy area
around and above him was less and less of a
solitude.

Physicians who have studied the effects of various narcotics tell strange stories of their observations. Things incredible, but for the high character and pure motives of the narrators, and for the
scientific bearing of the data so gathered. The
longer Fred Heron lay and looked, that night, the
more distinctly he seemed to see, although not a
solitary gas-jet was increased above the dull blue
glimmer of the midnight watch.

At last his attention seemed to concentrate itself, without any will of his, upon a narrow bed, at
some little distance, where lay a prisoner whose exact condition and requirements had been a puzzle
to the hospital authorities.

" He could not move an inch when I left him.
Was he shamming? He seems to be rising, now.
Delirious? No, he had no fever. And how comes

it that he's all dressed? What's that? A Prussian army uniform! Where did he get it, and all those medals and decorations? Standing on the cot and looking down at it, I declare. Where's the man on duty. If he can't keep a better lookout, I'll attend to it myself. Hallo, where's he gone?"

Fred was on his feet, now, but all things around him were in so deep a shadow that, but for the whiteness of the couches, he could hardly have made his way among them.

He did, however, as rapidly as he could, and with a feeling creeping over him which he did not remember to have had before.

It was nearly half a minute until he stood by that particular cot.

There was a head on the pillow, a massive, well-made head, such as belongs to a grand physique, but Fred half doubted if there were any body for it, under the coverlet.

So he slipped his hand under the bed clothes and passed it across the iron ribs of the body till it stopped, suddenly, of itself. It was just over the heart, and there was no need for it to go any further.

The broad chest had forever ceased to rise and fall, and the heart to beat.

Fred withdrew his hand and walked softly to the other end of the ward.

In a few minutes afterwards a rough voice aroused the surgeon in charge.

"No. 18's dead, sir."

"Dead? When did he die?"

"Just now, sir, all of a sudden, like."

"Heart disease, eh? I thought so, this afternoon. I'll be there in a minute." And then, as he slowly arose, he added: "Dead. Well, there are those who will be sorry, and those who will be glad. For once the extradition treaty has been fairly beaten. But I'll have a report to make, and there'll be no end of bother."

Fred Heron had done his duty, and, somehow, when he returned to his own couch, he speedily fell fast asleep, and not so much as a dream disturbed him till morning.

He needed all the rest he could get, and Miller had to shake him more than once before he could be made to understand that he was "a man under authority," from whom obedience and prompt service were required by those into whose hands he had fallen.

"Another day?" he said. "Well, and then I suppose there will be another night to follow it."

Day it was, but all the sunlight of it failed to make clear for him his experience of the previous night.

"What did I see?" He asked himself, again and again. "How do I know I saw anything? Was it a ghost? No, I don't believe in ghosts. Besides, I know what's the matter with me. It isn't as if my brain and nerves were in good order. I saw a good many other things I know were not there. He wasn't there, either. But that's the very thing that puzzles me. He was dead. And what's that, I'd like to know? Pity I can't ask some such man as Tyndall, now, or Huxley, and have it all explained in a twinkling. How those fellows have delivered the world from superstition. There isn't a grain in me. I mean of superstition. No, nor of anything else, and I'm glad of that."

CHAPTER XIX.

TRAVELING EXPENSES AND A VERY EXPENSIVE JOURNEY.

A MAN of Dr. Milyng's experience, thoroughly well acquainted with the manners and customs of mountains, was not likely to be long in finding his way across any given range. It was of little use for them, the mountains, to rise and station themselves across his intended path, with their elbows touching. He was well aware, however, that the force of discipline and long habit would make them keep their ranks in that precise order, like Russian infantry, until he should have more than time for bringing his pony and its precious freight through and beyond them.

There they stood, when he reached the easterly slopes, only they seemed to have faced about, and to be frowning down upon him, as if they would have said:

"You have done it. We are not unwilling. But here we stand, now, between you and your wonder-

179

ful mine. You will never repass us, and beyond
you are the deserts."

A good distance beyond him, as yet, and the immediate vicinity was rich in pasture-valleys where
the abundance of game suggested the propriety of
laying in an ample supply of "jerked meat," before
he struck out into the arid solitudes beyond. Nor
was he the man to disregard so plain a dictate of
prudence.

Of course, the hunting and the other operations
consumed time, days and days of it, but there was
no help for it, and the doctor's solitary explorations,
in the performance of his duties, brought him something more than dried venison.

"I can't afford to load myself down with it," he
said, after a hard day's work in the bottom of a
sandy ravine, "but some of the pockets are first
rate, and I'll need a little ready money when I get
to the settlements. It can't be there are many
placers, here away, but this is a good one. There's
pay-dirt enough for a season's work, with a sluice.
If I had supplies I'd stay here for a month. It'd all
be so much capital towards working the other mine."

That's the way of it. All our best windfalls in
life are apt to be treated in precisely that way.
They are only regarded as so much "capital for
working that other mine." And, nine times out of
ten, that other mine had a great deal better be left
unworked, so far as we are concerned.

But the doctor was not now going through his first "placer" campaign, and his judgment as to the value of the "claim" he had struck was likely to be correct. He would wash, therefore, and sift, and dig around, until he had laid in his expense-money, against his return to civilization, and then he would pack his pony and move on. So he did, and the pony himself seemed to consider it in the light of a desirable summer vacation, and grew fat and frolicsome, up to the very day when he resumed his load. Then, indeed, he discovered that his master had not been idle, and that provisions and other things are subject to the tyrannical law of gravitation.

Even now, however, the doctor was in no wise disposed to exhaust either himself or his horse by too long and rapid marches.

"We'll have to call on all we've got in us, by-and-by," he remarked, "and we might as well keep a good stock on hand. Those two antelope skins'll hold water fairly well, now, but if I take on any more load I'll use up the pony."

It was now about ten days since he left the mountain ranges behind him, and, for the last three, the ravines in which he found water enough to camp by had been separated by long reaches of hot desert, almost devoid of either vegetable or animal life. Still, he had been able to take very good care of his pony, and that sagacious animal had reciprocated by a degree of docility which might easily have been educated and ripened into affectionate obedience.

"Muddy, but sweet," was the doctor's comment upon what was left of the pool he was preparing to leave, one of those mornings. "Reckon I might as well fill up my skins. There's no telling what the next drink'll be sweetened with."

But the "next drink" did not come in the way of that day's journeying, nor of the next, and the slender provision he had been able to lay in had to be husbanded with the utmost care.

A man is better than a horse, for he can endure thirst better, and the pony's wants were invariably cared for before those of his master. He was permitted to avail himself of every eatable bunch of grass, and every possible moment of rest, and his parched mouth was washed out with fluid for which every corner of the human organization in charge of him was clamoring.

"It isn't so much mercy as it is selfishness," remarked the doctor. "If I can manage to keep him on his feet for twenty-four hours more we're pretty safe to strike water of some kind, even at this season."

Very possibly his four-footed friend only partly comprehended him, but he took his allowance, and whinnied pitifully for more. A proper knowledge of his "rights" might have induced the latter to "strike," or even to trample out whatever water was left in the skin-bottle, but he was too much of a brute for any such exhibition of lower-class intelligence, and the thirsty march went on.

Towards the close of that third day, however, Dr. Milyng's own eyes began to brighten over sundry indications which he discerned in the distant horizon, and he turned to say, in a voice which was husky with heat, fatigue, and a thirst-swollen tongue :

"One more pull, old fellow. It can't be more'n fifteen or twenty miles, now. We'll strike it before midnight."

But the pony halted by the side of a withered sage-bush, and stood panting with outstretched head, and bloodshot eyes, in the hot sun.

"Come to that, has it? I've been afraid of it, all day. There's only one thing to do, for I can't give ye up."

Every ounce of load was promptly removed from the pony and stacked under the sage-bush. The end of the long lariat was fastened to the latter. And then the last pint of water was squeezed down the throat of the worn-out pony.

"Best I can do, old fellow. If I ain't mistaken I'll be back for ye before morning."

Somewhat relieved and refreshed although he might be, the hardy and faithful animal seemed to comprehend that he was to be left alone, and looked after the retreating steps of his master with a mournful, reproaching neigh.

The doctor took with him no ores, no gold, no provisions. Only his weapons and one of the antelope-skin water-bottles on which he had expended so much tallow and ingenuity. He had suffered more than a little, in that long test of endurance, but he strode away towards the sunrise with an elasticity and rapidity which could hardly have been expected.

That is, not from any ordinary man or under any ordinary circumstances, but the doctor was no ordinary man, and a walk for life can scarcely be termed an ordinary circumstance.

Mile after mile of sand and gravel, with here and there a sage-bush or a dismal acacia, with patches of soil interspersed that were whitened with alkaline salts, and then the sun went down behind him, but still the doctor kept up that steady, unfaltering gait.

The moon came up, hot and red, and then the doctor could not keep his resolute mouth shut any longer. If he did any soliloquizing the sound of his voice was lost in the harsh rattle of his dry breath.

A tough pull, but he had had precisely such an experience before, and he did not seem to yield, for an instant, to the manifest horrors of his situation. If there was any of the thing called faith in his mental operations it was of that strong, unconscious kind, which does not throw its vitality away on disabling doubts.

Forward, till the moon was high in heaven, and then, at last, the doctor stumbled.

"Bunch grass, eh?" he whispered. " Now, that's good. What's that ahead?"

He regained his feet, with an effort, and pushed forward for a couple of hundred yards.

Willows. A clump of them. Sumach bushes. Some young cottonwoods. Short grass. A ravine. Tall, bright, fresh blue grass. Hurrah, the bed of a water-course, with standing pools at intervals! He knew that the desert, or the worst of it, lay behind him, and a hope of life before.

He had kindled no fire for days, and it might be dangerous now, but when he arose from his first long, delicious draught of that yellow water, there stood before him, on a knoll scarce thirty paces distant, a shape which brought his rifle to his shoulder, as if without his volition.

"Splendid buck," he muttered, a moment later. " I must have a square meal before I take the back track."

A fire was built, therefore, and the venison was cooked and eaten—all that one man could eat. The rest was swung up to the lower branch of a cottonwood.

A long sleep now, as a matter of course?

It would have been for some men, but Dr. Milyng was at work in the blue grass with his long knife.

Men do not eat grass, but he did not rest until

he had cut and tied up quite a bundle of the forage, and then he procceded to fill his "bottle." A good deal of a load they would make for weary shoulders, but the bottle and the grass were lifted unflinch-ingly, and once more the man of iron turned his footsteps westward.

Slower, now, for he had to follow the trail he had made and marked, and not many white men could have done that, even in broad daylight.

To miss it would be serious, indeed, but he had no notion of missing it.

All distances are longer, too, to a hungry and thirsty man, than to the same pedestrian after a hearty meal. Even the forage and the water did not cover the difference.

Still, the night was far spent when the doctor once more stood beside the sage-bush to which he had tethered his pony.

"Not any too soon," he muttered. "He's lying down. I'll have to work carefully with him."

And so he did, for hours.

Water and rubbing. A handful of grass, and some more water. More rubbing, and then the pony got upon his feet and took some more water. Then he lay down for awhile and considered the matter, and seemed to think well of it, for he got up again of his own accord and whinnied for re-freshments. A careful process it was, but by the arrival of daylight the doctor declared:

"He's safe to stand it now, but I'll give him a day's rest when we get there. He's a good one."

The pony was compelled to resume his load, but he stood fairly well under it and plodded on without a stagger until he planted his own happy hoofs among the blue grass at the border of the pool and took a long, sweet draught in his own way.

But the doctor made another attack on the venison, and then picked out a shady spot among the bushes and lay down.

After such a strain as that had been, sleep had to come, peril or no peril, and for twelve long hours the weary veteran was as much at the mercy of all comers as if he had taken a smoke with the Big Medicine of the Apaches. Even the pony's precious burden lay unprotected on the grass, and that hardy animal solaced himself for the trouble it had caused him by giving it as wide a berth as possible in his pasturing. To tell the truth, a civilized horse, unaccustomed to that kind of vicissitude, would hardly have survived the amount of feeding and watering he did before his master woke up.

CHAPTER XX.

WHEN Mr. Daniel Brown ordered his carriage for that errand of mercy, with Mrs. Boyce and Mabel Varick to bear him company, his ideas of what he had better do in the premises were somewhat vague. In fact, the more he examined them, the more dim and undecided was the shape they assumed, and he said so.

"But, Mr. Brown," remarked the widow, "I thought we were to go to your legal adviser, first?"

"And so we are."

"Well, won't he be very likely to know how it is best to proceed?"

"I suppose so. He'll recommend something. They always do. But then we'll have to decide, after all."

In any ordinary business matter Mr. Brown was

188

just the man to disgust his "counsel" by deciding for himself, instead of agreeing with them, but for once he discovered that the situation was master of him.

A sharp-eyed, well-fed, resolute little man, was Mr. Allyn, when he smiled around the little circle of his distinguished visitors, that morning, and he seemed to take the deepest interest in the case presented, but when Mr. Brown inquired:

"That's the whole sad story, Mr. Allyn, how are we to get over there?" he quietly responded:

"Riotous and disorderly conduct is the surest way, my dear sir."

"But we must see her at once. It isn't a matter to be trifled with."

"Please do not mistake me, my dear sir, but you surely do not think of going over, yourselves, you three?"

"Certainly. We cannot do less. May I ask, why not?"

"Because you would thereby defeat the very object I suppose you to have in view."

"How do you mean?"

"By, in the first place, making sure of the most disagreeable publicity. It would be in all the papers. In the second place, I fear you would prevent my securing Miss Dillaye's immediate release."

"I do not see that. It's an outrage. A gross outrage. I'm not without influence, Mr. Allyn—"

"Can you bring it to bear without stating your case to some one, or perhaps to a number?"

"Ah—well—no—I suppose not."

"What if I say then, that no sort of influence, such as you can wield, is required, and that, of the kind which is required, there are saloon-keepers and dog-fanciers who have twice as much as you. Not to speak of humble members of the bar."

"Such as yourself?"

"By no means, but such as I shall retain, with your permission. Please write me a letter, of introduction and so forth, to Miss Dillaye, and I will guarantee her prompt release and delivery at your house."

"But can we not meet her, at some place?"

"On this side of the river, my dear sir. Your carriage can be in waiting at two o'clock, this afternoon."

"But can you not explain?"

"Not till I know more myself. I shall do nothing improper, you may be very sure of that."

"Mrs. Boyce," remarked Mr. Brown, "what do you say?"

"Why, Mr. Brown, Mr. Allyn certainly knows more about it than I do. I should not dream of trying to improve on his advice."

"O uncle," exclaimed Mabel, "it surely is the better way. I will come down with the carriage and wait for her."

"So will I, then. Beg your pardon, Mr. Allyn, but I believe I have got myself excited over this matter."

"No wonder," replied the lawyer, "but men of our profession have to avoid that. Our first lesson is to keep cool. If we fail to learn that, our other lessons do not amount to much. I will telegraph in a couple of hours or so, where you had better wait for us. I do not think you will be disappointed."

Very politely he bowed them out, but they were hardly gone when he sat back in his office-chair with a dry little chuckle.

"Pretty kettle of fish he'd have made of it. Stirred up the courts and the city departments. Made a big row. Got the reporters after him for a week. Shouldn't wonder if the whole family had their portraits in the illustrated weeklies. The poor girl never'd have heard the end of it. Get her out? Of course I can. They'll be only too glad to have it done without any unpleasant fuss. They've too many awkward things on their calendar already to be hungry for another just now."

Mr. Brown had not neglected, before departing, to pen a hasty note of "authority" to Carrie Dillaye, and, armed with this, Mr. Allyn put on his hat and sallied forth. To do him justice, he was quite willing to let other matters look out for themselves while he devoted himself to such an errand as he had now in hand.

There were not many "wires" to be pulled, or
at least it did not require any more time to pull
them than Mr. Allyn had given himself, and the
promised telegram was duly sent and received.

A little to Mr. Brown's surprise, Mrs. Boyce decidedly declined making one of the party for the
second trip.

" I've thought it over," she said, "and I am sure
Miss Dillaye would rather meet no one but you
and Mabel, under such disagreeable circumstances.
Especially if she is ill or nervous it will be better
so. I will have everything ready here when you
return."

And after Mr. Brown was in the carriage he said
to Mabel:

"What good common sense Mrs. Boyce has.
Genuine delicacy. I can see that her decision was
a wise one, but most women would have come right
along, without thinking."

· Mabel assented, but she did not seem disposed to
talk much. Probably she was thinking and feeling
too deeply about her cousin Carrie.

She could not, of course, have helped admiring
Mrs. Boyce.

It was about half-past one o'clock of that day
that Fred Heron, after struggling desperately with
the restless spirit which possessed him, took it into
his head to manœuvre for an errand to the female
ward of the hospital. He was anxions to have a

word with the matron, but he was not very clear as to what he wanted to say to her.

It must have been something about Carrie Dillaye, for no sooner had he crossed the supposed-to-be impassable boundary of that section of the sick-prison than he looked quickly around for his acquaintance.

He searched in every direction, but he found her not.

Could she have been taken down sick again? Or could anything have happened to her? Could she have been removed to the common ward?

He knew there were traditions of dreadful things connected with the history of that noble institution, and all he had heard, and more, came trooping through his mind as he looked, and looked in vain.

It was the matron's voice at his elbow, as hard and as harsh as ever.

"It's all right, Rogers. She's been gone these ten minutes. They came down fairly well, but I expect you to look out for me a little when your own turn comes."

"Gone?" exclaimed Fred.

"Yes, didn't you know they were coming? The lawyers? Mum's the word, though, for they're awful nice about it. What's her real name, any way? The one she gave me was Dillaye. Of course that's a blind."

"Blindest sort," replied Fred, "but I can't give you any other, not without lying."

"You can't, eh? Well, I don't care. One's as good as another. I hain't got much curiosity, no-how."

But Fred Heron went back to his own limits, with a great buzz of doubt in his head.

Had the right parties come for Carrie Dillaye? Was there no fraud about it?

He would have been glad to be sure about that, and it half-way seemed as if she ought to have sent for him before going.

And yet, why should she?

What was the hospital assistant, that she should remember him in such a moment of excitement as that in which Mr. Allyn handed her Mr. Brown's note, and said he had come to take her away.

"Home?" she had said. "My father?"

"I've not seen him, Miss Dillaye, but Mr. Brown's own carriage will be waiting for you. I believe he means to take you to his house."

"O I'm so thankful! But nobody will see me? Nobody will know?"

"Only Mr. Clark, here, and myself. You can trust our prudence, Miss Dillaye. Shall we not go at once? The boat is ready for us."

And so it was. Not a ferry-boat, nor yet the "tug" which plied between the Island and the shore, at useful intervals, but a good-sized yawl, manned by four oarsmen who seemed very decent fellows for convicts, and commanded by an official whose face struck Carrie Dillaye, if not the lawyers, as decidedly the worst one on board.

So difficult it is to judge by a man's face whether he should be in prison in one capacity or in another.

A sweep of the oars, and the boat darted away from the landing into the strong rush of the tide, which instantly called for all the muscle of the four convicts.

A long, slender, waspish piece of land, was the Island, with its various temples of charity and correction strewn irregularly over its surface, and on either side of it the tides poured back and forth with their ceaseless ebb and flow, stronger there than anywhere else, because pent between such narrow barriers of sea-wall and pier. And beyond the swift currents, on either shore, were the endless streets and squares of the great city which is by that water split in two.

A great city, and through all those endless miles of stony thoroughfares the tides of human life ebb and flow with a velocity and turbulence they attain not elsewhere, because nowhere else are they pent between such narrow barriers of unyielding circumstance.

But Carrie Dillaye had not yet begun to think of the city. She was looking back at the Island.

"O sir," she suddenly exclaimed, "I ought to have seen him, before I came away. I ought at least to have said good-bye to him."

"To whom, Miss Dillaye?" politely inquired Mr. Allyn.

"Mr. Rogers, one of the hospital keepers. He was very kind to me. The only person who was. Seems to me I owe him my liberty. He told me he should write to Mr. Brown."

"O he knows your uncle? It's all right, then. Of course we could not go back, now. Mr. Brown and Miss Varick will be waiting for us."

"Will they, indeed? I would not keep them waiting one moment. But I must not be ungrateful. I do hope I shall see him again."

"Never fear about that, Miss Dillaye. If you don't see him, Mr. Brown will. That sort of man is never backward to report himself if he has any good excuse."

"He is not that sort of man, I'm sure he is not," began Carrie, half-indignantly, but there was a smile of derisively superior intelligence on the lips of the polite lawyer, and the young lady somehow called to mind the fact that she herself was but just escaping from the horrible grasp of a prison hospital, and she subsided into a pale and anxious sort of silence.

The channel between the Island and the city is a narrow one, but it is not to be ferried in a hurry by a row-boat when the tide is running strong, so that Carrie Dillaye had plenty of time to collect her thoughts, or to scatter them, before the yawl

was pulled in at the bottom of a little flight of
movable wooden stairs.

" Let me help you up," said Mr. Allyn, and Carrie
felt that she needed help. She had never in all her
life stood at the bottom of so tremendous an elevation as that between the boat's gunwale and the
level of that rickety, dirty pier. It seemed to contain all the moral distance between the Island and
the city, and Carrie did not know how delusive a
thing that might be. Her trembling steps were
aided in their task right vigorously by Mr. Allyn,
for that gentleman was on a strictly business errand,
and would have reproached himself for any neglect
of the least part of it, and in a moment more she
was conscious, dimly, that the boat had instantly
been rowed away by its convict crew, and their un-
convicted captain.

A long, narrow pier, longer, by hundreds and
hundreds of miles of shame and suffering, than any
which Carrie Dillaye had ever before seen or heard
of, but a close carriage, drawn by a very stylish pair
of horses, was waiting at the shore end.

Mr. Allyn must have been a gentleman as well
as a lawyer, for not one word was spoken as the
door of the carriage came open, and Carrie was all
but lifted through it, and it was banged behind her
instantly, and the driver whipped up his horses,
and all she knew or cared to know for a few minutes was that a pair of strong arms received her.

She knew whose arms they were, although Mr. Brown struggled in vain to unchoke a kindly word or so from the glut of them which were struggling so fiercely in his riotous and disorderly throat.

She knew it was her uncle, and then she had no doubt whatever by whose side he had put her down, on the back seat, for another, not so strong a pair of arms, was round her now, and the voice of Mabel Varick sounded slightly defiant of somebody, if not of everybody, as she exclaimed:

"You're going home with us, Carrie, dear. Don't be afraid. Don't cry. We'll take care of you."

CHAPTER XXI.

PRINCE AND THE WIDOW TAKE A SURVEY OF THE SITUATION.

A VERY wise woman was Mrs. Boyce, and gifted with a high degree of that kind of philosophy which refuses to break its heart over the inevitable. Her business affairs, she knew, were in better hands than her own, although she was well pleased with the fact that her several boxes were safely stored, and that her personal trunks, with her wardrobe and so forth, were under the protecting ægis of Mr. Daniel Brown's hospitable roof.

The past was secure, and so, to all appearance, was the present, but she had hardly as yet had a day-light opportunity for quiet contemplation of the latter. The first chance came when Mabel Varick and her uncle drove off together on their errand of mercy and hope, leaving the widow looking after them from the open window of the library.

Prince followed them to the gate, for he had
been blessed with an increase of liberty since his
adventure with the tramps, albeit with the melan-
choly drawback of a wire-cage on his muzzle. That,
to be sure, was only meant as a protection against
improper food which might again be cast in his
path, but the sorrow of it was none the less de-
pressing to the mind of the dog.

There is probably no created thing that is satisfied with its muzzle, no matter what the reason for
strapping it firmly on.

Prince looked at the departing carriage with a
low whine, as much as to say:

"Gone. So they have. And the only protection this world has from its tramps and things is
left here with his faithful nose in prison."

And then he turned and strode back along the
gravel-walk, up the front steps and through the yet
open door. He might as well have a whole house
over his head as that intolerable wire-cage.

Mrs. Boyce had not hitherto succeeded in acquiring the confidence of Prince, but she was well
aware of his importance. Of small account in any
household must be that member whom the house-
dog refuses to recognize as "one of us," and Mrs.
Boyce knew altogether too much not to know that.

When, therefore, the stately quadruped marched
into the library and looked around him so wistfully, he was greeted with a degree of cordiality

which ought to have gone to his very heart. It must have done so, more or less, for not only were the usual effects visible in the corresponding sway of his heavily fringed tail, but he came forward, more and more slowly, until his wire-bound head was thrust into her lap.

Absurdly forlorn was the look he gave her, and her own eyes suddenly lighted up with a half-triumphant expression. It seemed as if all the indications were so completely in her favor,—even Prince—

But the one great enemy of the profoundest human wisdom is its proneness to that haste which makes the present the enemy of the future. Such a perpetual infanticide of hope goes on at the hands of that same haste! Mrs. Boyce had permitted her too-ready hands to fumble with the strap and buckle of Prince's muzzle, as if she had it in mind to earn his gratitude by a temporary gift of freedom.

He knew what she meant, there could be no doubt of that, but all the brute fidelity within him arose in prompt resentment. That was an act of sovereignty which belonged to his master alone, or his known and accredited delegates, and its usurpation by unauthorized fingers called for so gruff, husky, threatening a protest, and so green a gleam in his sagacious eyes, that Mrs. Boyce drew back her touch as if from something very hot.

"You ungrateful fellow. Wear it, if you want to. I'll never offer to help you again."

Prince wagged his tail, but did not remove his head, and the widow was a little puzzled what to do about it. She had duties before her, all over the house, more than anybody else knew anything about, and here was this monstrous animal right in the way of them all. Especially in her own way. There, too, he seemed disposed to remain, for minute after minute passed, and Prince continued his unwavering study of her face, with his upturned eyes, except when, now and then, he yawned as widely as the confining wires would let him. In those brief moments Mrs. Boyce obtained a clearer idea than she had ever had before, of what is meant by "the jaws of destruction." She concluded that they must be lined with ranges of long, white teeth around a cavern of vivid red, shading into black streaks, here and there. It was a great improvement in the situation, whenever Prince again shut his mouth.

How long it lasted, that mutual study of dog and lady, were hard to say, with exactness, nor could its further duration have been prophesied, but at last the front-door went to with a great bang, when a passing servant discovered how carelessly it had been left open, and Prince was compelled to go for a look into the hall. Mrs. Boyce was on her feet in an instant.

"Was I afraid of him?" she said to herself. "He could not have bitten me. I declare, it seemed to me as if I could not have moved. Have dogs any mesmeric power?"

One would say not, at least if they are well muzzled, but under some circumstances, at the foot of a fruit-tree with a boy in it, for instance. But then that may not be considered genuine mesmerism.

Once delivered, the widow had no notion of returning into bondage, but Prince was by no means disposed to deprive her of his company.

Slowly, thoughtfully, as she passed from room to room, mentally grasping the contents and capacities of each as only such a woman can, just so slowly, thoughtfully, and with even greater dignity, the great and solemn dog, with his wire muzzle on his head, paced from room to room behind her. He knew she belonged in the house, and perhaps he saw no special objection to her present pilgrimage, but whatever article of furniture, of art, of curious antiquity or other attraction, the widow paused before, on that same piece of property were at the same moment concentrated the eyes and interest of the sagacious Prince.

In one room on the second floor, a large corner room, there stood an elegantly carved ebony cabinet between the windows. It was surmounted by a mirror, but was evidently more of a writing-desk than dressing-table, although it might have served for either or both. A curious ancient sort of an affair, and the key was in the lock, as much as to say, "No secrets here, certainly none from you."

Mrs. Boyce put out a white, plump hand, on which were lovely rings, and it rested a moment on a little carven dragon, just above the key. Then it was quickly and sharply snatched away, although the ebony dragon had neither moved wing or claw nor uttered a sound.

No, not the dragon. The growl came through the meshes of that wire-cage on the head of the house-dog.

"You foolish fellow," she exclaimed, " I shall not steal anything."

But Prince only wagged his tail and yawned. There was much about his self-assumed duty which he did not clearly understand, and he knew that good manners were required of all in that house. As much tail-wagging, therefore, as politeness might suggest, but not too much investigation, and all that sort of thing. His mind was clearly made up on that head, whatever might be the temporary disabilities of his own.

Certainly a noble mansion, elegantly and tastefully furnished in every part. Even the servants' rooms were models of neatness and comfort. Mr. Brown would have despised himself if he had permitted them to be otherwise, and Mrs. Boyce was compelled to remark: "The housekeeper is a good one, no doubt, but there is more in Mabel Varick than I had imagined. This is not all housekeeper. There's more than a little mistress about it. I'm glad to have learned so much as that, in spite of this horrid old dog. I'll make a friend of him, though, soon enough. He'll get used to me, and then it'll be only a question of bones. Dogs are all alike."

That is the prevailing superstition, but there is a tremendous fallacy in it. One dog is no more like another than one day is like another. No, not so much, for the days are nominally of the same length, while the dogs are not. Even clipping their tails will not make them so.

Back to the library, now, and Prince went about his other business, and left Mrs. Boyce to the enjoyment of the book she picked up from the table. There was one occupation, at all events, which he considered entirely innocent, but in which he took no interest. Even if he had known more about such things, it is possible he might have retained his opinion without any loss of reputation for wisdom. He would simply have continued to vote with the majority of his fellow-beings.

But Mrs. Boyce had not picked up that book with any intention of reading it. Something to hold in the hand while gazing out of the window and following a very wandering train of thought, that was all. There was a good deal in her present circumstances

which called for careful thinking, and even the conduct of Prince may have had its suggestiveness to
so keen a mind as that of the widow. Her survey
of the house had been conducted leisurely, and had
consumed a good deal of time for her, and patient
waiting by the window ate up the rest, until there
came a sound of rapid wheels up the street and Mr.
Brown's carriage stopped in front of the gate.

Mrs. Boyce had at first intended to open the front-
door for them, in person, but she had now thought
better of that, and she did but pull the bell for a
servant. When they came in she could be just a
little in the back-ground, at the library door.

It was admirably done, for Mr. Brown did not
have to ring the bell, and when Mabel and Carrie
came in, the latter was just able to perceive, in a dim,
cloudy sort of way, that she was "received" by Mrs.
Boyce. Such a kindly sweet-voiced, smiling welcome, a good deal more friendly than motherly, but
with a subtle absence of any undue expression of
feeling, for which Carrie could not help being grateful. It seemed so to ignore the suggestion that
there were any unpleasant things connected with
her coming, and such a delicate desire to make her
feel at home. Mabel Varick had been trying to
school her cousin into that state of mind, all the
way, and she too would have been grateful if it had
not been for the self-possessed completeness of
that reception. It was not only self-possessed, it

seemed to her, but almost house-possessed as
well. And good Mr. Brown thought he had never
witnessed anything so nearly perfect in all his life.

Very likely he never had.

"Would your cousin not like to go to her own
room, dear?" asked the widow, of Mabel. "It is
all ready for her."

"Her room? O—yes, she is to room with me.
Come, Carrie, I'll order lunch, and we'll be ready for
it. Uncle Daniel can stay and talk with Mrs.
Boyce. I know she won't mind our leaving her."

"Certainly not, dear. And I'll see about the
lunch. Is there anything special you and your
cousin would like?"

"Never mind them," exclaimed Mr. Brown, his
strong, honest face all aglow with the enthusiasm of
his inner purposes. "Run right along, girls; I'll
see to everything. I'm just happy all over. You
are safe, now, Carrie."

Miss Dillaye had arisen, while he was speaking,
from the sofa upon which she had sank on entering,
and Mabel had put an arm around her, as if she
thought some sort of assistance might be needed,
but there was a great light on her cousin's face as
she leaned towards Mr. Brown and murmured:

"Uncle Daniel, I am safe, indeed I am. It would
never have happened if I had been here. I see it
all, now. Quick, Mabel, I must go with you before
I say any more."

And there was a half-frightened look on Mabel Varick's face as the two hurried out of the library, but it had chased away something very like a cloud.

If Mr. Brown expected to be plied with questions concerning what had passed since he left the house, he was agreeably disappointed, but the account he gave the widow was amply sufficient. He told all he knew, before lunch was ready, and she listened with the utmost sympathy and appreciation. He was absolutely sure of her admiring approval. Nor was there the least touch of hypocrisy on the part of Mrs. Boyce. She was just the woman to comprehend the vigorous unselfishness of such a man. The one thing she failed to see, perhaps, was that very little weakness displayed itself, after all, in what seemed to be the soft spots of Mr. Brown's character. A moderate pilgrimage among his business acquaintances would have enabled her to discover many things to which she was as yet disposed to be a little blind. Even her own self-knowledge should have taught her that a woman like the widow Boyce could not possibly have so admired a man who was the least bit of a fool.

What she wanted to ask him about, after all, was the nature of his purposes, rather than the history of what he had already done, but Carrie herself had said enough to suggest the idea that those purposes would require more than a little close thinking.

"Can there be," she said to herself, "a skeleton of any sort among the closets of a family like this?"

If so, Daniel Brown was just the man to string the loose bones of it together and secure them a decent burial, without setting up any unnecessarily descriptive monument.

CHAPTER XXII.

RAW VOLUNTEERS AGAINST REGULAR TROOPS.

THERE is no other corner of the habitable globe so entirely hidden and unexplorable as the private chamber of a young lady, unless it may be the inner room of her own heart. But Bessie Heron sat by her table, that evening, with her pen in her hand, inditing a somewhat minute confidential picture of both kinds of privacy to her former hostess, Mrs. Baird. That is to say, she gave a reasonably full description of her present surroundings, and ornamented it with graphic settings forth of her state of mind.

Nor could Mrs. Baird have complained of any lack of truth to nature on the part of the artist, for Bessie was a good hand with a pen.

But she was not contented to stop there. Other states of mind and heart required analysis and description, especially those belonging to her erring brother Fred, and if Mrs. Baird had never before obtained a clear idea concerning the needs and disqualifications of that luckless wanderer, she received one now. That is, if Bessie's picture made its due impression on her mind. It was all done so lovingly, too, with such a perpetual ripple of sisterly sorrow and hope, as ought to have been in the highest degree satisfactory to Fred, or even to his wife, if he had had one. Pity he had not, and that she could not have received that letter. How it would have opened her eyes. And Bessie thought it not unlikely Fred might meet Mrs. Baird, some day or other, and she desired to interest that good and kindly lady on his behalf. She, in turn, might interest others, and they ought to know all about him, and how very much he stood in need of constant surveillance. She had helped him, in that way, had that good sister of his, more times than once, already, and one striking proof of the depravity of his nature was that he had not only shown no appreciation of her kindness, but had even manifested a disposition thereafter to separate and conceal from her his ways in life. He had gone so far as to take pains that she should not know or come in contact with any of his present friends and associates.

It was hard to understand, and Bessie said as much, in a long letter she wrote him, after completing the one to Mrs. Baird.

Many things she had to endure, in the inscrutable course of Divine Providence—could that have been Bessie's Sunday name for Blind Luck?—but the lack of her brother's sympathy and confidence had been one of the bitterest drops in the cup of her earthly discomfort. She felt for him, and she wanted him to understand it, but she had neither care nor thought for herself—she had never had— and she freely and frankly told him so. For his own sake, however, the sooner he aroused himself and began to care somewhat for others, not for her, in- deed, for she had friends who loved her and cared for her, and acknowledged how much they were indebted to her, but for Augustus, and for—well for quite a list of more or less able-bodied men and women—the sooner he would realize what a dis- graceful failure he had made of his life thus far, and that would be a tremendous blessing.

So it would, but it might be Fred had a tolerably clear notion of the sort already.

Bessie's philosophy of help differed somewhat from poor, old, stupid John Bunyan's, not to speak of some of the writers from whom the tramp in Bedford jail was so fond of quoting. He, and some of the rest, talked of their pilgrim as finding a means of casting off his burden. There was even a place for it to fall into, so that he saw it no more, but marched on rejoicing, but Bessie understood clearly that no such thing would have done for Fred. If she had known, that night, in what ward of what hospital to look for him, she would, no doubt, have, wept profusely, but she would have consoled herself with the hopeful thought—

"I expected some such thing. But will it be enough? Will it teach him what he really is? It's only for sixty days. O if he would but come out subdued and in a frame of mind to listen to me, I would not care how much he suffered. It would all be well put in."

Yes, if she had known it all she would have borne it, for she had a good deal of that sort of heroism in her composition, as Fred had more than once discovered.

Even such a case as that of Carrie Dillaye would have had its bright and comforting side to a mind like Bessie's, and it was a pity the two were so widely separated, that evening. As it was, the course of events at Mr. Brown's had been led by the nose in a way the wisdom of which was open to question.

Mabel and Carrie remained in the latter's dressing-room an unconscionably long time, considering what had been said about lunch, and only the faintest outline can be given of what they had been up to.

"I'm so glad," Mabel remarked, "that we are so nearly of a size. My things always fitted you. Never mind the colors being a little wrong for you."

"Do I look very badly?"

"No, not even pale. You must have had enough to eat."

"So I did, but I could not eat at all, at first.
Then, I must say, my appetite came back, and I'm
ever so hungry now.   I wonder how I shall get at
my own things!"

The two girls were standing by the dressing-
bureau as she said that, and the thought that came
with it certainly did make her pale.

Her father? His house? Her future? What
about them?

Mabel heard all the questions that were not asked,
for she quickly answered.

"Dont speak of it now, Carrie; Uncle Daniel will
take care of it all. I know he will. Don't you
suppose he loves you as well as he does me?"

"But my father!"

"I suppose I mustn't say what I think, Carrie, but
he cannot have his way in everything, even to
please your stepmother. Uncle Daniel will see
about all that, too. I believe they will be afraid
of him."

"They do not like him any too well. I know
that. But, Mabel, what about Mrs. Boyce? Is she
here on a visit?"

"O Carrie, that's another of Uncle Daniel's good
deeds, I suppose. She's poor, now—"

"Poor? Mrs. Boyce?"

"O you've not heard. Well, I'll tell you—"

And so she did, and it was very well told, too, for
before the story was ended Mabel herself knew

more than when she began it. There is nothing occult or uncommon about that, as everybody knows. If you want to understand a thing, try to explain it to somebody else. The result will sometimes surprise you. It did Mabel, for it brought from her, at last, the exclamation:

"And now I've another reason for being glad to have you here. It seems as if I had an ally."

"Why, Mabel! Is it war?"

"Hardly a skirmish yet, but I feel as if the invader had already passed the frontier and was beginning to fortify herself."

"She can't be starved out."

"No, Carrie, but I'll tell you what we can do."

"What's that, dear?"

"We can take care of Uncle Daniel. Think of what a change there has been in your own house—"

"It makes me shudder to think of it. But what can I do, Mabel?"

"You can throw off all the prison air you brought with you, and come down to lunch as if you and I owned all this part of the city."

It was a grandly good thing for Carrie Dillaye to have something besides herself to think of, just then. She certainly was looking well, and her selections from Mabel's ample wardrobe fitted and became her admirably, in spite of any criticisms on "the colors."

The latter seemed to suit Carrie's darker style almost as well as they did the sunny hair and fair complexion of her cousin.

No higher compliment than that could have been paid to colors or fabrics by any young lady. But then neither Mabel nor Carrie belonged to that large class of females whose obstinate and ill-tempered beauty seems in a perpetual death-grapple with its surroundings. Sometimes the dress is killed, and sometimes the beauty, but not uncommonly they both perish, and their unfortunate owner might almost as well not have had any dress at all.

That is, nothing but clothing.

Clothing does not imply dress, and an inspection of a grand ball or a royal reception will promptly establish the fact that dress, on the other hand, by no means implies clothing—at least, for the lady part of the human beings on exhibition.

Mrs. Boyce had met Carrie Dillaye more than once, in days gone by, and believed herself to have formed as clear and correct an estimate of her as of Mabel Varick, but her face put on a puzzled as well as delighted look when the two girls sailed into the dining-room.

If the widow had proposed to herself to relieve Mabel of the irksome duty of presiding at the lunch table she was not quick enough in making the offer. It took several seconds too much time for her to tell Carrie Dillaye how very greatly she

was improved in appearance already, for Mr. Brown
joined her in the pleasant business, most exuberantly,
and he had to be made to feel how entirely he had
the womanly sympathy of his accomplished guest.

In not neglecting that impotant matter, Mrs.
Boyce temporarily missed the control of the coffee-
urn and Mabel Varick was able to remark:

"Come, Uncle Daniel, Carrie is hungry. You
must be, also, Mrs. Boyce. Sorry we kept you
waiting so long, but we could not help it. After
this you won't have to wait. Carrie can take my
place when I'm not here."

"It will be so pleasant," softly responded Mrs.
Boyce, but Mr. Brown was vaguely conscious of a
formless and soulless idea, vainly scratching for entrance at the bare spot on the top of his mind. It
is every bit as well for all men that they are not
endowed with feminine perceptions. It would only
make them miserable, every time they blundered.
Even as it is, a good many of them are more fully
posted than they need be concerning their occasional
short-comings. But that is generally owing to ex-
cess of loving zeal on the part of the best woman
in the world.

Mr. Brown had not blundered, nor had anybody
else, perceptibly, and the nearest thing to it was
when he said something about his house being a
better place for a hungry young lady than the hospital on the Island.

"Is there such a place, Uncle Daniel?" exclaimed Carrie. "Have I ever been there? It seems to me as if I had been just waked up from a dreadful dream, but I cannot recall much of it, just now."

"Do not try," suggested Mrs. Boyce, with something arch in her smile. "The best we can do with ugly dreams is to forget them."

"That's it, Carrie," said Mr. Brown, very heartily. "Nobody knows anything about your dream. If any one should ask me where you are, I should tell them you are visiting your cousin Mabel at my house. You and she may be planning a summer tour together, for all I know."

"Or we may not," suggested Mabel. "What shall I do about dinner, Uncle Daniel, after so very late a lunch?"

"Dinner? O—well—I suppose I shall not be here. Doubt if I'm home before it's quite late. I have some very important business on hand."

"Then, if Mrs. Boyce does not care," said Mabel, "we will only have tea, and it's almost too warm for even that."

"Me?" said Mrs. Boyce. "I shall be glad to be rid of the responsibility of eating a dinner. It will be so much time saved for my inspection."

"Your inspection?"

"Yes. If you and Miss Dillaye will come to my room with me, after your uncle goes, I will get you to help me."

Either Mabel Varick or Carrie Dillaye would have scorned the idea that she could be influenced by so base a motive as curiosity, but Mrs. Boyce had won a move on them, for all that. She was by all odds a more experienced player, and it is quite possible she was taking a deeper interest in the game than either of Mr. Brown's nieces.

That gentleman himself was momentarily putting on more and more of the accustomed wrinkles of his business face, and it was evident that not all of his thoughts were pleasant ones. They cut short his lunch for him, at all events, and, late as it was, he was speedily hurrying away on some errand about which he was exceedingly in earnest.

Mrs. Boyce was left, therefore, to make such an explanation of her "inspection" as she might choose, and it was pretty sure to include such an unselfish effort to amuse Carrie Dillaye as would keep her and Mabel within the reach of the widow's eye and tongue for the remainder of that evening, whatever might be its other and more remote consequences.

CHAPTER XXIII.

A GREAT city like that has many neighborhoods, although the greater part of its population never by any chance get into one of them. It is only the very poor, the very rich, and the socially capable and designing, who succeed in discovering neighbors among a crowd so vast. When a city gets to be a millionaire it is apt to be a trifle careless as to how its varied thousands are invested and arranged. That's one reason so many of them find their way into bonds of one kind and another, and so large a percentage is annually wasted and lost.

Mr. Brown's neighborhood was a good one, full of old families, some of whom could even show the pictures of their grandfathers, though very few of them would have freely exhibited said portraits, if authentic. Strange that the best thing in oil should be shut out of a portrait gallery, if the name of the subject goes with it, and it should represent a man with a pack on his back, a tinsmith's hammer in his

220

hand, a broken flat-iron on a leather apron in his lap, or even a robust and motherly woman leaning over a wash-tub, with a pipe in her mouth. But such is one of the latter-day tastes of the old families in the great city.

Did you ever see, in one of those galleries, the portly ancestor with the ribbon in his button-hole, and did you take it for so mean a thing as a decoration accorded him by some royal numbskull beyond the salt, salt sea?

That was your own blunder, then, for it was fairly won him by his proud, prize pig, at a great and memorable show in the good old times when pork was less generally diffused through our social structure than it now is.

But in the vicinity of Mr. Dillaye's own residence there was just as creditable a sprinkle of old families as in Mr. Brown's neighborhood, with the difference that the houses were more closely packed together, and some people even lived next door to one another. Fewer opportunities, of course, for the disreputable doings of tramps, but fewer also for the acquisition of honorable distinction by canine heroes like Prince.

The distance between the two settlements of wealth and aristocracy was a long one, and the church attended by the related families was about half-way between, and only to be reached, comfortably, by either, in their respective carriages.

And neither Mr. Brown or Mr. Dillaye had ever been known to express any feeling of regret over this feature of their circumstances in life.

On this particular evening, at the very hour when the former was getting away from his home as fast as he could, the latter was expanding the courteous chill of his presence as respectably as he could around the dinner-table of his own.

He was assisted by a tall, large, showy-looking woman, who did not seem the least afraid of him, but who absolutely appeared to be absorbing information from him through her rusty brown eyes, even when he was not saying a word.

It is the nature of sponges to absorb, but at last she concentrated enough of what she had obtained to squeeze out:

"I see how it is, Mr. Dillaye. Not a word concerning that unfortunate young woman?"

"Not a word."

"I've had all the papers brought in, and I'm positive they do not contain the slightest hint."

"Not the slightest. It is really a very great mystery."

"Every day renders the certainty more absolute. We shall never see her again."

"You forget yourself, Mrs. Dillaye. She is my daughter—"

"I hope I forget nothing, Mr. Dillaye. Have you heard anything more from Mr. Brown?"

"No, and I do not think I shall. He is too wise a man to give unpleasant publicity to a strictly family affair. As to any other kind of meddling, he has not the smallest pretext for that."

"Of course not. We have done our whole duty, and we can prove it."

Something like a wince passed over the well-dressed frame of Mr. Dillaye as his wife emphasized this last remark, but he was momentarily passing more and more completely under the influence of her absorption.

It was not difficult to see who was the controlling sponge of that table and house.

Would those two have sat every whit as comfortably over their tea-cups, at the close of their stately meal, if they could have known, by telephone or otherwise, just what was passing, during those long, aimless minutes, between Mr. Daniel Brown and his deeply interested counsel?

Perhaps not, for Mr. Allyn said, among other things:

"Certainly, my dear sir. She is of age, and mistress of her own movements. She is entirely competent to select her business agent, and to give him full power of attorney to manage her affairs. I will draw one in due form before you leave the office. She will execute it?"

"Undoubtedly. Her father has declared to me that she can never return to his house. In that state of things she must assume control of her property, obviously. Any other course would be out of the question. It is in precisely the same condition as was that of my own wife. You have attended to that, and know the terms of the old gentleman's will."

"Exactly, but your wife left no children. Did her sister have any other besides Caroline?"

"None, so that her right is beyond dispute. The very house he will not let her into is her own unquestioned property. So also is a good share of the income that runs it. I only wish I knew just how Dillaye has been doing, financially, of late years."

"None too well, I fancy. Hardly anybody has. But will he not try to regain control of his daughter? It's likely he will."

"I'd like to see him, then, that's all. The first information he gets of her whereabouts ought to be a somewhat formal one."

"Trust me for that, my dear sir. He is the last man to want any public row made. Unless he is in a pretty tight place, I think a demand will be enough."

"You do not know Stephen Dillaye, then. That's all I've got to say. Nor his wife, either."

"We shall see. There's no possible loophole for him to escape an accounting. Take it altogether, it's one of the most remarkable cases I ever had anything to do with. Even your discovery of your niece is not the least singular part of it. How does she explain it? Did she ask some one to write to you? She said something of the sort to me."

"No, and that makes me think. No hurry about it, of course, but one of the hospital assistants was very kind to her, and he must be hunted up. A young man named Rogers. He wrote to me, she says. Seemed to know her, and me too. Very queer, but I must not forget a favor from a man of that sort."

"He won't forget it, if you do, my dear sir. Hospital assistants on the Island are the very men to report themselves, in such a case, the very first time they get a day off and can visit the city."

"You think so?"

"Well, if he does not, we can find him in an hour, any day we want him. We know exactly where to look for him."

So they did, but that does not surely imply that they knew just where to find him. Especially if they should wait till his sixty days ran out before looking for him.

The lawyer and his client had a good many things to talk about, and the more confidentially they talked the less they said which would have been pleasant hearing for either Carrie Dillaye's father or stepmother. If there is anything in the old up-country superstition worth noticing, there were at least two left ears that should have been uncomfortably warm. And yet even Fred Heron-Rogers did not experience the least degree of fever on the right side of his head.

There must be something wrong about the superstition, or, at least, it is like some men's piety, and does not always work.

Fred Heron, indeed, was not thinking of himself, that evening, and cared very little whether other people were talking good or bad concerning him. Ever since he had ascertained the departure of the young lady patient who had so deeply interested him, he had been in a decidedly uncomfortable state of mind. He would have given almost anything to be sure that his own epistle had fallen into the right hands, and that she had followed it with consequent security. It was too bad that he should be deprived of that small consolation.

"I've done all I could, anyhow," he said to himself. "A fellow in jail is a trifle limited, that's a fact. I never fully appreciated my liberty before. And yet Miller tells me the tramps come back regularly, some of them, and get themselves shut up for the winter. Freedom less desirable in cold weather, eh? I think I shall try and keep mine when I get it again. I wonder if I can stand it here till then? Got to, I suppose. At all events, I'm not shut up very closely. I believe they'd hardly say a word if I strolled all over the Island."

A doleful day, with a doleful night to follow it.

Fred could not have imagined that such a sense of utter loneliness was possible in a crowded ward of a great public institution.

Crowded, indeed, for after the lights were turned down he peopled the dim spaces around him with all the forms and faces he had ever known.

He even brought in, at last, the library at Mr. Brown's, and imagined himself again seated at the book-strewn table. It was not a very difficult mental feat, but then, when Mabel Varick came in, as on that memorable evening, he could not shape Miss Dillaye as entering with her and was compelled to turn anxiously to Mr. Brown with:

"Where is your other niece? I wrote to you about her."

And then, without any imagination at all, he turned over on his pallet and muttered:

"I hope it's all right. Bessie would say she is in the hands of Providence."

CHAPTER XXIV.

OLIVER PROTECTS THE MINE IN THE DOCTOR'S ABSENCE.

ALL these things came to pass in the great city a good while before Dr. Milyng reached or passed the thirsty desert, nor had the veteran mining explorer the least idea that he was at all concerned in them or in anything else beyond the reach of his own hawk-like vision. When he awoke from the long, refreshing sleep called for by his protracted exertions, he found himself a trifle stiff and sore, but this soon passed away, as he busied himself with preparations for his breakfast.

The pony was at work among the blue grass around one of the pools, and seemed entirely satisfied with his occupation. So much so that he gently and suggestively edged away when his master drew near, as if he would have said:

"There, now, don't you see I'm happy? Why disturb me, then? Let's rest awhile."

"Rest it'll have to be," remarked the doctor. "I can't say exactly where we are, but there's a good long pull before us, yet. I think the worst is over, but I must get him in good condition before I move on."

Prudent, but difficult, for the doctor's thoughts were busy with his one tremendous enthusiasm and the conviction was growing upon him that, in mining matters, delays are dangerous.

"I wouldn't care so much if it were a little later," he soliloquized, "but there's time yet, this season, for almost anything to turn up. The luck of it has followed me pretty close, thus far, but there's something going wrong, just now. I'd like to take a look at that ledge of rocks, I would, if only to know they're all alone. Poor old Oliver! I'm afraid the coyotes have picked his bones clean before this. But then his very bones might help point somebody the way to that claim. Pity he tumbled down right where he did."

But Oliver and his bones had nothing to do with it. Nor had any other living thing, human or quadruped. It was just that ungovernable chance, which exercises such a mysterious control over the affairs of men and rocks, which led those three ragged men into that valley while Dr. Milyng was eating his broiled venison, so many miles away. The valley itself looked a good deal as it did when the doctor marched out of it, and the mine was there, or rather the wonderfully promising place for one, just where chance had gathered the ore for it in the first place, and where the doctor had chanced to find it. There, too, was his worn-out pick, just where he had chanced to leave it, but the chapter of accidents did not include the bones of Oliver. A wonderfully calculating brain has the thing called " chance !"

And those three men had as many mules of their own, with a couple of very spare ponies, and they too, the men, were manifestly of the mining and exploring persuasion.

" Wall, boys," said one of them, " we've tracked him good, and if he's lit on anything yer like he did in the other places, we hain't followed him for nothin'! And we won't be the first lot that's made thar pile by pickin' up what he's throwed away."

" Wall, thar's his marks," replied another, " and we mought jest as well take possession. He'll never come back for it."

" What if he does? Hain't he abandoned it, I'd like to know? What's minin' law good for, if a man's to let a thing lie and not work it? Besides, he's bound to lose his hair, some day, foolin' round the Sierras all alone."

Very strong and hearty were the expressions of assent, but already busy hands were getting out tools from the packs on the starved-looking animals, and it was evident that Dr. Milyng's precious claim was about to be investigated.

That was not all.

It was about to be jumped.

A man of ordinary agility could have cleared the traces of the doctor's solitary toil at a single bound, but that was not the precise duty in hand.

Terrible are the misuses of human speech, and one of the worst is perpetrated when a hardy miner is said to " jump" the bit of rock belonging to another man which he feloniously settles on and digs into.   That was what these ragged three were about to happen to do.

They were men of experience, and the remarks they dropped, from time to time, showed that they not only knew Dr. Milyng, but had an unbounded confidence in his judgment as a mining expert.   A claim on which he had wasted such an amount of labor as he had there expended hardly needed any additional recommendation in their eyes.   If it had, however, their own rude tests would have given it, before they had worked three hours.

" This 'll do, boys.   This yer's the biggest thing out o' doors."

" It's too good.   It's a sure thing the doctor 'll come back to look after it."

" Don't you believe it.   And what if he does? How's he to prove anything?   Wasn't he all alone?

I'd like to see how he'll work it, and we in possession."

No wonder the doctor felt a sense of anxiety
creeping over him as he cut another slice of venison and went to the pool for another cup of yellow
water. Chance, and the luck of the mine, and the
whole chapter of scientific probabilities were arranging themselves dead against him. There was not a
single thing for him to do to protect his interests,
and those three enterprising adventurers were having it all their own way.

Everything, mine and all.

Everything but Oliver, and they knew nothing
whatever about him.

He was worth all three of their mules to them,
however, with the two spare ponies thrown in, for
Oliver's bones were his own, that day, and the Big
Medicine and a whole swarm of his devoted con-
gregation were following him to convince him that he
had made a mistake.

Oliver had made good time over that same
ground, once before, to his own and his master's
sorrow, but that had not prevented him from taking
advantage of the temporary carelessness of Big
Medicine and trying another race.

If men of another race had been behind him, indeed, he might have been sooner caught, but the
Apache hunters were warriors as well, and it speedily
occurred to them that Oliver's motions were guided

by some kind of knowledge. They had not at all connected him, in their own minds, with the daring thief
their braves had driven over the precipice, and yet
somebody, they knew, must have lost him. What
if he should now guide them to something worth
their stealing? More than one squad of their out-
ranging buffalo butchers joined them as they pushed
forward on the heels of their medicine-mule, and by
the time he entered the wooded valley they were
full two score, with the Big Medicine at their
head.

Oliver knew his ground, and he could hardly have
managed his business better if he had been acting
under instructions from his master. Whether or
not he had any idea of recovering the doctor himself is a question for those who know what passes
in the mind of a mule.

There was but one way, that one, into that
strange amphitheatre, or if there was another prac-
ticable pass nobody then present knew anything
about it. And so, when Oliver led his Apaches up
the narrowing ravine he thereby shut up the only
hope of escape for any one who might just then
happen to be investigating, or jumping, mining
claims in the ledges beyond.

It was a singular chance, for on any previous day
the Apache hunters would have found nothing more
valuable to them than some odds and ends of worn-
out mining tools, and a heap of broken rock for

which they would not have given the scalp of a jackass-rabbit.

But now, there were three men, and only three, with mules and ponies, and nothing in the wide world to prevent an immediate application of the true intent and meaning of the last treaty the Apache tribes had made with their Great Father at Washington.

Nothing whatever, except that the three miners dropped their tools and picked up their rifles as if they intended making some species of seditious protest.

If there had but been a few more of them, or if greater time had been given them for preparation!

Men who venture into the mountains as they had done are not likely to be backward in matters of self-defence, and the first whoop which came echoing up the valley had warned them that the treaty was in full force. They made no futile attempt at a parley, therefore, but each man sprang towards the best cover he could see, leaving the quadrupeds and the mine to take care of themselves.

It was a sad thing for the Big Medicine, just then, that he was not mounted on Oliver, or at least on a swifter pony. The sorry animal he rode was so slow of foot that almost every brave of the faithful flock went clean past his pastor before any of them were within rifle range of the miners. It was best so, for what place has a chaplain in a charge? None

at all. His duties come afterwards, when the dead
are to be buried and their effects divided. The
Big Medicine's slow pony was of special value to
the tribe, just then, for the whooping rider whose
bounding steed really did make him the foremost
man rolled off upon the stony level at the first
crack of those three rifles. All three of them had
been pointed at him, and no amount of medicine,
big or little, could have done him any good.

His fall, however, did not check the rush of those
wild horsemen, and a storm of arrows and bullets
went before them. The three white men had
taken cover behind the same bowlder, and it was
big enough for twice as many, but the closing scene
of the little tragedy was thereby concentrated within
very narrow limits, both as to time and space.

Forty men on horseback, all well armed, against
three on foot, and the latter a little taken by surprise.

They were not taken prisoners.

They had been congratulating themselves on
their luck, a few minutes before. Fortune had
never smiled on them so liberally in all their lives.
Such wealth was theirs!—but that Oliver chanced
to get away from Big Medicine just when he did,
and so many yelling red men happened to follow
him.

And now, three corpses reeking in the hot sun.
Three scalps at as many belts of savage riders.

A mining expedition entirely obliterated, and a

great claim left to take care of itself without so much as a single man to " jump" it.

Not even Oliver, for, having accomplished at least as much as he set out for, that excellent mule fraternized with those of the miners and permitted Big Medicine to mount and ride him homeward in triumph. For on this occasion also the great man calmly took to himself the credit of leading the way to the exploit which had ended so gloriously. Nothing was said, however, about the dead brave being charged to his account, or the half-dozen shrewd hurts which the doomed miners had distributed among their other assailants. These things were all in violation of the treaty, and Big Medicine had nothing to do with them.

Dr. Milyng did not know a word of it all, but his claim had been taken care of for him in a remarkably opportune way. There was some kind of luck about that mine.

CHAPTER XXV

A PARADE AND INSPECTION ON THE SKIRMISH
LINE

IT has long been one of the standing marvels of
art and literature that Cornelia should have been
so offensively proud of two little heathen Italian
boys. Mrs. Boyce, however, had given herself to the
collection of jewels of quite another sort, and it was
with these, rather than even with her very interesting wardrobe, that her proposed inspection had
to do.

There was no unseemly haste or urgency in her
management of the matter, but it was not a great
while after lunch that Mabel and Carrie found themselves smiled all the way up-stairs, and into the
ample front chamber set apart for the uses of the
widow and the stranded wreck of her former pros-
perity.

If Mabel Varick was really beginning to organize
herself upon a skirmish line with reference to her
uncle's fascinating guest, her presence in that chamber, after those caskets and cases were spread upon

237

the centre-table, was a grave strategical mistake. Neither she nor her wondering cousin, nor their mothers before them, had ever possessed the tithe of such a collection. In good truth they had never seen anything like it, outside of a shopkeeper's show case.

The mere pecuniary value was no small consideration, and would have made quite an item if transferred to the column of assets of the late firm of Boyce, Millington & Co., but there it did not belong by any known rule of law, or any practised rule of equity.

Some of the stones were superb, and all were fine, well selected, well set, and in perfect order and condition. The exposure of each in succession to the strong light now thrown upon them called forth from the two girls the most enthusiastic expressions of admiration. Mrs. Boyce had pulled down the window shades and lighted the argand drop-light on the table and the effect was all the most experienced salesman could have asked.

"Lovely!"

"Exquisite!"

"Perfect! O Mrs. Boyce what will you do with them all?"

"Have them put away in a safe place now. I wanted you to see them first. One of these days I must sell them. That is, the greater part of them."

"How sad—"

" Sad, Mabel, dear? Yes, it makes me sad enough at times, for I fear I am a very worldly woman. But it is the more costly of them that I can part with most easily. Perhaps they will help me keep the keepsakes."

" Are many of them keepsakes?"

" Yes, Carrie, I was a bride, once, and some of these came to me then. Some before marriage. Others came afterwards. They have little histories of their own, my dear—"

And then, with the matronly calmness which so well became her, Mrs. Boyce repressed her feelings and softly rehearsed to her young friends the little romances of some of those jewels. Such sacred names came up as she did so!

Father. Mother. Betrothal. Marriage. Husband, —others, of relative and friend. A favored woman had she been before the tide of her life began to ebb and its good things were drifted away from her. And yet, from beginning to end, she uttered no word of foolish complaint, and gave way to no single spasm of false sentiment. Her auditors were compelled to confess to themselves that they were listening to no ordinary woman. They even failed, in their admiration of her and her treasures, to obtain any information as to how she came to possess so many mere diamonds without any history at all. These, indeed, had come with later years and a more intimate acquaintance with her husband's business affairs, and she had never so much as worn them. They were quite sure to bring their value, or very near it, should their sale be properly managed at some future day.

There was little or nothing said about this, however, and when Carrie Dillaye remarked:

"If I had such things I don't believe I could help wearing them," Mrs. Boyce replied:

"You must wear this garnet cross for me, dear. It suits your complexion exactly. There is its exact mate in torquoises, Mabel; that is for you, unless you would prefer this pearl cluster—"

"O Mrs. Boyce—"

"Indeed, I cannot—"

"My dear young friends—"

There was a little cloud of pain on the widow's face, and her plump, white hand unconsciously shut down the cover of a casket wherein a diamond necklace rested.

They looked at one another for a brief second, and she added:

"I did not dare to offer you anything more valuable. If you would let me I would give you your choice of all, but I was afraid—"

The least possible tremor in the clear soft voice, and Mabel Varick picked up the torquoise cross. An elegant thing it was, and richly set, but not of too large a mere pecuniary value. Just the precise thing to be selected as a present from among its

more showy companion gems that were for sale, by-
and-by.

"It is beautiful. I shall prize it ever so much.
It is prettier than even the pearls."

"I never saw such perfect garnets," exclaimed
Carrie. "The color is so rich, and they are so very
clear. So exquisitely polished, too. Thank you,
ever so much!"

And even while their two pairs of hands were
busy with the crosses at their respective throats,
the captured girls leaned over, one after the other,
to kiss the graceful donor of the jewels. They
could see, as they did so, that they had been but
just in time to keep the tears from her eyes, and
they remembered that misfortune has its privileges,
and that one of them is to be a trifle sensitive at
times. It would have been dreadfully unkind
of them to have refused her presents. Mabel,
indeed, went a step further, in the reaction of
her feelings. She had removed a small ruby
brooch to make room for the cross, and now, with
another kiss, she pinned that upon the widow's
bosom.

Somehow it seemed to make both of them feel
better.

Mabel, oddly enough, felt less of a burden of
obligation, and Mrs. Boyce felt better assured that
her torquoises had been wisely expended.

Carrie had stepped before the mirror to complete

the location of her garnets, and she could but be proud of them.

"Some day, my dear," said the widow, "you must make your husband get you earrings to match. I never had complete sets of either of those crosses."

"I hope I shall not have to wait as long as that," said Carrie, merrily.

"Your brooch is such a sweet little thing, Mabel," said the widow, as she took it off and held it to the light. "I've another keepsake, now. They are the only jewels I shall ever care for or wear. I wish the rest of them were all sold now, but I must wait awhile for that."

And then the talk rippled on, and the two girls were astonished to find how much the widow knew about the general subject of precious stones. She told them more than they had ever known before, and in so interesting a way that they ceased to wonder at her for having gathered such a collection.

The caskets were closed, one by one, and packed away in their boxes, and those were placed in the bottom of a trunk, and clothing filled neatly in above them.

"O Mrs. Boyce," said Mabel, "I should think you would be afraid of robbers."

"What, in your house, and with Mr. Prince in the front yard? Well, so I am, and so I shall be, till Mr. Brown helps me put all these away, somewhere.

I shall ask him in a day or so. Meantime I will show you something, if you will never tell. Remember, I have been a lone woman for two years, not even so well protected in my own house as I am here."

And, as she spoke, she pulled open a little upper drawer of the bureau, and there, reposing in their case of Russia leather and velvet, was a richly mounted pair of revolvers. Not too small for service, nor too large to be carried in one's pockets, if need should be, but with a decided flash of possible danger on their blue barrels and gilded handles.

"You must not tell."

"But can you use them?"

"I will show you, some day. I can hit a visiting card, across this room, almost every time."

"But in the dark?"

"A burglar is larger than a visiting card."

"How would you ever get to the bureau, for them, if you heard a noise? I should cover my head up."

"O they go to bed with me."

"But would you really dare to shoot at anybody?"

"I fear I should be too much of a coward not to. It must require a wonderful deal of courage not to shoot sometimes."

The widow was right about that, but after the pistol drawer was closed the two girls began to believe they had remained long enough.

Still, even at the tea-table, afterwards, the conversation ran curiously upon jewelry and fire-arms and kindred topics. Mrs. Boyce had made a great point, that day, and her young friends little imagined how difficult it would thenceforth be to set up again the barrier they had thus permitted to be thrown down.

There came a later hour, however, in the retirement of their own room, when they felt called upon to re-examine and admire again their respective presents from the widow.

"They are more beautiful, now we cannot compare them with the other things," said Mabel.

"It's always so. That's what makes shopping of any kind so difficult. I get bewildered, and half the time I pick out the wrong thing."

"Mrs. Boyce would not. She'd get just the pattern she went for, in spite of anybody."

"I believe you are right, Mabel. Which of us has she picked out?"

"Carrie Dillaye! I wish she had her crosses back again."

"I do not, then. I shall wear mine. If I had any brooch on when I left home I can't guess where it is now. This is a beauty."

"I shall wear mine, too. She would feel hurt if I did not."

"Hurt, Mabel, are you sure of that?"

"Why, she is certainly not heartless, and she has plenty of pride. I must not be unjust to her."

"But then, if one gets it into one's head once, that any other person is designing, it goes through every idea one has about them."

"Good people may be designing."

"So they may, but it isn't easy to see always, just where the good leaves off and the designing begins."

"Not with women like Mrs. Boyce, at all events."

CHAPTER XXVI.

MR. BROWN HOLDS OUT HIS HAND WITH AN INVITATION.

DAY after day went by, containing, as all days do, a great many matters of interest. That is the difficulty of it. All matters are of interest, but they cannot all be recorded. Life is both too long and too short for that.

The papers prepared by Mr. Allyn were signed by Carrie Dillaye, without a thought of demur or hesitation, and the lawyer had his instructions from Mr. Brown to lose no time in taking the steps required.

Mr. Dillaye's down-town office was in the rear of the warehouse in which the greater part of his commercial business was transacted, but he had so fitted it up that it wore, like himself, a thoroughly well-dressed and respectable air, particularly his own little den in one corner of it.

It was into this little den, one day, that there entered a spruce and active-looking young gentle-man with a paper in his hand.

"Mr. Dillaye?"

"That is my name, sir."

"All right. I am instructed to deliver this to you, personally."

"Any answer?"

"To be sent as directed in the inclosure, I suppose. I am not aware that I am to wait for one."

"Very well. I'll examine it at my leisure."

The young man had been even hasty in his withdrawal, and Mr. Dillaye's eyes were absorbed by the large envelope he was tearing open.

When he began to read, however, his absorption became every moment more and more intense. It took all the color out of his face, and then put it all back again, with interest at a high rate. Then it brought out a more profuse perspiration than even the heat of the day could have developed upon a man of Stephen Dillaye's organism. It made his hands tremble and his lips quiver, and finally made him drop the paper and bow his head upon the desk before him.

"Ruin! Ruin! Disgrace!" he muttered. "The black-hearted villain. He has planned all this. The deep, deceptive scoundrel. Turning my own daughter against her father. And that man calls himself a Christian!"

Severe language, to be sure, and yet it had been applied to no less a man than Mr. Daniel Brown, and had been called forth by so very simple a document as a formal, legal demand, on the part of one Caroline Dillaye, for an accounting and delivery to

her, or her attorney in fact, the said Daniel Brown,
of certain specified and described properties, real
and personal and mixed, to her belonging, and
formerly a part of the estate of her mother, and so
forth, and so forth, now deceased.

He recognized his daughter's signature, as well
as that of Mr. Brown, for the papers served upon
him were originals, to prevent question or denial
on his part. He saw that either would be impossible.

"But where is she?" he exclaimed, springing to
his feet. "Where has she been, all this time? I
am the rightful custodian of my own child!"

When a child becomes of age it ceases to have
any rightful custodian, but for all that Mr. Dillaye
seized his hat, and in a very short time, for a man
not accustomed to fast walking, he stood, still covered, in the office and presence of Mr. Daniel Brown.

"Ah, Brother Dillaye? Glad to see you. This
is the right course to pursue. We can settle everything between ourselves, and the world be none the
wiser. Take a chair."

"No, sir, I will not. Nor your hand either.
Where is my daughter Caroline, Mr. Brown?"

"I believe she is visiting with some friends, at
present, Brother Dillaye. She has put all her affairs in my hands, meantime. I merely propose
to take possession of them. That's all."

"Take possession of them?"

" Every dollar's worth. You have yourself told me she can never come back to your roof. I shall see to it that she has one of her own to cover her."

The merchant looked his visitor calmly in the eyes while he was talking, and was himself astonished at the effect his words seemed to produce.

Could it have been that then for the first time Mr. Dillaye received a clear perception that his daughter had any rights in the premises which he, her father, was bound to respect?

If so, he was not unlike a great many other fathers, to whom their children never assume the attitude of fellow-citizens, their equals before God and the law. Many a man, who would scorn the thought of depriving any human being of aught which belonged to them, will nevertheless pitilessly rob and plunder his own flesh and blood, cursing them if they murmur under the operation. As if he failed to recognize them as human beings.

But, if Stephen Dillaye was then and there in the act of learning something, his feelings towards the man by means of whom he was learning it lost none of their bitterness as the new ideas came to him.

They were not pleasant ideas to receive, and they came with such a dreadful pressure of Daniel Brown behind them. Had he been a weak man, a poor one, a man who could be argued with, cajoled, threatened, pooh-poohed, in any way, it would not have been so bad, but when Daniel Brown held out his broad palm to anybody and said, "Settle!" it was well understood by all who knew him that some kind of a settlement was among the sure things of the future.

"Mr. Brown, again I ask you, where is my daughter?"

"You have not tried so hard to find her that you have much to say on that head, Brother Dillaye. I assure you she is in the hands of friends, who will not only take good care of her, but will see that she is protected in her rights. I shall send for her wardrobe, this very day, and I may as well say to you that the gentleman who comes for it will be provided with proper authority. Whatever he asks for had better be surrendered to him without any nonsense. I do not think you would care to get into the papers for refusing your daughter her clothing."

Bitter words, to be spoken so calmly, but Mr. Dillaye had heard all he could hear at one hearing. His hands were clenched till the nails pierced the skin, and his teeth were grinding audibly as he turned on his heel and strode out into the street.

There is nothing so galls a proud and self-willed man as a sense of utter helplessness in the hands of another. The sense of wrong-doing on his own part does not by any means ease the smart of it, and any degree of personal hatred is the worst kind of an aggravation.

Dillaye had it all, and with it a sense of shame concerning his treatment of his daughter which had never visited him before.

And for this also he was indebted to the calm eyes of Mr. Brown.

He did not return to his own place of business, though there must have been matters there which needed his attention, but, calling a cab, he ordered the driver to make his best speed uptownwards. He felt that it was a good time for him to have a consultation with his own wife.

And Mrs. Dillaye herself had been having a busy morning of it. Day after day she had grown less and less anxious concerning the whereabouts of her missing stepdaughter. Whatever remarks she had felt called upon to make in that connection had been merely such as were calculated to sustain the just indignation of a respectable father whose unworthy daughter had got drunk and run away from home. Day after day, too, she had realized the obligation resting upon her to make things generally cheerful for her husband, so that he might not dwell too gloomily upon his heavy affliction. But, for all that, Mrs. Dillaye had never before, since her marriage, realized as she was now doing, the fact that she was once for all mistress of that mansion. A sense of proprietorship was creeping over her, and she had more than once muttered to herself:

" Even if things went wrong in the business, none

of Mr. Dillaye's creditors could touch this property. I'm glad he has never compromised it in any way. She will never come back after it."

It was under that impression, doubtless, that Carrie's stepmother, on this particular morning, performed such a remarkable piece of housework in and about Carrie's own room.

"Better pack them all up and store them away, for the present," she said, as she put article after article of dress and ornament into the great trunks she brought in.

"I wouldn't touch a thing of 'em, not if the moths ate 'em all up. But I won't have 'em lying around where her poor father can see 'em. Even if they were put in the closets, he'd be sure to stumble on to them some time."

It is likely, moreover, that Mrs. Dillaye flattered herself that something of a sentiment of personal honesty entered into the considerations which led her to pack those trunks so carefully. It was no small job, albeit Carrie's wearing apparel had not been at all scattered around the house, but was contained, on the contrary, within the narrow limits of her own private domain.

When all was done, and Mrs. Dillaye sat down on one of the ample "Saratogas" to think about it, she remarked to herself:

"What a terrible thing wine is. To think of her inheriting such a taste for it that she could

not keep her hands off from my own brandy flask
when it happened to come in her way. And it
couldn't have tasted very good, either, with what
was in it."

Wine. That was what she called it.

And yet Carrie Dillaye had not inherited a taste
for "wine," and there had not been a drop of it in
the fatal flask which came a little more than "in her
way." And many a human being goes down to the
gutter, and lower still, and he and his friends lay
the curse of it upon "wine," a liquid of which
neither he nor they know the taste.

But Mrs. Dillaye was about to comfort herself
with some additional remarks upon the subject of
intemperance and its manifold evils, when she heard
the sound of a well-known foot on the stairs, and
hastily slipped from her not very graceful perch on
the Saratoga. Even for a tall woman, it was a
pretty high seat.

"Mr. Dillaye! Why, what can have brought you
home?"

"This did, and I think you may read it for yourself."

"This" was the legal document he had received,
that morning, and it was no wonder he preferred
his wife should read it, rather than himself unfold
to her its unpleasant contents.

Rapidly her rusty-brown eyes ran from line to
line, down more than one long page, and at first

it seemed as if she were trying to hold her breath till she got through. That proving an impossibility, she still employed so little air in her reading that when, at last, she crushed the paper in her hand she could only gasp:

" Mr. Brown! Stephen. Mr. Brown!"

" The old villain! Yes, it's his work."

" Have you seen him? Where is Caroline?"

" I've seen him, but he refused to tell me."

" Then she's at his house. We must see her, Mr. Dillaye."

" I would not cross his threshold!"

" But we must make her cross it. Why, she has not even her clothes—"

" I expect a man here for them any minute. There's the door-bell, now. I hurried home to tell you."

" Not a stitch of them shall go out of the house till she comes for them."

" We cannot help ourselves, my dear. It is a legal proceeding. If we do not give them up they will be taken by force. Trust Daniel Brown for that. The cast-iron old scoundrel."

The servant who answered the door-bell was coming up now, and Mr. Dillaye's surmise proved correct. The young gentleman from Mr. Allyn's office had brought a carman with him, and had his employer's instructions to permit no trifling.

" They are all ready for her," exclaimed Mrs.

Dillaye, with a suddenness of acquiescence which astonished her husband. "Everything is in these trunks. You'd better take them all."

"Mrs. Dillaye, will it not do as well to send one of them?"

"And have her accuse me of holding back something? No, indeed. She shall have every rag. And then we must see her ourselves. I tell you she is there."

There was work to be done in getting those trunks on the dray, for they contained old clothes as well as new, and winter outfit as well as that adapted to the season, and, by the time the young man from Allyn's set out with his prize, Mr. Dillaye was already half-way to Mr. Brown's in the cab. Not that he had any idea of then entering the house, but, an hour and a half later, he was able to say to his wife:

"I did precisely as you requested, and I saw the dray stop in front of Mr. Brown's gate."

"Then we must call there, to-morrow, just as if nothing had happened, and Caroline herself had sent for us."

Mr. Dillaye's face was a study as he listened, but discipline was fully vindicated in the fact that he made no open sign of dissent. If he made none then, it was safe to say that he would not on the morrow, but it is not always wise to put off until the morrow what can just as well be done to-day.

When Mr. Brown came to dinner that afternoon, almost his first question was:

"Mabel, did Carrie's things come?"

"Yes, uncle, and she and I and Mrs. Boyce have been sorting and packing, ever since. We will be all ready to start, in the morning."

"Well, dear, a few weeks in the mountains will be good for all of you. Sorry I cannot go right away, but you'll see me before long. I had a talk with Mr. Dillaye, to-day, but I won't say anything about it just yet."

He had to before the evening was over, and it was anything but agreeable, even though Carrie tried hard to seem composed, and kept most of her crying for her own room.

There was no change made in the programme, however, and when, the next day, while Mr. Brown was about his business, a lady and gentleman called to see Miss Dillaye, all the answer they could get from the staid servant at the door was:

"The ladies is all gone to the country, mum. I don't know when they'll be back. Not for some weeks, mum."

And "the country" is so very wide!

CHAPTER XXVII.

A VERY STORMY PASSAGE.

SLOWLY, one after another, the summer days went by, there in the city. Almost as slowly as to Dr. Milyng himself, among his rocks and deserts. But all the while Mr. Brown's plans and ideas were working themselves into a more magnificent system of confusion in that clear, practical and benevolent head of his. He saw more and more, as he studied the matter, what tremendous things he was capable of doing, if he only had money enough for them, and again and again were his growing trays of specimens brought out upon the library table to be studied over.

He was alone now, and the evenings were too warm to read with any comfort, and almost everybody he knew was out of town.

The matter of Carrie Dillaye's estate was going forward, but a little slowly, for he still hoped to secure a settlement without the business getting into the courts and the newspapers. As to the

257

Boyce affair, that required little further attention, as there was no prospect that the widow would ever receive any other consolation than a release from any claim upon her, individually. That would come, as a matter of course, in due time, and Mr. Allyn would see that nothing was overlooked.

But Mr. Brown had more than a little business of his own, which required attention and settlement, especially if he was ever to do anything with those philanthropic dreams of his. Even if he should not, these were times when careful men looked closely to their investments, and were disposed to trust as little as might be to the hands and brains of subordinates.

But if time travelled slowly elsewhere, his feet lingered with multiplied loads of lead and other heavy material among the wards of the hospital on the Island. Not even the most faithful and zealous discharge of his duties among the patients availed to relieve Fred Heron of the intolerable sense of duration which seemed to be crushing him.

The days had already lengthened into weeks, and these were a good deal more like centuries to look back upon, while those which were yet to come before the termination of his sentence were ages and ages to face.

"What an awful thing a life-sentence must be," he muttered, as he lay awake in the growing light of one cloudless morning. "And yet there is one

relief there. The very absence of hope must be
something. One could get a sort of resignation
out of that. I'm used to being forgotten, but I
haven't acquired the faculty of forgetting myself.
That's what's the matter. I'm looking forward to
some sort of life to come. This isn't life. And
yet I've done what I could for these poor fellows.
Even the surgeon told me he hoped I'd get myself
convicted again as soon as possible. So I shall, if I
see another policeman pounding a sick man. But
what's this? I haven't had a touch of it before for
a fortnight. Perhaps a cup of coffee will help me
throw it off."

Perhaps. It had done so, in part, at least, on one
or two occasions, for "this" of which he was conscious was simply a return of that old inward
opium-gnawing with which he had wrestled so often.
He could have gratified it now, without much difficulty, for there were all sorts of things in the dispensary, and the hospital assistants had their privileges. Hardly any one seemed to remember, nowadays, that he was a convict, and Miller treated him
with a half-way sort of respect, as a man who must
really be somebody, if ever he should get out of his
bad luck. Miller had known all sorts of men to
take a brief vacation on the Island, and the great
world they had left be none the wiser for it.

One of the consequences of Fred's hospital occupation, as well as of his exceptional steadiness and

good behavior, had been that he was now a privileged character, not the only one by a good many, with a pretty free run of the whole water-guarded area.

And pretty well the water guarded it, too, with its strong tides, its powerful eddies, its absolute certainty of drowning nine men out of ten who should fall into it, and the added certainty that lynx-eyed policemen were patrolling the opposite banks to whom a man in convict garb or even in wet clothing would surely be an object of curiosity.

But Fred was not in convict garb, and he had more than once gazed into that water at the "slack," when the eddies were still, and the straws on the surface barely moved, and he had thought how short a swim would give him at least a chance of liberty. And with it, too, a chance of being sent back again for a longer term and under less favorable circumstances.

Reason had repeatedly urged him to wait, those few remaining days, and he had waited, heroically, and perhaps he would still have waited if it had not been for that singular return of his malady.

It is one of the curious phenomena of chronic narcotic poisoning, so to describe it, that the return of the hunger itself, after long abstinence, brings with it some of the mental and physical effects more or less fully developed, of a dose of the poison. That is one reason why precisely the same antidote may often be employed with effect.

The same is true, to a less degree, with alcoholic poisoning. The symptoms vary so much, however, in different cases, that there is little wonder professional men are at such loggerheads about it all. Each man reasons from his own experience and observation, and sometimes these are worth a good deal more than they are at other times.

In Fred Heron's present case his cup of contract coffee gave him a little temporary relief. It might have given him more if there had been more coffee in it, but it was a species of Java and Mocha, mixed, of which the vender might truthfully have declared:

"No chiccory in this. Give you my word. This is the genuine bean."

So it was, but not all beans are alike in the effect of soup made from them upon the disordered, or ordered, human system.

And so, as Fred proceeded with the punctual discharge of his daily duties, his old enemy grew to larger and larger proportions within him, till his hand shook and his step became uncertain. He made a tremendous effort, for he knew he would have a chance for a breath of fresh air, by-and-by, and he longed for a look at the walls and spires of the city.

A busy day, with a number of new arrivals, some of them very interesting cases, and it was later than usual before the opportunity came. When it did, he had to take it carefully, so that no man's attention was attracted to him as he drew nearer and nearer the unwalled, unguarded edge on which he was so hungry to stand. As yet, not a thought of anything more had entered his mind, for it was still broad daylight, and the tide was rushing out with even more than its usual violence.

O how beautiful the city looked—the great city, by which such men as he were so utterly forgotten on principle. He drew in his breath painfully as he stood there all alone, and it seemed as if he had never been so much alone in his life. Forgotten by even the keepers of the prison. He wondered if indeed any one really remembered him. And then he felt the rising within him of a strong, painful, almost agonizing exhilaration, and with it came a thought that was full of despairing temptation.

"If it were only night! If it were but dark! I could not more than die, and that would surely bring me a sort of freedom. Would it, though? How about suicide? Would it be suicide if I got drowned? I wonder where they go to—"

He had not been looking up, or he would have seen that, even before he left the hospital, the summer sky had begun to exhibit symptoms of an approaching change. There are no storms so terrible as those which gather in the hearts of men, but now and then an August afternoon will give the world a very fair material imitation of them. One of these

was coming now, and any sensible convict would
have sought the shelter of his prison, as every
keeper and patrol had already done, for the sky
was as black as the cap the old-time judges wore
when they sentenced men to be hung for sheep-
stealing.

Fred had noticed nothing of it all, but he saw
that the angry flood before him was growing
strangely dark and menacing, except where it was
streaked with livid lines of foam. The air was
charged with electricity and all his nerves were so
many galvanic points prepared to receive it.

Does not the mind as well as the body sometimes
take in from an outer atmosphere of its own some
subtle fluid which prepares it for explosive action?

Fred Heron felt as if he were full of something.
Full to bursting.

There was a vivid flash of lightning, followed by
such a stunning thunder crash as made him start
back from the edge of the water and look around
him.

Had night indeed come?

Something like darkness had, and in a moment
more not only the city over yonder, but the gray
buildings on the Island were hidden from him by
blinding sheets of plunging rain.

He stepped forward again.

It was less than four feet from the level of the
bank to the surface of the water, but he could only

see the hissing, foaming rush, as the torrent from above smote the offended torrent below.

Fred Heron was a good swimmer, with enough of practice to know precisely the nature of the risk he was running, but he never thought of either his own skill or the terrible danger.

The thunder pealed again, in a long, continuous roll, and the lightning made blue clefts in the glittering walls of the falling rain. That was the last thing he saw as he yielded to the storm within him and without him, and sprang with a fierce shout from the stone sea-wall of the Island.

It was well he made a leap, for the impetus of it carried him to the further side of a somewhat dangerous eddy, and within the power of the out-rushing tide. What a power that was when he felt it grasp him.

No living swimmer could have done more than keep himself on its surface as it bore him swiftly away.

"It'll carry me out to sea if I let it have its own will," he thought, as he strove to direct his course towards the opposite shore. "If it isn't running six miles an hour and more, I'm mistaken."

More than that, just there, but not so fast in the wider waters below. It was one result of the heavy rain, however, that but little sea was running, in spite of the wind. There was very small danger, or hope either, that he would be seen by anybody.

" I must look out for ferryboats and other craft," he said to himself. " If I go under one, or if one goes over me, it'll be all day with me."

It was hard work, for even a good swimmer, and Fred was beginning to feel anxious. He had not the least idea how far he had been carried, but he was keenly aware of one other thing—every trace of his unpleasant internal sensations had disappeared and he felt like shouting:

" Victory !"

Just then a huge, misty object loomed up before him, and he was compelled to pull with all his remaining strength to avoid being swept against the hull of a vessel, moored in the stream. He saw no one, and he had not made up his mind whether or not to shout for help, when, as he reached the stern, he saw a yawl-boat fastened to it by a painter.

That would do, admirably, but when he clambered over the side he was compelled to throw himself flat on the bottom, utterly exhausted, although the water was several inches deep. It was a very grateful feeling, that of having something buoyant between him and death, and he lay as if the mere pelting of the rain were a luxury.

Just how long it was he could not have told, precisely, but he became conscious, after awhile, of another motion than the rocking of the waves, and he raised his head.

There was no ship in sight over the prow of the

boat. The painter was free. It had been carelessly secured, and he had helped loosen it in climbing in. There were oars in the boat and he knew how to use them, but nothing could have been more hopeless than an effort to restore that yawl to her owners, just then, and he did not think of such a thing. It would have been a more hopeless task than even Fred himself imagined, for she had been in the temporary service of the tramps of the harbor, and when the crew of that ship returned on board, after the storm, they had small difficulty in capturing three half-drunken river-thieves who had been trapped at their vocation by giving the painter of their stolen boat so very tipsy a hitch. But Fred Heron knew nothing of all that. His only ambition was to get ashore somewhere without attracting too much attention, and he knew he could do that best, if he got ashore at all, while it was still raining hard.

CHAPTER XXVIII.

A PERMANENT PROVISION MADE FOR TWO OF THE MINOR CHARACTERS.

THE one peculiar thing about a clock is that it ticks right on, without the slightest reference to the human experiences, few or many, which may or may not be crowded into the hours it measures.

There were clocks, for instance, in the western home which Bessie Heron had provided for herself, and they continued to tick for her after she had written every letter which her sense of duty called for. And after that, of course, she felt called upon to do something for the clocks. That is, she determined to make the best possible use of her time, and so she said to her hospitable friends.

She had soon discovered that they had responsibilities and connections of their own. Strange as it seemed, at first sight, their family relations had been planned for them in gross disregard of such possibilities as the advent of Bessie Heron, and they were in grave danger of other visitors to come.

Had Fred been the man he should have been, and never exposed himself to the wretched casualties of war and sickness and consequent disability of all sorts, this would have made no difference, but as it was, Bessie foresaw a coming necessity for action on her part. And she was a young woman of action. She had always been. She was fond of saying so. She had taken care of herself, at the expense of others, for ever so long, in spite of the misconduct of various members of her own family. She was ready, now, to continue her glorious work, and all she asked for was her work room.

If there was one thing in which she was without a rival, it was the management of children, provided she could have unobstructed control. In spite of all manner of obstructions, she had brought up her father, uncles, brothers, and quite an extended list of her male connections, not to speak of outside parties, and now she was absolutely hungry for a fresh engagement. Nor could one be long in making an offer, in a western city, where young women of her stamp must necessarily be like the visits of other angels, far and few between. Very few.

A middle-aged widower, with children on his hands. A good house, plenty of money, business to attend to, frequent absences from home. That was a mission field for which Bessie Heron was willing to have sacrificed anything except the duty and privilege of writing to and talking about her erring relatives, and she entered upon it with a great sigh of admiration.

Not of the mission field, but of her heroineism in undertaking it.

She wrote about it to Mrs. Baird and to other of her friends in the east, and, if they did not melt into tears of some kind over those letters, it was no fault of the mistress-hand by which they were written. Every justice was done, assuredly, to the virtues— and the failings—of the widower's four children, and the terrible defects of their bringing-up before the arrival of their good angel. That is about the usual way with missionaries, home and foreign. Trust them to count and classify the weeds in their respective vineyards, but who ever heard of one finding so much as a wild vine?

But Bessie's time went by for her in her new vineyard, more rapidly than for others, and she was so thoroughly ingrossed with her weeds and other things that she hardly wondered at not receiving an answer to her letters to Fred. And yet he had always been a good correspondent, and she ought really to have wondered a little.

Perhaps she may have felt, with Dr. Milyng, that she had crossed her desert, and that it really mattered very little what became of the pony which had carried her over. He would be pretty sure to find pasture, somewhere.

And yet, to do him justice, Dr. Milyng did care. His day of rest by the summer remnants of the far-western " river" was not prolonged for an hour more than was necessary, and his quadruped companion was called upon for all the working power he had in him, when they again moved forward. But when, some few days thereafter, the borders of civilization were reached, within "staging distance" of a railway terminus, the doctor made no effort to sell that pony.

The " dust and nugget" part of his precious luggage was promptly turned into ready cash and eastern bills of exchange. Saddle and bridle and even weapons were transformed into available greenbacks, but the doctor steadfastly refused more than one good offer for the full value of his mustang. He had his eyes about him, nevertheless, and he seemed at last to have found the man he wanted under the tattered sombrero of a veteran New Mexican herder.

Tattered as was the sombrero of Senor Jose Vallejo, he could have drawn his check for an amount which would have startled many a better dressed man, and he and the doctor understood one another at sight.

"You see," said the doctor, " I stole that pony of the Apaches, 'way beyond the Mogollan Sierras."

" Si, Señor."

"And I worked him across the alkali plains and I risked my own life to save his."

"Si, Señor."

"Now he's come through with me, and I can't take money for him."

"Of course not. I understand you. It is the feeling of a true caballero."

"Will you give him the freedom of your range, not to be worked or branded?"

"One of my peones will lead him to my ranche to-night, if you say it."

"Will you oblige me by accepting this repeating rifle? I assure you it is a perfect weapon, Senor."

"You honor me, Señor. I esteem it a great privilege to accept your favor. The pony will live and die without a saddle-mark. May I ask your kind attention to some little matters for me in St. Louis? A caballero of such distinguished sentiments is a man I can trust. I beg of you to give me your considerate friendship."

A very ragged miner was Dr. Milyng, at that day and hour, and an equally remarkable person was the man he was conversing with, but the former had been a United States Army Surgeon, and was now the owner of endless mining claims, besides the very good sum in his pockets, while the latter was lord of uncounted herds of cattle, sheep and horses, as well as of "land till you can't rest."

There was little doubt but what the Apache

pony's latter days would be better for him than his first, for Señor Jose Vallejo would have used up his last mustang before he would have called for a day's labor from the beast he had so received "in trust."

And yet Dr. Milyng discovered that the business entrusted to his management in consequence of the pony matter carried with it "commissions" which materially increased the moderate store he had digged and washed from the placers "this side the mountains."

From that time forward, however, the doctor's movements were governed by a very different phase of human progress from that against which he had been struggling since he was compelled to part company with his faithful Oliver. A couple of days of swift staging brought him to one of the rays of the great railroad spider-web which has been woven over the Western Continent, and he had nothing to do then, but to slide along that ray towards the central den where the spiders themselves abide. There were stoppages, brief ones, of course, especially for the care of Senor Vallejo's interests in St. Louis, but very little time was really wasted before he found himself once more bewildered by the rush and roar of the great city by the sea.

He had been there before. He had visited many another great city, in his time, but never had he so deeply felt the unfathomable difference between that awful hive of human life and the solitudes among which he had been seeking the "Golden Heart." He could hardly make it real.

The streets were ravines which ought to lead to either heights or depths, and they only opened into other ravines as helplessly regular and aimless. The crowds were an intolerable burden, for among them all he saw no man whom he cared to either seek or avoid.

He had had something like a similar experience, in days gone by, but it all seemed new to him now, and he found himself possessed with a strong desire to flee from it and be at rest again among his peaceful mountain ranges.

He had had in mind, as he whirled along over the railways which brought him, the names of more than one man to whom he meant to open the subject of his mining discoveries, and that of Mr. Daniel Brown had been among them, but, on the very morning after his arrival, he found his first choice made for him.

He had selected his hotel, hit or miss, and had made himself remarkably at home, as the hotel clerk thought, over-night, but he had risen, bright and early, with the idea that what he needed most was an "outfit."

A clothing store, a bootmaker's, hatter's, and various other establishments, were visited, with such a result that Oliver himself would not have known his master, not to speak of matters which were ordered to be sent to his hotel. If he had been preparing for a season of fashionable operations among the summer watering-places, now so soon to close, he could hardly have been more liberal. But the doctor's notions of what belonged to the armor of a mining warrior about to assail the strongholds of eastern capital included something more than mere clothing. He must have weapons as well as uniform, and he entered a jewelry store. He knew what he wanted. A seal ring, some diamond studs, sleeve-buttons, a watch and chain, and something curious to hang on the chain.

That was all, but when he came to pay for them the loose paper in his wallet, already drawn upon for many items of expenditure, was hardly sufficient.

A trifle, to a man who could offer western bills of exchange to so comfortable an amount.

"Are you Dr. Charles Milyng?"

"Of course I am. Just give me a pen and I'll endorse that draft. You can give me your check for the difference. It's all right."

"Haven't a doubt of it, my dear sir, but you can easily identify yourself?"

"I identify myself? Do you mean to dispute my word?"

"Certainly not. It's a mere matter of business. We can't deviate from our rule, you know. Somebody that knows you must identify you."

The doctor's black eyes flashed, and he felt for his revolver.

It was not there, and it was just as well for the jewelry salesman that it was not.

Then he looked at the watch and chain which he had already put on, and he thought for a moment.

"City ways," he muttered, and then he added, aloud, "Do you know Mr. Daniel Brown?"

"*The* Mr. Brown? Merchant, and all that?" replied the clerk, running over several items of the business connections by which the world knew of such a man.

"That's him. He knows me."

"He'll do. One of our men will go with you to his office. He'll cash your bill for you at sight, if he knows you."

"Knows me? Well, I guess he does. Send on your man. Tell him to come right along with me."

"Queer customer," remarked the man of gold and watches, as the doctor sailed out of sight, "but I guess he's the right sort. I'd like to sell a few more watches and things to-day at those figures. Old Brown's check'll do for me."

And so it did, but Dr. Milyng himself was hardly prepared for the exceedingly hearty welcome he received from his old acquaintance, the city merchant. His bill was cashed, as a matter of course, but he himself was forbidden to leave the office un-

til he did so in Mr. Brown's own carriage, and be‑
fore the evening was over, burned out like a candle
to the very socket, the doctor had discovered that
he was under no necessity of hunting around among
eastern capitalists. The man whose soul was all
gunpowder for the kind of sparks he had brought
with him was already on fire. The tray of speci‑
mens had been brought out, as a matter of course,
but they, the specimens, were mere mud compared
to the evidences of mineral wealth which Dr. Milyng
laid beside them.

, " We can have any assay you please to ask for,
Mr. Brown—"

" Don't need any, my dear old friend. You say
it's the best mine you ever found ?"

" Found, sir? I didn't find it. There's no such
thing about it. It's the centre of a system. I
reasoned it out, years ago, and I've been working
down to it, ever since. The gold region is no hap‑
hazard work of luck and chance. It's governed by
laws, and I've discovered the operation of those
laws, that's all. Every system has a heart. Our mine
is the heart, not a mere vein. Veins play out; use up;
all that sort of thing. What we are to work on is the
golden heart of the continent. The golden heart of
the world. All we want is the money to work it."

" I've got that," said Mr. Brown.

" Then we'll form our company, and I won't look
any further."

CHAPTER XXIX.

SOMETHING LIKE A MODERN CASE OF META-MORPHOSIS.

M R. BROWN had been wise in sending the ladies of his household into the mountains for the remainder of the hot weather. Thereby he placed Carrie Dillaye beyond the reach of annoyance from other members of her family, pending the proceedings for a settlement, now in the hands of Mr. Allyn. Thereby he relieved Mabel Varick from a responsibility which threatened to be a trifle too heavy for a young lady of her few years and small experience. Thereby, too, although he hardly confessed as much to himself, he prevented the sojourn of Mrs. Boyce at his house from putting on too permanent an aspect. As it now appeared, she had but accompanied his two nieces for a vacation in the country, and he was in less of a hurry to join them than the widow herself expected or could, perhaps, have desired.

The locality selected for them was sufficiently fashionable, and they were under no bonds to re-

277

main there a day longer than pleased them, and the
two girls themselves were speedily ready to declare
to one another that they would not have been without Mrs. Boyce for the world. She did not in any
perceptible degree curtail their freedom, and yet
her matronly presence did supply such a tremendous
element of propriety and protection.

He would have been a singularly bold social free-
booter who would have ventured on any, the slightest, act of piracy, under the guns of such a woman-
of-war as Mrs. Boyce.

She deemed it proper, on more than one occasion,
to come out, in company with her young friends,
resplendent with such jewels as made them proud
of her, and effectually prevented any notion, on the
part of anybody, that she was other than a "great
lady." Even those who failed to bow to her
matchless manners were ready to prostrate themselves before her diamonds.

It was a regular campaign for the widow, and she
would have won every battle of it, but for one thing.

Mabel and Carrie called it a peace, or at least a
truce, in the absence of Uncle Daniel, and there was
really nothing to be won from them during so complete a cessation of hostilities.

Mrs. Boyce began to understand it, after a while,
and she longed for, although she was too wise to
hasten, a return to some sort of debatable ground.
It was altogether too much like a defeat to have her

position as "elderly friend of the family" so frankly and unreservedly conceded to her.

"Could it be," she thought, "that Mabel Varick was anything more than a mere girl, after all? There is no doubt about Carrie. She is even too ready to get up flirtations. Mabel has not flirted with a soul since we left the city."

That was a bad sign, as every matron knows. It always means something, and it is not always easy to discover what it means.

There was nothing for it, however, but to see it through, and Mrs. Boyce herself had but a faint idea of how little would have been gained by a transfer of operations to the city.

Mr. Brown's business affairs, of themselves, would have been enemy enough to meet, just then, with his fifty-odd years to back them, not to speak of Mabel Varick and other considerations, but now— the arrival of Dr. Milyng!

The doctor himself had no idea how often his face had returned to the merchant's memory and his name to his lips, during the dreamy evenings spent over those fragments of ore at the library table. Still less did he imagine the effect actually produced by the exhibition of his few but weighty evidences of the wealth of his new discovery.

Talk of boys.

If you care to know what enthusiasm is, wait till you see a man of mature middle-age throw him-

self away on a hobby. Henry Berg, Cyrus Field,
Dr. Livingstone, all the rest of them, how they do
shame the cold-blooded, cautious, calculating shiver-
ers of twenty-one. Now and then some sophomore
gets up gas enough to blow out his cork, but then it
is only a cork, after all, as a general thing, and the
world never joins in a grand rush to pick it up.
They know there could not have been anything
wonderful in that kind of a bottle, no matter how
large a kind of beer the bottle may think of itself.

It is a grand thing to capture a genuine hobby
and break it in for your own riding. If it does not
throw you and break your blessed neck—you
must take your own risk of that when you mount
it—it will be sure to carry you somewhere, where
neither you nor anybody else ever went before.

Mr. Brown's hobby was yet a trifle indefinite as
to form and features, and was likely to develop a
good many of both, in time, but he felt the bounding motion of it under him, from the moment when
Dr. Milyng entered his office. The doctor was compelled to transfer his baggage and headquarters
from his hotel to the merchant's residence, that first
night, bringing with him the ores which had been
such a weariness to the pony during that thirsty
third day on the alkali plains.

The next morning the two rode down town together, and Mr. Brown never stopped talking about
mining affairs until he reached his office. That

was the reason he never till then asked himself the question what he should do with Dr. Milyng for the remainder of the day.

It was a question which had to be asked and answered, nevertheless, and the doctor could give but a very partial and insufficient solution of the conundrum.

Ores could be taken to an assayer. That would be something, and would consume a little time.

There could be a consultation with Mr. Allyn as to legal formula relating to a mining company, of which the members and corporators were yet to be selected. Then there could be a hunt for a map-maker, by whom a more or less accurate profile of the region around the Golden Heart should be put on paper. All that was very well, and the merchant and the miner stopped there, as if exhausted in laying out such a programme for one day's operations.

But all that was mere antelope-shooting to a man like Dr. Milyng. He could have seen twenty lawyers, fifty assayers, a hundred map-makers, killed them all, and then complained that the hunting was poor. When and where he got his lunch, he could hardly have reported correctly, but in the course of the afternoon he found himself exploring some of the wild and unknown regions in the lower part of the city. He knew there was salt water in that direction, somewhere, and that some of those red-brick ravines and passes led down, through the ranges of warehouses and lager-beer shops, to wharves, and shipping, and he had pene-trated within a hopeful distance of a discovery when he became aware of a change in the weather. No such thing could have taken him by surprise on the plains or among the mountains, where storms give fair warning, but now he had barely time to spring past a wooden Indian, of no tribe with which he was familiar, before the rain came down. It was no hardship for a man who smoked, to be driven into a tobacco shop, but if it had been he could have consoled himself by gazing out at the familiar violence of that " cloud-burst."

There was nothing for it, having respect to his civilized clothes, but to wait, and he waited.

And it happened that, at the end of that very street, there was a boat-landing. A pier not alto-gether given up to big vessels. There was hardly another like it on the whole water-front of the city, which is like life, with few places where small craft can land their cargoes with comfort and security.

Just before the deluge ceased, there came a yawl-boat, rowed by one man, leisurely pulling towards that boat-landing, and the only wonder was that the oarsman should be in no greater hurry to get ashore.

" Had a tough pull, I reckon," said a policeman under an awning as he saw the boat pulled in.

"Hullo, mister," shouted a small boy, "forgot yer umberelly, did yer?"

But the drenched boatman made no sign or sound as he fastened his boat, nodded to the pier-keeper, and he hurried away up the street.

He moved very much like a man who was wet and wanted a change of clothes, and everybody looked at him as if they thought he was just that kind of a man.

Certainly no one thought of inquiring how he happened to have come ashore in that particular yawl.

The rain was holding up, now, and the sun was coming out again as the boatman strode rapidly forward. It was a hot sun, too, such as comes after thunderstorms, and well adapted to make men and things dry again.

"Beg your pardon, sir."

A wet man has no business to run against a dry one, especially one so glossily dry, so shiningly unmoist as the gentleman addressed, but he showed no sign of bad temper.

"Got soaked, did ye? Hallo. Look here, is it you? Fred Heron! How d'ye do, old boy? If I ain't glad, now. Give us your hand."

"Dr. Milyng—"

"That's me. I'd have given anything to meet you. You're just the man I want. Where'd you come from? Never mind your wetting. That's nothing."

Fred Heron had taken the doctor's outstretched hand, almost mechanically, and he had let him shake it half-loose, but he withdrew it, now, remarking:

"You're the first man I've met, Dr. Milyng—"

"Am I? Are all the rest dead? I ain't, then. What are you up to? I'm just glad to have met you."

Fred's face had been changing color rapidly for those few moments, but there was a firm expression gathering about his lips.

"Dr. Milyng," he said, now half-huskily, "you're an old friend, and I must tell you just how it is with me. I've just escaped from the Island."

"The Island? What's that? It's a kind of jail, isn't it?"

"It's all kinds of a jail."

"And you got yourself corralled by the lawyers, did you? How did they get in on ye? What was the matter with your lookout?"

There was not the slightest cooling in the cordiality of the doctor's manner. On the contrary, his interest seemed to be growing, as if his young friend had come out of a sharp brush with some tribe of Eastern Apaches, and was about to tell the story of it. And so he was, for Fred could but see and feel that anything but the utmost frankness was out of the question. His wet clothes were of less consequence in the warm sunshine now pouring down upon him, and his story was not a long one, for he confined it mainly to the manner of his getting in, at the Island, and his remarkable exploit of that very afternoon. He told it all well, but his modest way of presenting the facts did but bring them out more clearly, and the doctor came very near throwing his arms around the very damp narrator.

If Fred Heron had had a friendly hold upon the heart of the mining veteran before he told that story, he had fastened him now as with hooks of steel. The English language itself ran short of words to express the doctor's enthusiastic admiration, and loose fragments of half a dozen others were called in to make up the deficiency. He wound up with:

"You shall go right along with me, my boy. You shall be the secretary of our mining company. We will go right straight to old Brown's office and I'll tell him I've engaged you."

"What, in this rig?"

"That rig? No, indeed. He's a very particular man, and—well, if I ain't an old fool. Come on, Fred, we'll get you an outfit first thing."

"But I've no money, doctor, and I can't borrow, even of you."

"Can't you, indeed? Well, then, I'll divide my pile with you, and I'll break your neck if you make any dispute about it. Don't be too proud, now. It's only an advance on your salary as secretary of the company."

"But I don't know anything about the company. What is it?"

"You'll know, soon enough. Come along, now."

The ideas entertained by men of Dr. Milyng's stamp about money matters are apt to be a little vague. No others set so small a value on the treasures they hunt for, once they have found and pocketed them. All their greed of gold seems to cool off as soon as the metal takes the form of coin, and is at zero when it is expressed by mere paper.

Fred went with the doctor, but was compelled to interfere continually as a moderator of the profuse liberality of the latter's notions of what became the secretary of the Golden Heart to wear and shine with. As it was, he feared that at least three months' pay must have disappeared before their shopping was completed. All their packages had been ordered to a hotel, selected by Fred, and when, after an hour spent in his room, the escaped convict reappeared arm in arm with the now radiant miner, all the keepers on the Island would have walked by without knowing him.

There was one thing more, which tended to make the young man walk firmly and look all men in the face.

While his outward seeming had undergone so great a change, a wonderfully fresh and joyous feeling crept over him, through nerve and vein. A feeling of freedom. Not of mere freedom from stone walls and water-guarded Island limits, but from the torturing grasp of that old enemy within.

He had broken the last fetter of his bondage when he sprang from the sea-wall into the foaming tide.

Dr. Milyng knew nothing of all that, however, and he urged his companion to a tremendously rapid rate of walking as they left the hotel.

"It's four o'clock," he said, "and old Brown 'll be bound home before a great while. We must not run the risk of keeping him waiting."

Risk, indeed!

Mr. Brown had been waiting and fretting and fuming for an hour, and imagining that his friend had lost himself somewhere. The carriage was waiting, too, to take them home to dinner, and the merchant's face clouded a little, when he saw that his wanderer had not returned alone.

"I've found him," exclaimed the doctor, as he marched in. "My old friend, Mr. Fred Heron. Knew his father, and his mother, and his whole family. I'll tell you all about him. He's to be the secretary of our mining company."

Somewhat to the doctor's astonishment, the merchant was on his feet before the queer introduction was over.

"Mr. Heron. Glad to see you, sir. Been wondering for a month and more, why you did not keep your promise to call on me. How do you do, sir?"

"Very well, thank you, Mr. Brown. It has been impossible for me to call. I've not been in the city."

"Tramping, eh? Well, it has done you good, I should say. You must tell me about it when we get to the house. You will dine with us?"

"With pleasure, Mr. Brown. I am anxious to know more about the company."

"You know each other, then," slowly remarked the doctor. "I didn't suppose anybody knew anybody else, here-away. Why, Fred's face is the only one I've met all·day, that I could fit a handle to."

"Big crowds, eh, doctor? Well, the carriage is waiting. We'll drive right to the house."

Fred walked out of the office with them, like a man in a dream. He had waked that morning, a prisoner, on a pallet in a hospital on the Island. He had fought for his life with the angry waves and the storm. He had landed from a stolen boat, with a feeling that the world did not contain a more hopeless, helpless, half-drowned castaway. And here he was, now, better dressed than he had been before for years, and whisking through the streets of the great city in a stylish turnout, the guest of a great merchant, a strong friend by his side, and the opening dawn of a new career before him. Let somebody moralize.

CHAPTER XXX.

THE HARD FATE OF AN ENTERPRISING PUBLIC SERVANT.

DURING all those lengthening days following their fruitless visit to the Brown mansion, Mr. and Mrs. Dillaye found the world growing dark to them.

Not that they were visibly annoyed by those whom Mr. Dillaye termed "the hired minions of Brown's infernal malice."

In fact they knew only too little of the steps which were steadily taken by that astute and cautious gentleman, Mr. Counsellor Allyn. All they knew was that he was moving, and that nothing they could now do could hinder him. The condition of Mr. Dillaye's own business affairs rendered him quite willing that such should be the case, since that which was unknown to him must also be a secret to the financial gentlemen who discounted his notes.

All the more vexatious was it, one morning, to find in a journal somewhat given to the mysterious and sensational in the manufacture of what it called its "news," an item under the head of "mysterious disappearance," setting forth that the daughter of one of the city's first families, the heiress of large wealth, a young lady of singular beauty and accomplishments, and an ornament to the society in which she moved, had been for some weeks among the missing. Her relatives had offered fabulous rewards, so it was stated, and the entire detective force had been employed, but without avail, and the darkest suspicions were entertained of foul play.

"Can they mean Carrie?" he mournfully exclaimed, as he passed the sheet across the breakfast table to his wife.

She read the item carefully through.

"Don't care if they do. What can they make of it? We can give a perfect answer to all inquiries."

"But they have not inquired. They have printed it at once. What they want is something to fill up with."

"Wish it would poison them, then."

But poison does not work on constitutions daily accustomed to it, and the reporter, who had overheard an incautious conversation between two of Mr. Allyn's clerks in a restaurant, was not disposed to let the matter rest there. Not even the contemptuous snubbing he received at the lawyer's office, in spite of his credentials from the influential journal he represented, served to cool his professional ardor. He had struck a trail, and he would

follow it, like a red Indian or any other blood-
hound, for he had even caught the names of individuals with those long, keen ears of his.

Failing to find Mr. Dillaye when he called, in the
course of the day, at that gentleman's place of business, he proceeded at once to his residence.

"My daughter, sir? Mr. Dillaye's daughter?
What have you to do with her?" was the curt
and severe response of the lady who entered the
parlor in response to his card, and who listened so
grimly to his smirking statement of his errand.

"Beg pardon, Madame. A very painful case, no
doubt. Sorry to intrude on family matters, but
the public interest is greatly excited, and it is the
duty of the press to meet the popular demand.
We must really ascertain the particulars, or some of
our unscrupulous rivals may print a false and garbled
account of it."

"Let 'em, then. Miss Dillaye is visiting with her
uncle, Mr. Daniel Brown. You'd better see him, I
think. Good-morning, sir. John, show the gentleman the door, and keep an eye on the hat-rack. See
that no more of his kind get in."

Unbroken was the metallic smile on the reporter's
face as he bowed himself out of the parlor, for he
was used to that sort of thing, and had little doubt
but what he should come again, with a certainty of
a better reception "when the secret leaked out."

And he knew, too, that a hundred other warriors

of his tribe were even then scouting in all directions
for some traces of the very trail he was following.

At the Brown mansion he made even a more
complete failure, for he failed to pass the threshold,
and Prince himself stood calmly by while the housekeeper repeated her assurances that "the ladies is in
the country, sir."

Further questioning was made difficult by the
thickness and strength of the door which was closed
in his face, and any prolonged survey of the premises
was vetoed by Prince. The reporter discerned that
there had been some carelessness in fastening the
wire muzzle, that morning, and he had doubts of
Prince's appreciation of the privileges of a free and
untamed press.

"Old Brown himself. I'll make him disgorge.
See 'f I don't."

And his next descent was upon Mr. Daniel Brown.

"Disappearance? My niece? Miss Dillaye? O
yes. She is my niece, and she has disappeared.
Gone very mysteriously to the Bald Mountain
House, in company with my other niece, Miss Varick,
and her friend, Mrs. Boyce. Remarkable, is it
not? Glad to give you any information, sir."

"But, Mr. Brown—"

"Excuse me, my young friend, that's all. I've no
time to bother with your blunders. Good-morning."

Another very open door through which he somewhat sadly made his exit, but he felt more sure than

ever that he had a good thing on his hands if he could only get at the bottom of it. So strong and so unerring is brute instinct, especially when its brutality is well trained and well rewarded.

There was no throwing him off in that way, and the Bald Mountain House was not so far from the city that the afternoon train could not carry there a man who represented so many puffs of so very many summer hotels. A few hours by rail and boat, and he was there.

"Lo, 'twas a gala night," and the ladies were dressing for the dance which was to come as soon as the dining-hall could be transformed into a ball-room. All the parlors were filling up, already, but the reporter had help from the landlord and the clerk, and Mrs. Boyce's party were duly advised that a gentleman from the city was waiting to have a word with them.

"Will you see him, Mrs. Boyce?" asked Mabel. "I do not know the name on his card."

"He sends word especially to Miss Dillaye. Do you know him, Carrie?"

"I think not, but I will not see him alone. If it were any law business we should have heard from Uncle Daniel or Mr. Allyn."

"If you wish it, dear, I will see what he wants," said Mrs. Boyce, for she had completed her toilette, and in a minute or so more the gentleman of the press felt a throb of triumph at his heart as the stately lady sailed into the reception-room where he waited and hoped.

"Miss Dillaye? I am grateful indeed, and sorry to trouble you about so unpleasant an affair, but I represent the most widely read and influential journal in the country, and we are desirous of lay· ing before the public the particulars of your late mysterious disappearance. I wish particularly to know all that happened, and under what circumstances you returned. I assure you it is not generally known that such is the fact."

Mrs. Boyce listened, with an expression of the deepest interest.

"Certainly. But may I ask when I disappeared?"

"That's precisely the first thing I wish to know. The public is deeply interested."

"Very sorry to disappoint you, but I really do not know. This is the first I have heard of it. If you would only tell me, now."

"Why, Miss Dillaye, you certainly will not be so cruel, so unwise. The most dreadfully incorrect reports might get in circulation—"

"Permit me to correct you, sir. My name is Mrs. Boyce, and you will please address me as such. I beg leave to decline any further conversation upon the subject of your errand. It is a strictly private affair. Good-evening, sir."

A flood of light broke in upon the soul of the reporter as the elegantly-dressed lady swept from the room. He saw through it all, now. Not even the shallow subterfuge played by the landlord and his cunning subordinate were proof against such sagacity as his. He would not let them know he had seen through it. Not he.

"O if I could only get a glimpse of Boyce himself!"

And so he lingered at the door of the dining ball-room, until, the centre of a brilliant group of ladies and gentlemen, the widow passed him. He entered, he watched, he made his unerring selection.

Mabel Varick and Carrie Dillaye had begged Mrs. Boyce to relieve them as much as possible of that particular young man, but they had never guessed what would come of it by reason of his being so skilfully detained at the widow's side.

Another day, and the great journal announced the solution of its social enigma.

The supposed disappearance had been an elopement, no more, no less, and the lady, "who, though very beautiful, is quite old enough to take care of herself, has evidently married for love. Nothing else would compel any woman to tie herself to such a red-haired noodle of a boy as Mr. Boyce, whoever he may be. It is rumored, by the way, that he is enormously wealthy, but, of course, that has nothing to do with it. Her family and friends are evidently a good deal discomfited by the match and the manner of it. The happy couple are spending their honeymoon at the Bald Mountain House, the accomplished proprietor of which popular resort is doing his utmost to make it pleasant for them."

There was half a column of it, and there was no question but what it was news, pure and simple, and the reporter had won a glorious triumph, as usual, over the obstacles thrown in his way by the absurd scruples of private delicacy.

When, however, that article was perused by Mr. Daniel Brown, he picked up his pen with a very red face.

The first thing he wrote was a telegram. The second was a note, which was carried to the editorial office of that newspaper by Mr. Allyn, and was therefore printed.

It was a bad thing for the reporter, for it called the attention of his superiors and the public to the facts that, " My niece, now visiting with me, did not run away or elope; is not married; was not seen by your reporter, or conversed with; and her friend Mrs. Boyce, whom he seems to have determined to misrepresent, is the widow of the head of the late house of Boyce, Millington & Co. You have been very absurdly victimized."

And then everybody laughed at the great journal, except the ladies whose names had been bandied about so freely, and the discharged reporter himself. The latter was dropped, as his chief informed him, "for being made a fool of by a woman." As if, indeed, he was to blame for his likeness to Adam.

But the telegram brought to a sudden end that pleasant vacation among the mountains, for Mr. Brown wisely concluded that the best way to prevent any mystery was to have his household under his own roof.

A busy man was he, and the little mess provided by the reporter did not tend to clear his mind, so that he might well be pardoned if he neglected to inform Dr. Milyng and Fred Heron of the change in his family arrangements. The former was the very man to have rejoiced at it, but the latter had congratulated himself only too heartily on the existing state of affairs. He had said to himself:

"If Miss Dillaye has told him anything about Rogers, she has not been able to mix me up with him. I'll keep away from the house after she gets home."

He had his misgivings, even then, about what might possibly come to pass, and the more friendly and confidential the treatment he received from Mr. Brown, the more he felt disposed to give him the truth concerning his recent "absence from the city." He spoke to the doctor about it, but the veteran of the mountains had his little streak of worldly wisdom.

"I wouldn't," he said. "It's none of his busi-

ness. He wouldn't see it as I do. He never was
in jail in his life, and he'd be prejudiced. No more
was I, but I've done what would have put me there
if I'd tried it on in the settlements. Why, the last
thing I did, before I came east, was to steal two
horses and a lot of other things. That's a heap
worse than interfering with a policeman."

And so, sure of the sympathy of his admiring
friend, Fred had let matters drift, and Mr. Brown
took a stronger liking to him every day, insisting
on his coming to the house for his dinner and for
the talks about mining matters, not to speak of
social, political, and religious questions, which the
rush of down-town business rendered impossible at
the office. But it was the very frankness of the
manner in which the merchant treated him which
was beginning to trouble him, and, on the day after
the sending of that telegram, he went through Mr.
Brown's front gate with a mind made up. Come
what would, he would make a clean breast of it. No
man should be able to say of him that he had obtained social recognition under false pretences.

"I ought to have told him before," he said to
himself, "the doctor to the contrary notwithstanding."

And so, perhaps, he ought, but there had been a
great many other things to talk about, during
those few days after he came ashore.

CHAPTER XXXI.

EVEN A GOOD DEED SOMETIMES REQUIRES HUMBLE CONFESSION.

MR. BROWN and Dr. Milyng were in the library when Fred Heron arrived, and were busy over some drawings which had that day been sent in from the mapmaker's.

"They will do," remarked the doctor. "What do you think of them, Fred? We will all be out there the first thing, next spring. There's never any winter there, but we must do our travelling before the hot weather sets in. Especially if we are to have lady company."

"Lady company?"

"Yes, Mr. Brown says it's likely we may. We shall not take our machinery with us, you know. Only a strong working party to make a good beginning and complete our surveys. The machinery can follow us. We'll have a grand time."

Fred's face grew gloomier with every word, for the mention of the ladies drove and clinched the last nail in his determination.

"Then, doctor, it's high time Mr. Brown knew precisely what sort of a fellow he is dealing with and bringing into his house in this way. Mr. Brown, I should have said it earlier, but I say it now. I have been a prisoner on the Island."

"You? On the Island?"

"All the time, sir, from the very night I first entered this room until the day Dr. Milyng brought me to your office."

If one of the quartz specimens on the table before him had touched itself off and exploded, Mr. Brown's face could hardly have put on an expression of greater astonishment.

"On the Island, Mr. Heron?"

"And what is more, sir—"

Just then the door from the hall swung open, and Fred heard a great rustle of silk and the like behind him. He had not been seated, and he turned on his feet to face the unexpected interruption.

"Miss Dillaye!"

"Mr. Rogers! O Uncle Daniel, I'm so glad you have found him. Has he told you? I have so much to thank him for."

She held her hand out frankly as she spoke, and Fred saw no reason why he should not take it, although his face was crimson as he did so, for it looked still more like a case of false pretences.

" Was that the name under which you were con-victed," sternly demanded Mr. Brown.

" It was—"

" But, uncle, it was he that wrote you about me. He was the only friend I had there."

" There was no name signed to the letter I received—"

"Carrie," suddenly exclaimed Mabel Varick, " why do you not tell Uncle Daniel all you told me? He ought to know why Mr. Heron was arrested. Tell him. If you won't, I will—"

And Mabel went on like one who could not wait for any other tongue, for never in her life had any-thing appealed to her like the story her cousin had told her of the young hero of the hospital, locked up for his knightly interference in behalf of the helpless against the strong. She forgot that the hero himself was standing there by the library table, and she told the tale with flushed cheeks and flashing eyes.

" There is more in that girl than I thought there was," said Mrs. Boyce to herself. "I'm on the young man's side as strongly as she is. Good for Mabel, but it ought to have come from Carrie."

So thought Carrie herself, and she added all the emphasis she knew how to her cousin's swift recital. As for poor Fred, his head was drooping humbly enough, now, as if he longed to hide it somewhere, and then, to complete his discomfiture, Dr. Milyng capped the story of his incarceration with that of his superlatively daring escape.

The merchant had not lost a word.

" Saved my house from burglars," he muttered, "and my niece from prison and worse, and not a stain upon him that ought not to be set in pearls!"

Getting poetic in his old age. as sure as shooting.

It was the doctor thought that, but Mr. Brown was holding out his hand to Fred, with a light on his face that the discovery of another mine could hardly have brought there.

" I'll hear your explanation of it all some other time, my young friend. This'll do for once. We'll go into dinner now. Mrs. Boyce, Mr. Heron. Mrs. Boyce, Dr. Milyng."

" Both hands, please," exclaimed the widow, as she held out her own to Fred. " I'm glad there are such men. I don't care if you've been in fifty jails, if you got there in such a way."

" My only experience of the kind, I assure you. God keep me from such another."

That was a dinner-table, indeed, and the girls could hardly eat for sheer excitement. It was less to be wondered at in Carrie's case, for all the realities of her terrible adventure were brought back to her most vividly, but it was odd for a young woman like Mabel Varick to be stirred up by the fortunes and misfortunes of a man whom she had first encountered as an avowed tramp, rescued from a dog-

watched tree in her own front yard. But then the
lives of well-bred young ladies have so few ripples
of genuine disturbance in them, and these two had
returned from the country in no very equable frame
of mind.

Mrs. Boyce was in her element, and Mr. Brown's
close observation of his young guest more than ever
convinced him that the "tramp" felt very much at
home in the character and associations of a gentleman.

Very modest was Fred, for the attentions he received were by no means easy to bear, and he con-
stantly sheltered himself behind the free, exuberant
talk of the thoroughly delighted doctor.

Such tales of mountain life and western adventure as the latter did tell!—all of them true, beyond a doubt, but losing nothing by his telling.

"And I tell you what it is, ladies," he said,
"there's nothing I've told you that called for any
more courage than Fred's jump into the river to be
swept out to sea by the tide. There are not many
men I know of that would care to try that. I'm
going to give Fred a mining claim for every hundred yards he swam."

And, after dinner, there were the wonderful ores
to be examined, and the story of the Golden Heart
to be told, and all the thrilling adventures of the
long, perilous, lonely march to the settlements,
over mountains and deserts. And when, late in the
evening, Fred Heron took his departure, he left

behind him enough of red-hot mining enthusiasm
to have furnished forth a dozen companies instead
of one.

To be sure, the summer was over, and bad weather
would be sure to come on before preparations for
active operations could be completed.

The doctor and his friends understood that well
enough, but they could prepare, just the same.
Machinery could be bought or manufactured and
sent upon its long way westward. All eastern business which might otherwise interfere could be steadily closed up or set in order to take care of itself.
In short, the proposed mining and exploring expedition could be rendered all the more complete and
sure of a comfortable success by reason of not
sending it out in a hurry.

Meantime, the Golden Heart would wait, in the
centre of its supposed "system," whether or not
that had any existence outside of the feverish brain
of its discoverer.

There was no doubt about the quality of the
specimen ores he had brought with him, as the report of the assayer abundantly testified, and Mr.
Brown's other dreams took on an aspect of something like reality as he perused that same report.

Fred Heron slept more soundly than might have
been expected the night after that dinner at Mr.
Brown's, for a considerable load had been lifted
from his mind. He had less and less doubt, too,

about his own future, whether or not he should turn out a successful miner. It would be hardly fair to expose the peculiarly mixed character of some of his dreams, however, or the extent to which they were confused by the entry of enthusiastic females in rustling drapery. He could but confess to himself that Carrie Dillaye looked wonderfully improved, in her city surroundings, from the sorrowful girl he had known on the Island, but for all that he was compelled to add, and this when he was wide awake, and not in any dream:

"But she does not compare with her cousin. She was splendid, to-night. Handsomer than she looked, at the window, the first time I saw her. I'm on better terms with Prince, now, than I was then."

And that meant a good deal, considering whose dog Prince was, and what sort of a dog.

CHAPTER XXXII.

FRED HERON RENEWS SOME OF HIS FAMILY TIES.

FRED HERON was a man of what are called "strong family instincts," whatever may have at any time appeared to the contrary, and one of his first doings on finding himself restored to the world had been to write a long letter to his sister. Another had been to hunt up his brother Augustus.

In his letter to Bessie he had a good deal to say, of course, concerning his new employment, although he somehow failed to give the names of those with whom he found himself associated.

"Just Fred's way," she said to herself, when she read the letter. "I've no means of learning about them. I'd write to them on his behalf if he had only given me an opportunity. Anyhow, I'll write to Mrs. Baird. I'm sure Mr. Baird would not mind hunting the matter up for me. Poor, foolish boy. What will become of him? To think, after all the mistakes he has made, of his mixing himself up with gold-hunters and such people. I'll write and tell

306

him what I think of it, anyhow. He shall never say I did not do my duty by him."

And so she did, copiously, and her brother was fully warned, so far as faithful words could warn him, of the character and purposes of the disreputable sharpers who had drawn him into their wild and visionary schemes.

He must at once, she said, shake himself clear of his fresh entanglements, and take some honorable and lucrative position which would enable him to do justice to himself and to others.

"Yes," he had remarked, when he came to that, "I guess I'd better take a bank. Nothing better than that, unless it is a large landed estate. Either would do. The only difficulty is that when fellows take those things other fellows make a terrible fuss about it."

What would Bessie have thought and written had she known that there were ladies in the case, and that her brother was likely to be thrown a good deal into their society? If there was one danger against which she had persistently warned him it had been the designing character of her own sex, and thus far he had seemed disposed to be more or less guided, in that particular. She could at least congratulate herself upon her success in breaking up and dissipating the most serious peril of the kind which had ever taken hold of him.

But Fred's second letter, like his first, preserved

a sphinx-like silence concerning those "mining evenings" as he called them, which he was now so frequently passing, with Dr. Milyng and the rest, over Mr. Brown's library table.

To be sure, the talk did not always run upon mines, for the doctor himself had an endless fund of other reminiscences, and was by no means ignorant of books, and Fred.

Well, the more they knew him, and the more he unfolded to them the facts of his history, the more they were disposed to deal charitably, to say the least, with their strange acquaintance.

"He's a wonderful fellow," said Mrs. Boyce, "and I don't believe we've heard a tenth of what he must have gone through. There are matters he does not mention, depend upon it, and I do not believe they are at all discreditable to him."

"What sort of matters?" said Carrie.

"Well, family matters, for instance. He has told us nothing about his immediate connections. I'd like to know about them."

"He must have some."

"Yes, indeed, and I'm not sure but I have a sort of a clue. I've waited for some word from him before mentioning it, but I heard of Fred Heron before I ever saw him."

"You did?" exclaimed both of the girls, as if with one voice.

"Yes"—and then followed a detailed account of

the widow's call on Mrs. Baird, and her meeting with Bessie, and all she knew of that young lady. There could be no question of Fred's identity with the "erring brother," but the interest attaching to him was none the less. Certainly not by reason of any lack of accuracy in Mrs. Boyce's estimate and description of Bessie Heron. For once in her life Bessie had really given Fred a lift, and it was a great pity she could not have known it, and known, too, just how the lift was given.

"O Mrs. Boyce," said Mabel, "if you would only call on Mrs. Baird and see if you can learn any more. I'd even like to know about his sister, and what she is doing now."

"I do not believe she half appreciates him," exclaimed Carrie.

"People who appreciate themselves too well rarely get correct ideas of others, my dear. But I have already seen Mrs. Baird. There was very little she could tell me. She was glad to hear that Fred was doing well. His sister is in the west, and seems to be quite comfortable. It is my belief, from what Mrs. Baird told me, he sent her his last dollar, just before he was put on the Island."

"It would be just what I would expect of him," said Carrie. "Think of his giving me those lemons when he was so sick himself."

"Any Christian ought to have done that," remarked Mabel, severely.

"And how many of them would have given away both lemons? Besides, Mr. Heron is not a Christian."

"Isn't he? How do you know?"

"He has such queer notions—"

"I wish some other people had 'em, then—"

"I'm not so sure as I used to be, what it takes to make a Christian of a man," interrupted Mrs. Boyce. "At all events, if Mr. Heron does not wish to talk of his family, we have no right to make him. He may, some day."

"I hope so," quietly remarked Mabel.

But they were to meet with one of Fred's relatives, at least, before a great while.

When he went to Mrs. Gibbs's boarding-house for his trunk, to remove it to more convenient quarters, he tried in vain to obtain the present address of his brother Augustus, and he remained in ignorance of it until he met him in that great world's reception room, "the street."

A good looking, well-dressed fellow, was Mr. Augustus Heron, and he seemed as much delighted as surprised to meet with his even better-dressed, if not quite so handsome, elder brother. If the good clothes were anything of a puzzle to him he made no mention of the fact. He may have been accustomed to expecting unexpected things from Fred.

A good deal was said, on both sides, in a very

few moments, but Augustus learned nothing concerning the Island, and little more than the name of the mining company.

As they talked they walked, and when Augustus remarked:

"Hold on, Fred, I've some business in here at Brown's. Won't keep me three minutes," Fred simply responded: "So have I," and entered with him.

The business which had brought Augustus had made necessary a note of introduction from the very reputable house in whose employ he was, and this, when handed to Mr. Brown, elicited the inquiry:

"Heron? Any way connected with my young friend Frederick. Ah, Mr. Heron, is that you? Come in."

"My brother, sir," responded the astonished Augustus, as Fred leaned over the desk assigned him as secretary and so forth, and began to examine some papers and open a letter or two.

"Brother, eh? Is that so, Fred? Glad to know you, sir. Know your house very well. Senior partner is an old friend of mine. You must bring your brother to the house, Fred. Why can he not come this evening?"

"Give me sincere pleasure," remarked Augustus, before his brother could say a word, and the latter could only add:

"Thank you, Mr. Brown. We will be there soon
after dinner—".

"Come to dinner, both of you. It'll be a great
deal pleasanter."

So it would, not only for the young men, but, it
might be, for others. As for Mr. Brown himself, he
might well be pardoned if under his cordial hospitality were concealed a vague idea of acquiring information.

Fred Heron would hardly have planned precisely
that arrangement if all had been left to him, but
his brother was precisely the man to understand
and appreciate, yea, and to grasp, the social advantages involved in an invitation to dinner at so excellent a house as that of the great merchant. He
had his social capacities, too, of a very respectable
order, and before that evening was over he had
done for Fred at least the service of confirming
Mr. Brown's opinion of their birth and breeding.
He hardly knew how much more he had told to
such keen eyes and practised ears as those which
had been around him during what he described as
a "truly delightful time."

The worst accusation brought against many people is that they "do not improve their advantages,"
and Mr. Augustus Heron may have been one of
these, in times past. In fact, his sister Bessie had
more than once dimly hinted as much under the
form of accusing Fred of not improving them for

him, but he did not propose, evidently, to throw away the good- things of his immediate present. In fact, he was disposed to stretch them into the future as much as possible.

His employers, next day, were well enough pleased to find where he had spent his evening, as well as to learn that:

"Mr. Brown's a great. friend of my brother Fred, you know. Fred and he are working some mines together."

It was about as good as a promotion for Gus, and secured him a very good report when next their senior partner found himself in conversation with the merchant.

It is curious how our friends do improve on our hands when we find, or think we are finding, how very creditable to them their other friends are.

From that time forward, however, the Brown household found it more difficult than ever to comprehend their first acquaintance.

While Augustus was fond of society, of amusements, and always at the service of his lady friends, Fred persistently refused to go anywhere or see anybody. He even came less and less frequently to the house, and never except in company with Mr. Brown and the doctor.

The latter saw less to wonder at in it all, for he knew with what patient and successful assiduity Fred was devoting himself to his new profession of

miner. He knew of lectures attended ; books de-
voured ; geological cabinets ransacked and studied ;
chemists consulted ; all sorts of mechanical and engineering information gathered and stored away,
with marvellous rapidity. It was, in the doctor's
opinion, precisely the course which ought to have
been pursued by a man in such a position, and he
said as much to Mr. Brown.

The merchant very warmly assented, but he somehow neglected to explain the matter at home, perhaps not thinking any explanation necessary, and
it was the less to be wondered at that the ladies
sought for one of their own. Mrs. Boyce did, at
least.

She had employed Fred, very confidentially, to
dispose of some of her diamonds for her, and he
had done the business remarkably well, and she
was saying as much to Mabel Varick, and adding :

" He's a very trustworthy fellow. Not the sort
that are ever favorites with young ladies, but none
the worse for that."

" I do not see why you should say that; Mrs.
Boyce. I'm sure we have treated him very well.
It is not our fault if he does not come here. He
is a proud-spirited young gentleman. Anybody
can see that, and there are reasons we know of for
his avoiding society."

" Have you never thought of anything else,
Mabel ?"

"No, indeed," said Mabel, with a slight flush on her cheek. "What else should there be?"

"Have you forgotten under what romantic circumstances he became acquainted with Carrie?"

"So they were, and I have heard her express her gratitude and respect a hundred times."

"Gratitude and respect? And see how she has taken up with Augustus. Why, it almost seems to me as if I ought to speak about it to Mr. Brown."

"She is of age, and Mr. Heron comes here by my uncle's invitation."

"I know that, but that is not everything. Augustus Heron is a very handsome fellow."

"But what has all that got to do with his brother? Frederick is worth a dozen of him."

Cunning Mrs. Boyce! How very much she thought she was gathering from that frank and unembarrassed expression of opinion. She did not know, however, how relieved Mabel Varick felt after she had succeeded in making it. She even succeeded in concealing the effort, and that is sometimes the very hardest thing to do.

But if Mrs. Boyce did not learn a great deal from Mabel, neither did she from Fred himself. She did not even know that he had felt called upon, already, to speak pretty freely with his brother. So freely that something almost akin to a coolness had sprung up between them.

Mrs. Boyce thought she discovered signs of that, indeed, although she had a somewhat incorrect idea of the possible cause. The most skilful physicians err, at times, in the diagnosis they make of internal difficulties, and there are none so deceptive and misleading in their symptoms as are affections of the heart.

What is described before death as something else, or as an " enlargement," turns out, on a *post mortem*, to be only an ossification.

What curious discoveries will be made concerning the hearts of most of us when the angels make our final *post mortem* for us. Such " cases" as they must have, from time to time, and with such marvellous " complications," displacements, lesions, and such curiously obstructive " fatty deposits."

Of course it was impossible that Mr. Augustus Heron should not gradually become acquainted with the peculiar relations existing between Carrie Dillaye and the other members of her family. In fact, he one day astonished the astute and cautious Mr. Allyn by a conversational revelation of the extent and accuracy of the information he had acquired on that head. So much so that the lawyer felt himself almost compelled, from that time forward, to take the young man into his confidence, after his own sagacious and unconfidential manner.

The open-heartedness with which some men will

permit another to tell them all he knows has something touching in it. Mr. Allyn was one of those
men.

Still, he was thereby enabled to make himself
reasonably sure against Mr. Augustus Heron telling
the same things to anybody else.

CHAPTER XXXIII.

MR. DANIEL BROWN was not the man to make an unnecessary secret of anything, and yet all that the business world knew of his mining plans was that he had somehow acquired an interest in some seemingly valuable claims, and proposed paying them a visit to ascertain their true character before putting any considerable amount of money in them.

"Just like him," said his friends. "Trust old Brown not to get his fingers bitten. He's going to make it a summer tour and picnic. Wish he'd invite me to join him. They'll have a grand time. He knows how to do up that sort of thing in style. If he doesn't make a cent out of his mines he'll make everything else he can."

It never occurred to one of them that their hard-headed emblem of commercial common sense had actually been bitten by the golden serpent as poisonously, almost, as Dr. Milyng himself.

318

Very few of them knew anything of the doctor, but those who had met Mr. Secretary Heron were compelled to admit that Mr. Brown had shown his usual good judgment in the very quiet, intelligent, industrious young man he had selected.

What if they had known that Fred swam over from the Island to enter Mr. Brown's employment?

That might have opened their eyes.

But, as the weeks and months went by, not the least important and difficult of Fred's duties and responsibilities was his care of Dr. Milyng himself.

There is nothing in the wide world so uneasy as a fish out of water.

Did you ever catch one?

The prevailing impression among ignorant people is that all his flopping and flouncing is occasioned by the suffering he endures on being snatched from his proper element.

Not a bit of it. He is taking in too much oxygen, and taking it in by the wrong way—from the air instead of the water, that is all.

Dr. Milyng was no longer among his ledges and placers, but he was as much possessed by his mining fever as ever. Day after day he came forward with some new "claim" or discovery, raked up from the maps and tracings of his wanderings among the mountains, and which he deemed it wise to add to the already enormous assets of the great company. Day after day, too, his notions of the proper valuation of those assets grew and flourished, until Mr. Brown told him:

"Now, doctor, I'm perfectly willing we should pay the national debt, by-and-by. It would hardly be noticed if taken from such a pile as ours. But suppose we do not print the stock and bonds for it till we get some of the bullion into our treasury."

The doctor could stand any amount of good-natured chaffing, but one thing he could not do, and that was to measure his current expenditures by the gold in his pocket rather than by that which was waiting for him in the Sierras. If he could have had his own way it would have required some car-loads, at least, to make good the drafts he desired the company's treasury to cash before a pound of its machinery had been shipped westward. It was well for him that Mr. Brown held the purse, and that he stood in very wholesome awe of Mr. Brown, as of a man on whom depended the future of the Golden Heart.

For the doctor's heart was there, after all, and not in the city. He would have starved himself and gone in rags rather than have thrown away the dazzling dream of conducting a working party to the mouth of that treasury of the world.

And now the time drew nearer and nearer, the set time for the departure of the expedition, and all things were assuming a prepared and perfected shape.

There was not a loose peg left in the arrangement of Mr. Brown's business affairs. The doctor could not think of an article of probable need which had not been either purchased, or at least declared unnecessary by Mr. Brown and Fred Heron. The heavier goods had all been shipped, even, and that which had for so long a time been a beautiful dream and a thing of the future began to put on more and more the semblance of a positive reality.

Only one matter somehow refused to be settled, and that was what troubled the soul of Mr. Allyn.

Do what he could, Mr. and Mrs. Dillaye managed to put him off, and they were aided and abetted to a certain extent by Mr. Brown.

They had counted on that, very deliberately, or at least Mrs. Dillaye had done so, and had courageously sustained her sometimes faltering husband. Of course they had not interposed anything like a refusal to settle, and a considerable part of the securities involved had been from time to time surrendered, but the "settlement" seemed as far away as ever, and there were no symptoms of a coming delivery of the real estate. Carrie herself had objected to any proceedings which would involve a public scandal, and the only one thing in which she had exhibited any feeling of bitterness was in her persistent refusal to hold any personal conference with her father or step-mother. So clearly had she stated her determination to this effect that even Mrs.

Dillaye had given the matter up as hopeless, for the present.

"She will be more easily reached after Mr. Brown goes west," she said to her husband, when the mining adventure was detailed to her.

"But suppose he takes Carrie with him?"

"With him? Do you mean there are ladies going?"   .

"Quite a party."

"Well, then, he will do nothing against us, more than he has done, before they get back. Every postponement is of value to us, now. If we can tide over the spring and summer, we shall be all right."

"But suppose Carrie should get married?"

"We must prevent that. If we hear of anything of the kind on foot, it will be our duty to let the party in interest know her history. That would always be enough, I think."

"I should say it would. Few men would care to have that kind of a wife."

"She has property."

"But nobody knows that. Even Mr. Brown cannot say much about that, just now, and he won't.

Hit or miss, that was the policy determined upon, and it so far succeeded that when Mr. Brown's other preparations were all complete he was unable to include among them a settlement of Carrie's affairs. And Carrie bit her lips over it, but of late she had seemed more sedate than formerly, with less of what Mrs. Boyce called "a slight tendency to frivolity."

The cares of the world sat lightly upon her at all times, but there had not been, since she entered her uncle's house, the least "out-cropping," as Dr. Milyng would have called it, of her unfortunate constitutional tendency.

"In many respects a most remarkable young woman," said Mrs. Boyce to herself.

But if Carrie was an enigma to the penetrating eyes and practised sagacity of the widow, she was a thousand times more so to the youth and inexperience of Mabel Varick. Much as she loved her cousin, Mabel could but feel that their relations were less intimate than at the first, and she strove in vain to account for it.

"Could Augustus Heron have anything to do with it? I don't believe she cares for him, but if she does, can she imagine I would interfere? I'd like to undeceive her, that's all. But what can have become of his brother. He's hardly here at all nowadays."

And Mabel had other perplexities which did not decrease with time. The interest which Mrs. Boyce had taken in the mining affair, and the energy with which she had identified herself with the expedition, had done as much as anything else to settle her position as a member of Mr. Brown's household until all that should be over, but Mabel could but ask herself, now and then, "How about the future?

Will she come back with us?   Is it to be a perman-
ency?   I wish I knew what Uncle Daniel thinks
about it."

And the question should rather have been, if he
thought at all about it.

How could it be otherwise?   A man of his age
and knowledge of the world?   How could he but
think?

Well, what if he thought that, with two young,
unmarried nieces in his house, it was an absolute
necessity they should have an older and wiser companion, a lady of discretion, education, high character, to advise them, and to play propriety for
them?   Especially if they were to travel, would it
not be needful that he should provide them with a
Mrs. Boyce?   And who so admirably fitted for the
position as the very Mrs. Boyce herself?

He may have had some such train of thought, at
some time.   He certainly did when he came to consider the "mining and exploring picnic," for the
"quite a party" referred to by Mr. Dillaye included
none besides the ladies of his own household.

No invitation was extended to Mr. Augustus
Heron, and it may be Mr. Brown decided, in a
friendly way, that it would not be well to take the
young man for so long a time from his business
pursuits.   If he did not neglect the invitation on
that ground, the result was all the same.

And yet, when the morning set for the departure

actually arrived, among the little crowd which gathered at the Brown mansion to say good-by, came Augustus Heron with a satchel in his hand.

"Am I not fortunate?" he said to Mr. Brown. "Our house has given me a commission for them in Pittsburg, and I can travel that far in your company. Combine business with pleasure."

And Mr. Brown smiled assent in a curious sort of way, for there were three others talking to him at the time.

Fred took his brother's presence a good deal as a matter of course, not seeming to be overjoyed about it, at all events, and he won golden opinions from Mrs. Boyce by the attention and thoughtfulness with which he prevented the least "jar" or oversight in the perplexing process of getting so large a party safely lodged in their own proper palace-car at the depot.

As for Dr. Milyng, a more uselessly enthusiastic individual never stood on two feet. He could hardly have sworn to that much on his own account, for it seemed to him as if he could already see the white-capped Sierras rising around him, and he half felt that it was time for him to be on the look-out for roving bands of Apaches and other of the kindly neighbors he and his friends were about to visit.

This too, although the latest news from the mining regions had been to the effect that the United States cavalry, under General Crump, had entirely

pacified the immediate locality of the Golden
Heart, in a succession of brilliant encounters, followed by a "very advantageous treaty."

If Carrie Dillaye felt sadly at missing either her
father or her step-mother among the "good-by
party," she made no outward sign of it. Neither
could Mrs. Boyce's eyes detect the least flutter of
either pleasure or the reverse when Augustus Heron
announced his good fortune.

"I really do not understand her," said the widow
to herself.

She was absolutely right in that, and so is any
woman when she says the same thing of any other.
Because why, there is no woman who does not contain
possibilities of which even she herself, let alone all
others of her sex, has but a dim and imperfect con-
ception. And these possibilities may be for either
good or evil, or both.

Men get over the difficulty admirably well by
giving it up to begin with.

But there comes to every train, whether composed
mainly of palace-cars or not, a moment when the
heartless conductor looks at his watch and shouts:

"All aboard."

From that moment the train and its passengers
condenses into a little world by itself, cognizant of
other worlds, indeed, but separated from them by
the very speed with which it rushes forward upon
its own curves. The inhabitants of that world, too,

are apt soon to become absorbed with either themselves or one another, with a perpetual undertone,
if the trip be a long one, of "shall we get there
without an accident ?"

And sometimes the unspoken question is answered
for them in one way, sometimes in another.

CHAPTER XXXIV.

A DESPERATE EFFORT TO GET EVEN WITH A GRASPING CORPORATION.

IT is a standing complaint of our public-spirited friends, the communists, that our lines of railway, the great highways of the nation, are constructed, by those grasping comorants, the capitalists, with sole reference to profits, that is, to dividends, and all that sort of thing, ignoring the undoubted right of the people, imported or otherwise, to have indefinite transportation in all directions provided for them by " government."

One of the consequences of this " monumental robbery" of the many by the few is that we have only a bare half-dozen or less of east-and-west main lines, which absorb to themselves the trade and traffic of a continent. Whether they do so with profit or not, is a point upon which the authorities differ. That is, the communists give a different account of it from that rendered to and remembered by the stockholders.

If the truth were known, however, it would probably appear that the fortunes of most of our great railway lines would not be badly represented by a costly section of one of them which penetrates, with many a twist and climb, the rugged ranges of the Appalachian chain.

After winding among great knobby hills of treeless stone, shooting through tunnels and burrowing in cuts which must have troubled the very souls of the constructing engineers, the track at last enters upon a steep down-grade, with a gorge of varying depth on one side, and a mountain round which it winds, on the other, and at the bottom of this grade there hardly seems a level, so quickly does the opposite ascent begin, with a steeper grade than ever. It is hard to tell which is the more difficult and perilous to train or corporation, the down-grade of the expense account or the up-grade towards the height of an honest dividend.

Be that as it may, the train on which Mr. Brown and his party left the great city reached that very section a little while after darkness closed in upon the varied experiences of their first day's travel. The snow lay deeply enough among the mountain gorges, for it was yet March. Dr. Milyng intended to reach the early summer which April would bring with it to the warm valleys and plains eastward of the Golden Heart, but winter had to be traversed at the outset.

A dark and cloudy night, but not stormy, and as safe for a railway train as the peacefullest Indian summer day.

Perfectly safe, for no road on the continent was better managed, or could boast of having fewer accidents. So long as steel and rock and sound timber could be trusted, with skill, experience and fidelity—

But what about human malice, greed, cruelty, callous indifference to the pain and loss of others? Are there no devils on the earth? Of course not, nor anywhere else, for is it not now settled that hell is a myth!

He was not a devil, therefore, but a mere human being, if anybody will kindly tell us what that is, and he was standing, in the dense gloom, just a little beyond the terminus of the down-grade. Those familiar with the spot will remember that the curve is a trifle sharp, but that the bank on the right is not more than thirty feet in height, while the ravine to the left is barely twice as much. Nothing about it, therefore, so far as mere feet and inches are concerned, that is very startling.

Neither was there about the man, but some recent "repair train" had unloaded a couple of new rails at the side of the track, and the man was prying strongly at one of these with a long crowbar. He moved it very expeditiously, too, as if his task were one which called for haste.

But could he possibly mean to leave it there—or had he only paused for breath—there across the track, at that treacherous angle with the permanent rails?

A train coming down from the east would surely be thrown from the track, with its iron head plunged hard against the rock, and then what would become of cars and passengers?

Down the gulf, at forty miles an hour, or fifty, or sixty, for who knows the speed of a lightning express at the end of a down run, with a stiff climb just ahead of it?

"Reckon that 'll fix 'em," huskily remarked the crowbar man, as he took a step backward. "Teach 'em a lesson. Other people's got some rights, as well as they have."

Other words, thick-voiced, hot, terrible words, strangely mingled with great names, sacred and otherwise.

If there were a hell, and any devils in it, one might expect to hear such expressions there and from them.

What a good thing it is for many human beings that there is no hereafter. If there were, and they were there compelled to associate with their kind, what a terrible realization of our most lurid dreams of hell would shortly result from that association. And somehow one cannot help thinking, at times, that the absence of any hereafter leaves the work of creation, or the "cosmos," if you will, dreadfully incomplete and unsatisfactory.

This man must have been a very complete philosopher, for, after setting his ingenious trap for that train, he calmly descended into the hollow, clambered up a few yards on the opposite side, and sat down to await results.

Foolish fellow, to have taken so much unnecessary pains, when sheer chance had been providing a surer trap, a more certain and terrible destruction, for that doomed express train, than could have been provided by a score of such as he.

He did not know it.

How should he have known the secrets of the rolling-mill and the forge, and the hidden things of all the iron bars and their weldings?

An hour before, another train of cars had passed that spot. A long, dark, heavy-looking train, laden with coal and with pig-iron, and drawn by two huge, hoarse-throated "camel-back" engines, whose utmost strength had barely sufficed to haul their enormous following up the long, steep grade beyond. They had done so, however, and had screamed with steamy satisfaction when they reached the summit, miles away, and pulled their grimy column of burdened trucks nearly out upon the side-track where they were to rest until the express train should pass them.

There was something almost human about it—

the locomotives gave their shout of triumph too soon.

Laborers and brakemen had sprung to the ground, after the brakes were thrown open again, for that was a lunch station for them, as well as for the engines, but the last cars had not passed the switch when, for some reason, the locomotives were "backed" a little.

Only one of the innumerable retrogrades incident to such work, but when the forward start was given again, the coupling broke between the seventh and eighth cars, back, and the great mass of the train was free of its iron yoke.

Safe, so long as it was on the track.

Well, it could not wander much, but it could slip along the rails, with momentarily increasing speed, and gathering in its solid bulk the resistless, measureless power of inertia.

That is one of the powers which the philosophers have exquisitely explained to us. They have traced it up to—yes, up, and up, and up, to the place where they could not trace it any further, and there they set up a triumphal tombstone and wrote "Nature" across the face of it. What more would you have, if you are a reasonable man, and do not believe in a hereafter?

But those awful car-loads of coal and iron, turned so suddenly into a "wild train," with that gathering power within them, and that sharp yell of human astonishment and fear arising behind them.

One man there had been, a brakeman, who sprang after his escaping charge, and followed it gallantly, in a desperate determination to get on board and apply the brakes, but he failed in his leap, and was now lying senseless on the track, well off in having nothing worse than a heavy fall and a broken arm.

Had he succeeded, not ten such men could have brought the runaway to a stand-still on that down-grade, and he would have shared the fate of the train. Considering the size of his family, it was well he did not succeed in boarding that rear car.

Faster, now, and with every second faster, on plunged the long line of cars, that had neither man nor any trained servant of man to drive them or restrain them.

The rails beneath them would do well enough for a guide, but the white-faced men at the station knew only too well what that guiding would be. There were those among the latter—strong men, too, with horny hands and weatherbeaten faces— who sat down and covered the one with the other, and did but groan when spoken to. One did say:

" Women! Children! Men! Ground to pieces! O it makes me feel faint!"

And then there was something said about a wreck, and sending for surgeons, but nobody seemed to know exactly what to do.

Faster and faster, on dashed the " wild train,"

attaining a speed rarely given or permitted to one of its kind with steam in control of it. A competent mathematician could easily have calculated that, with a given acceleration, and the speed of the express train approaching from the opposite direction being also known, the meeting of the two would take place precisely in so many minutes and at such an exact point. He could therefore have assured the man with the crowbar how entirely he had thrown away the free labor he had expended in slanting 'that rail across the track and assuming the responsibility of the coming crash.

CHAPTER XXXV.

ONE OF THE SERMONS THERE ARE IN IRON BARS.

THAT had been a very interesting day on board the western-bound express train. At least to a part of the inmates of one of its palace cars. One of the first and most interesting features of their position was that before noon they found themselves in sole possession of the car, which was about as good as it could be. There is nothing else in a republic half so princely as having a whole car to yourself.

Then there was a good deal to be seen from the windows, and all the eyes on board worked at that until they were weary of it and did not care what might be the name of the next town or of the river they had just crossed.

But the older portion of Mr. Brown's party found something to think of, after awhile, in the conduct and bearing of their juniors.

They had never before known Fred Heron to

336

come out quite so strong as he was now doing, so full of wit, anecdote, information, the very soul of the party, and yet, withal, so very unobtrusive, so politely considerate of others.

"He will be a treasure at this rate," soliloquized Mr. Brown.

"He puzzles me more than ever," was the thought of Mrs. Boyce.

Dr. Milyng regarded him with a sort of pride, as much as to say :

"That's another of my discoveries. You'd never have owned that claim if it hadn't been for me."

And no more they would. But Mr. Augustus Heron was not "panning out" as well as his brother, just then. He was almost as much disposed to be silent as was Carrie Dillaye herself, and yet he had left no angry, unreconciled father behind him. Could he have been dwelling, untimely, upon the sad fact that he was an orphan, or upon the other fact that he was a self-invited member of that travelling party?

Mabel Varick appeared most amiably in the character of a young lady willing to be amused, which was all that could be reasonably asked of her.

There were other interesting things to come, however, one of which arrived in the shape of a late dinner, served on board, and after that the gentlemen retired to the smoking-room and left the ladies for awhile to their own devices.

They had not a great many, but then they had their tongues, and that was a good deal, for they had a plenty to talk about.

"Carrie, my dear," at last said Mrs. Boyce, "what is the matter with you? You must not let anything you have left behind you prey upon your spirits."

Carrie's reply seemed in a manner to burst from her.

"It is not what I have left behind me, Mrs. Boyce, it is what I have brought with me."

"Brought with you? Why, my dear child, what can that be?"

"My secrets!"

And here Carrie covered her face with her hands and burst into tears.

"Your secrets, Carrie, dear," exclaimed Mabel Varick, "have you any that we cannot help you keep? Don't tell us anything we ought not to know—"

"I must tell you! I feel that I ought never to have any. You and Uncle Daniel and Mrs. Boyce are all so good to me!"

Mabel and the widow stared at one another as much as to say: "What can it all mean," but they waited patiently, considering the circumstances, for the termination of what became a long and somewhat awkward silence. The darkness of the cloudy March day was deepening, and the pause was prolonged by the entrance of the train porter to light the lamps.

They were not sorry, any of them, to have the stern and gloomy scenery of the mountains shut out for awhile.

When he had finished his duties and they were once more alone, Carrie suddenly began again with :

" You know my terrible adventure on the Island?"

No answer seemed to be called for.

" Well, that is one of my secrets. I do not mean only that it is a dark spot in my life which I must forever conceal from the world—from everybody but those who know it now—but there is something darker than that about it."

" Why, Carrie," exclaimed Mrs. Boyce.

" Yes—O so dark ! I refused to let myself think about it, at first. It was not my father—"

" Not your father !"

" No, it was my step-mother."

" Your step-mother ? Why, Carrie Dillaye, what can you mean ? Are you going crazy?" asked Mabel, with wide open eyes.

" Mean ? Why, I mean it was all a trap. A plan of hers. She meant it all, and I do not know, to this day, precisely how she managed it."

" Do you mean she sent you to the Island?"

" No, she could not have thought so far ahead as that. But she intended I should go wild and disgrace myself, so that my father and my friends should cast me off. She has always hated me. She knew I was proud. She believed if I once went away in such a manner she would never hear of me again. She was right, too. I should never have shown my face again to any one who had known me if it had not been for the manner in which I was rescued. I thank God for that. Next to Him, I thank Fred Heron, and my good, kind uncle. And then, to think I could ever be so base, so unkind, so ungrateful to him!"

"Ungrateful to Mr. Heron, or to Uncle Daniel?" again exclaimed the astonished Mabel, while Mrs. Boyce stared through the window into the now impenetrable gloom beyond.

There was a good deal of darkness gathering about that "lightning express" train, as it plunged along the rails on that down-grade around the mountain.

It is the way of human lives. Not a man or a train of us all, knows how far in the future a fellow with a crowbar may have been getting things ready for our coming.

Carrie turned her face full upon Mabel, a flushed face, into whose humility of self-accusation that question seemed to have brought a new and hardly so meek an element, and her lips were parted as if the remaining secret were about to come out, but just then the door of the smoking-room opened, and Mr. Brown strode through it, followed by the three other gentlemen.

They could hardly have finished their cigars so

soon, but there had been a mild breaking of bottled secrets among them also.

Not so very many minutes earlier, Dr. Milyng had turned upon Fred, with:

"I see how it is, my boy. The mines have got hold of you. So they have of me. I was never in such tremendous spirits in all my life, and yet I know there's something coming."

"The mines?" exclaimed Fred. "Well, I have been in pretty good spirits, to-day, and the mines have something to do with it, but not all. It's a family matter, and I've had no chance even to talk with Gus about it, but you are such good friends I don't mind telling you all. It's this—my only sister is now living at the west—and just before leaving the city, I received a letter from her, announcing her marriage—"

"Done well, then?" asked the doctor.

"Bessie married!" exclaimed Augustus.

"Married a gentleman named Gresham," continued Fred, " for whom she has been keeping house. A man of high character and some wealth, a widower, and so she has a home secured to her, whatever may become of me."

"Or me," remarked Augustus, and he too seemed affected to a greater degree of cheerfulness by the unexpected news.

But Mr. Brown arose, saying:

"I congratulate you, heartily, Mr. Heron. I can

easily understand your gratification over your sister's happiness. I think the ladies would be particularly interested. Come, let's be fair and give them the news. You and your brother can talk about it afterwards."

Neither of the young men could object, and it may be they were more than willing, while the doctor followed, as a matter of course. The very manner of their coming attracted the attention of the ladies, for Mr. Brown's benevolent face was full of news-bearing eagerness. Strange that Carrie Dillaye should turn pale at the sight of it.

"A wedding," he exclaimed. "A wedding in the Heron family!"

"Oh, Uncle Daniel," gasped Carrie.

What would next have been said it were somewhat difficult to guess, but at that moment the air was cleft by an exceedingly shrill whistle, and they were aware that the brakes were being applied with an energy which spoke plainly enough of some peril close at hand.

If they could but have known what a peril it was!

The scream of the engine was repeated, with what seemed a tremor of metallic fear in it, and the presence of danger must have been palpably felt in that car, for neither man nor woman uttered a word.

And yet the peril had passed, almost at the moment of its discovery, so swiftly had the train dashed on, in spite of all the power of the brakes and all the efforts of the engineer.

The man with the crowbar had been sitting in the snow, on the steep side of the narrow ravine, opposite his trap, a few moments before that, and he had ceased even to mutter profane words to himself as he peered into the darkness. He knew it was nearly time for the arrival of the express train from the east. It may be, too, that his nerves, and consequently his senses, were aroused to an unusual pitch of excitement and keenness. At all events they were not so completely absorbed by the awful watch he was keeping that they failed to catch the warning roar of the "wild train" coming from the west.

He must have been a railway man, perhaps a discharged *employee*, for he instantly understood the situation well enough to remark:

"Now won't there be a crash! I wonder which one'll get here first."

He had but a moment left for any speculation, and what was now the foremost car of the wild train was not armed, as a locomotive would have been, with a "cow-catcher" and a consequent hope of thrusting aside the slanting rail. The wheels of its truck caught fairly on the rigid steel of the obstruction, only to be thereby given a direction opposite from that intended by the man with the crowbar for those of the express train.

Over the sleepers that first car bounded to the right, with a great leap, and if all those behind it had been so many sheep they could not more closely and blindly have followed the plunge of their leader down into the ravine, and grand was the rattle and crash they made in doing so.

The rail, its work assured, was buffeted from one position to another, till it lay at right angles across the track, with six feet of its length extending over the edge. If any one can tell how the fragments of a wreck get into the places and positions they are found in he can do more than anybody else can. But the last car of the series was fairly bounced into the air by the force of the jerk which snatched it from the rails, and it came down, with its tons and tons of weight, on the projecting end of that fatal bar of steel.

A big bar and a heavy one, but the fillip it received was powerful in a full proportion, and it was spun into the air as boys at play will spin a chip of pine-wood. Had the blow been harder the rail would have been hurled farther, but, as it was, it was projected in a great arc, clean across the little ravine. There it was found by the wondering track-menders and wrecking-train hands, the next morning, and under it was the body of a man with a long crowbar convulsively grasped in his right hand.

"It struck him in front," they said. "Nobody

will ever know who he was by looking at his face."

Perhaps there were those, in the place where he was gone, who would be able to recognize him by other tokens than any his face had worn in life. That is, the face of his human body.

But the exploit of that last car of the wild train had cleared the track of all obstruction, and the rails were not so badly pried out of place but what a chance remained for wheels to keep upon them.

Barely that and nothing more, and the very speed of the express train was its safety. The engineer had heard the crash of that great wreck, if he had not at all understood it, and he had whistled "down brakes," but his entire train had passed the point of danger before any great degree of "slowing" had been accomplished.

A full stop was speedily made, and a hurried investigation revealed no reason why they should not try and reach the station on the summit. Something like an explanation would probably be obtained there.

The advance was cautious, for there was no assurance of finding the track on the up-grade clear, nor was the anxiety of the conductor and his passengers relieved until they heard the great shout with which their arrival was greeted at the station.

"It seems 'most like seein' dead·folks come to

life," exclaimed the man who had appeared to feel the worst about it. "I'm goin' to meetin' next Sunday. You see 'f I don't."

And now even the lady passengers were made aware of the nature and extent of the peril which had been so near them, and Uncle Daniel, after the shudder with which he told them of it, felt it imperatively necessary for him to give each of his nieces a hug and a kiss.

"It was God's providence," he said, although he knew nothing of the trap which had been set by the crowbar man, or of the precise manner in which it had been sprung by the wild train.

The young men looked at one another and at their lady friends, but seemed unable to think of anything worth saying, under the circumstances.

Fred Heron had a thought of his own in his head, however, and it led him to look up the broken coupling which had set free all those coal and iron cars, and Dr. Milyng went with him.

There was the flaw, in the centre of the bent bar, just where it had been ever since the liquid metal poured from the great crucible at the smelting works. No amount of subsequent drawing and forging had sufficed to remove that original defect, hidden as it was by the strong shell of iron around it.

"Do you see that?" he said to Dr. Milyng. "That coupling held to draw a good many trains. It held this one all the way up that grade, but it broke just exactly in time. How do you account for that?"

"S'pose it had broke too soon, or had held on a little too long?" said the doctor, with a dreamy look in his keen black eyes.

"I don't like to think of what would have happened to our party."

"But that's the way it turns out, now and then. Trains do get wrecked, and their passengers do get smashed up. Ships go down at sea, too, with all on board. What about Providence, then?"

"Well, I've been face to face with death a good many times. So have you. I never found anything in the looks of it that warranted me in suspecting God of a failure, in case He let it come to me. What's true of one man is true of a hundred, or a hundred thousand. I'm not half so much troubled about them as I am about this flaw in the coupling. The preparations for that flaw were made when the ore was packed away in the rocks of Pennsylvania, millions of years ago."

"Not a doubt of it," said the doctor. "When we get into the gold country I'll show you some points that 'll beat that. But I've made up my mind to one thing."

"What's that, doctor?"

"Death's nothing at all, and God knows it. Our mistake is that we think He hasn't found out yet, what a dreadful affair it is. I tell you what, Fred,

I ain't any too good, more's the pity, and I'm afraid I never shall be. Piety doesn't seem to thrive among the gold diggings. But if there's anything I'm sick of, it's hearing one kind of fool and another making apologies for God. He just don't need any."

"Reckon you've about hit it," replied Fred, thoughtfully, "but where did you get your theology?"

"Not a grain of it in me," stoutly exclaimed the doctor, "but, if a mountain can't preach a sermon, why then an alkali plain can. That's all. It ain't quite all, neither. I read more'n you'd think, and I tell you that when science climbs and climbs and climbs, till it reaches the level of a Digger Indian, about some things, it had just better let the Diggers do its loose whooping and yelling for it. That's what I say."

And Fred dropped the broken coupling, and he and the doctor went back to the car to ask Mr. Daniel Brown what he thought about it.

The train was quickly in motion, and before long the porters began to put the sleeping apparatus in order, so that the discussion had to be postponed, for the greater part, till the following day.

It lasted, with kindred topics, until they reached Pittsburg, and it served at least one purpose. Whatever may have been the state of Carrie Dillaye's mind and feelings, she made no further

reference to the subject of her "secrets," if any remained untold.

Neither her cousin nor Mrs. Boyce saw fit, whatever may have been their respective reasons, to ask
her any questions about it.

At Pittsburg Fred managed to write and post a
hurried letter to Bessie, with his good wishes and
congratulations, and with the news that he and his
friends were on their way to the gold regions.

"That'll startle her," he said to himself, "as
much as her marriage did me. And won't Gus get
some letters, after he reaches the city? I'd almost
like to read 'em."

They would be good letters, no doubt; the best
kind; but it seemed a difficult thing for Mr. Augustus Heron to break away from that party. There
was a serious flaw in his "coupling," somewhere,
however, and he had to go.

And after he had gone, and the train moved on,
Carrie Dillaye appeared, strangely enough, to recover her spirits and light-heartedness, as if her
handsome friend had himself been the incubus which
had weighed them down.

And Mrs. Boyce thought and thought about it,
and so did Mabel Varick, without arriving at a conclusion of any kind.

CHAPTER XXXVI.

A VERY LONG JOURNEY, AND WHAT WAS FOUND AT THE END OF IT.

APRIL, in the latitude of Dr. Milyng's great discovery, was the counterpart of June in less favored regions at the north, and mountain and plain were in all their glory when the mining-picnic party rested from the fatigue of their journey, under the oaks and pines near the mouth of the narrow ravine. The "wagoning" part of their trip had not been nearly so severe as the ladies had expected, rapidly as Dr. Milyng had pressed his teams, and every hour had brought before their eyes fresh wonders of unrivalled scenery.

Again and again did Mrs. Boyce thank Mr. Brown for permitting her to be one of the party, and just so often was he able to assure her, truthfully, that he and not she was the obliged individual.

For the remarkable capacities of the widow for all sorts of management came out with greater and greater strength as successive exigencies called

350

upon her for their exhibition. It was a grand piece of education for Mabel Varick that she found herself compelled to strive for the pre-eminence as a housekeeper, or rather as a camp-keeper, with so complete a mistress of all the arts thereof. They could but respect one another, those two women, while Mr. Brown looked on in an admiration which but feebly comprehended the facts of the case, and he and his friends got the benefit of it all.

If Carrie Dillaye were acting as an ally of either party, open or secret, she kept her own counsels, and received from the gentlemen all the attentions the other ladies gave themselves no time for. She seemed to have become, in the course of the trip, especially well acquainted with Mr. Frederick Heron, and Mrs. Boyce went so far as to remark to Mabel:

"That looks a good deal more like poetical justice, but what would Augustus say, if he were here?"

"Do you suppose Fred—Mr. Heron—would do anything in his brother's absence—"

"That he would not if Augustus were here? Certainly not, but I'm not so sure as I'd like to be about everybody else. There are some things I do not understand at all."

Mabel was silent. If she had anything on her mind, just then, it was probably not of a kind which she felt impelled to confide to the fair widow. Nor did Dr. Milyng tell her, as he might have

done, that Mr. Brown had said to him, that very
day:

"You are right about Fred. If they were my
daughters instead of my nieces, I could not more
heartily commend the respectful reserve of his behavior. I believe him to be a most honorable
young man."

"Sure as you live," returned the doctor, "but, I
tell you what it is, Mr. Brown, this expedition will
leave him anything but a poor man, and if I was
a girl—"

"Well, you don't look much like one, but what if
you were a girl?"

"I'd think twice before I turned up my nose at
Fred Heron, for fear I might go further and fare
worse."

"But, doctor—"

"I know, they kind o' look down on him. Perhaps they look down on a man like me, but I'd
have 'em know—"

"Come, come, doctor, who's been looking down
on you? Why, even Mrs. Boyce is enthusiastic
about you."

The color mounted richly in the veteran's bronzed
face, and his petulance departed like a summer cloud,
but Mr. Brown smiled most benevolently, later in
the day, at beholding the cavalier-like devotion
with which his friend returned from scolding a team of
mules, or giving orders to his men, to do the honors

of the journey at the side of Mrs. Boyce's ambling pony.

All that, and many another talk and incident, came to pass by the way, and ever, as they pushed forward, the mining fever warmed in their veins, until, at last, when the wagons were pulled in under the trees at the foot of the ravine, the whole party, with one accord, followed the lead of the impatient doctor, as he dashed forward, leaving to the teamsters and hired miners the task of going into camp.

It was not a long ride, but hardly a word was spoken until they reined in their several steeds at the side of their guide in front of the hole in the ledge where he had thrown down his worn-out pick, so many long months before.

Dr. Milyng's face was pale, and he had taken off his broad-brimmed hat to wipe the perspiration from his forehead.

"There it is," he said, slowly, in a deep voice, husky with emotion. "There it is, Mr. Brown. It's not a very big hole, but it leads to the treasury of the world."

"There it is," repeated Mr. Brown.

"And is that the wonderful mine?" doubtfully inquired Mabel.

"That's the mine, my dear young lady," said the doctor. "That brownish-white stuff lying there is almost half-gold, a good deal of it. Some of it doesn't belong to the pay-streak. That hole runs in, horizontally, for thirty feet, and the pay-streak widens all the way in. There's plenty of water, up among the rocks. We must set up our little mill and go to grinding. I can't wait till the stamps come."

If Mabel and Carrie found it hard to believe that they had come so far to see no more than that, not so with Mrs. Boyce, nor with Mr. Brown, and they were about to say as much, when the doctor, who had been looking curiously in all directions, suddenly exclaimed:

"Not a bone of him! I declare, the old rascal picked himself up and walked off, after I'd gone."

"Some friend of yours?" said Mabel.

"And a good friend he was. My old mule, Oliver. I thought he was so broken down he'd never get up again, and so I left him. But I might have known better. There never was such another mule."

"That's the one you've told us so much about? The knowing one?"

"Knowing? I reckon he was. I only wish I could have him back again. He'd come, too, if I called him, as far as he could hear me."

Meantime, Fred Heron had been prying around, in various directions, and he now came up again with:

"Well, now we've seen the mine, had we not better go back to camp and get some supper?"

The ladies felt themselves reminded of their

duties, and very promptly assented, and Mr. Brown wheeled his horse, for he had not dismounted, to accompany them.

"Doctor," remarked Fred, after they had ridden a hundred yards or so, "come back with me, a moment. There's one thing more I want to ask. We can rejoin the rest in a few minutes."

He could hardly have been accused of excessive gallantry, but the doctor caught from him a somewhat expressive glance which prevented any demur on his part.

"What is it, Fred?"

"This way, please—"

And he led him straight to the bowlder behind which the three ragged miners had taken their last stand after "jumping" the Golden Heart.

"Were those bones there when you were here before?"

"Picked clean! No, indeed. But they're white men's bones. Look at the bits of cloth and shoe leather. I ain't sure, but I can guess at 'em. Must have followed me, like they and their kind have done before. The luck of the mine took 'em. Reckon we're safe now."

"The luck of the mine, doctor? That skull's got a bullet hole in the forehead, and that other one looks as if a club had broken it in. Makes me think of red Indians, more than of any other kind of luck."

"That's it. Exactly. But did you ever read history, Fred?"

"Yes, I think I may say I have."

"Well then, can you think of any discovery, worth having, that hasn't got the bones of more or less dead men lying around the mouth of it? It somehow works that way."

"Why, are you superstitious about it?"

"Perhaps I am. I'm only dealing with facts, you know. I ain't smart enough to get behind them. Sometimes I wish I was."

"Well, doctor, all I've got to say about the luck of the mine is that we must look out and not leave our own skeletons here, and we must have these carted off and buried before the ladies see them."

"That's so. Don't want to give them such a scare as that would be. Spoil all their fun for them. That was the work of the Apaches. They're the only redskins here-away. Glad Crump has dressed them out for us."

"They may come back again?"

"Of course they will, but a party like ours is another thing from one man, or even three. Especially after the drubbings they've had. Still, I'm not sorry Crump promised to send an escort with the machinery."

Fred smiled. Even with reference to the Apaches, the doctor's anxieties went out to his mining affairs rather than to the picnic party. It was clear enough what was the state of his affections.

A squad of miners was sent up, that evening, with directions as to the burial of the three skeletons, and the ladies were none the wiser.

Six teamsters, eight experienced miners, Mr. Brown, the doctor, Fred Heron—that made seventeen well armed men, in case of necessity. Enough for all the work which could as yet be done, with spare hands for scouting and hunting and the care of the animals. None too many, but quite all that would be necessary until the hole in the ledge should be made deeper and broader and the heavier machinery should arrive. Mr. Brown had preferred too many, rather than too few, strong as had been the peaceful assurances of the military authorities.

The doctor deemed it only right to inform his friend concerning the bones behind the bowlder, adding:

"Now you see, Mr. Brown, we're sure nobody's been able to enter a conflicting claim for our mine. The Apaches have kept our title good for us, while I was gone."

That was one way of looking at it, but it helped Mr. Brown to a clearer view of the nature of mining titles, and he determined to add as much as he possibly could in other ways to the neighborly work of the Apaches.

That was a clear and beautifully moonlit evening,

and nobody felt like going to rest very early, in
spite of the energetic operations already planned
for the morrow.   It was pleasanter, after supper, to
stroll around under the trees, or look out upon the
misty plain, or away to the dim and cloudlike outlines of the snow-crowned Sierras.

Somehow, for the first time in their acquaintance,
this sort of feverish wandering brought Fred Heron
and Mabel Varick together, by themselves, a little
distance below the ravine, and although she said to
herself: "I suppose he would prefer Carrie," she
said aloud to him:

"Mr. Heron, is it not beautiful?   I would not
have missed it for anything."

"Nor I, Miss Varick.   I wish I could see how
those quartz rocks, up yonder, look under this
moonlight."

"So do I.   Why can we not make a party and
go up there?"

Fred thought of the grave-diggers, now at their
work, and the three skeletons, and he replied:

"Splendid.   I move we do so, some evening.
The moon will be full in a night or so more."

"Could we not go to-night?"

"I doubt if either your uncle or Dr. Milyng
would approve of it, Miss Varick, until we are a
little better acquainted with our surroundings.
There are no police here, you know, and the lamps
in the ravine are not lighted."

It was pleasantly, indeed, laughingly said, but Mabel could not help understanding that there was more of a reason than he gave for his polite refusal.

Acquiescence was a matter of course, but she was almost surprised at herself to find how much of a hurt and disappointed feeling she had about her proposed stroll.

Whether or not Fred was aware of it all, he suddenly changed the subject.

"Do you remember what Dr. Milyng told us, Miss Varick, about the ruins of the ancient city?"

"Yes, are they near us?"

"Across the prairie yonder. We can ride over there, some day. That is, if we find all things around us quiet and safe for such expeditions."

"Why, is there any doubt of it?"

"There are always doubts about such things in a region like this, and it does not pay to run any risks—" And then he added, with an energy that startled his companion:

"Risks? No, not for the world!"

His face was towards her, as he spoke, and the words seemed to say themselves, but Mabel saw something in the young man's eyes, which she had never noticed there before, and something very like it was quivering around his mouth. She could not analyze it, in that quick, flashing, moonlit glance, but the presence of one thing in that uncontrollable expression could not be mistaken.

That one thing was suffering—was pain.

Just then she heard the voice of her uncle, close at hand, saying:

"Mabel, my dear, are you there? Come, now, I think you have had enough for one day. Ah, Mr. Heron? A grand night, is it not? Come, Mabel."

And she turned away, with a kinder "good-night" than she would have said to him, but for seeing that strange ripple on the usually calm surface of his life.

Fred Heron stood still, for a moment, on the spot where she had left him, not following her with so much as a glance after returning her word of good will. But now the lines on his face grew deeper and more rigid, with that wonderful power of expression which surely follows upon long restraint—

"Glad to be alone," he muttered. "It is not the old agony, thank God! I thought, once, there could be nothing worse than that, and I ought to know, but I was mistaken. It is one of the penalties of a wasted life, I suppose. I don't believe even Esau succeeded in selling this part of his birthright—the power to suffer. He could still cry, with a great and exceeding bitter cry. Poor fellow!—Well, if that mine is what it seems to be, I'm likely to have a good deal of one kind of pottage before long. Will there be enough of it to buy me what I want? If it could be bought at all I should not want it."

CHAPTER XXXVII.

WILL YOU COME INTO MY PARLOR, SAID THE SPIDER TO THE FLY.

WHEN Augustus Heron returned to the great city his employers expressed themselves well satisfied with the manner in which he had performed their western errand for them. Nor were they left in ignorance of the fact that their young friend had made the first part of his trip as a member of Mr. Daniel Brown's party.

They were glad to be served by a man who possessed some sort of social position, as who is not?

They probably did not feel any special surprise, knowing Fred's relation to the mining company, but it was not many days before an event occurred which might have surprised them, somewhat, if they had known more about the circumstances of the case.

They had had occasional dealings with Mr. Stephen Dillaye, in times past, and of late he had shown some slight disposition to cultivate them, but they hardly knew upon which of his business

calls he had made the acquaintance of Mr. Augustus Heron. Nevertheless, it came to pass, one
morning, that the senior partner said to Augustus:

"Here's an order from Dillaye & Co. that we
can't make out. You know him. Just step around
and get his explanation."

A few other, and more minute directions, and
Augustus was on his way, with a momentarily
growing conviction that the real business he had in
hand was not altogether for other people.

He attended to the mercantile puzzle first, as in
duty bound, and was struck by the extreme cordiality of his reception, as well as by the further
fact that the troublesome order was very nearly
doubled on the spot, which would be a good thing
for him to report on his return.

"Must say, Mr. Heron," remarked Mr. Dillaye,
"I like your way of doing business. Quite confirms
what I have heard of you."

"Thank you, indeed—"

"And I have a reason of my own for desiring a
further acquaintance with you."

"I shall be most happy, Mr. Dillaye."

"You will excuse me from saying more, now, but
if you will do me the favor to see me at my house,
some evening, at your convenience—"

"Entirely at your own, Mr. Dillaye."

"Then, say to-morrow evening? Shall I expect
you?"

"Will eight o'clock do? Or earlier? Or later?"

"A good hour. But please do not mention it to any one."

"Certainly not. I shall be happy to come."

And it was not until Augustus had crossed the office threshold that his countenance betrayed the least token of any mental perturbation. He must have shared fully in the family capacity for self-control. That is, for face-control, which is not always quite the same thing. The report he made on his return was in all respects satisfactory, but, if he considered himself under a promise not to disclose his invitation to anybody he must have adopted the conventional view that a lawyer is nobody when a secret is in question. At all events he was closeted with Mr. Allyn, as soon as he could get away from business, that afternoon.

The learned and vivacious counsellor was a difficult man to take by surprise, but he must have been captured in that way for once, to judge by the expression of his face after the first half-hour of his talk with Augustus Heron. He had permitted his young friend to do most of the talking, up to that point.

"There's one thing very clear to me, Mr. Heron," he now remarked, "you must go and hear what they have to say. Then I think you had better come and see me again."

"That was my intention."

"Take it all in all, it's one of the most interesting cases I ever had in my hands. I wonder how many more complications there will be?"

"I do not propose to make any, I assure you. I am quite willing to be guided entirely by your advice."

"Then see to it, my dear sir, that neither Mr. Dillaye nor his wife obtains the smallest atom of fresh information from you. It might be injurious if they should. It might not, but the less they know, the better."

"I have no intimation of his purpose in having me call. It may be in relation to some business matter."

"Yes, very important business, to him. He's a good deal of a fox, Mr. Heron, but he's a baby compared to that wife of his. You will see, now."

So warned, Augustus felt in a manner forearmed, but there was a tantalizing bit of a surprise in store for him also. He called, he was well received by Mr. Dillaye, and more than well by the lady of the house. But there were other guests, including a couple of very fascinating young ladies, heiresses, selected from the choice preserves of that aristocratic neighborhood. Augustus was charmed, and his host and hostess appeared so willing he should be that the evening slipped away unawares, and at last, when he made some mention of the hour, Mr. Dillaye replied:

"Can it be so late? I beg you a thousand pardons. The ladies did it. Of course we cannot do anything with business to-night, but, if it would not be asking too much—"

"O don't speak of it. I have enjoyed myself exceedingly. Shall be most happy to call again, if you will be good enough to name an evening."

"This night week? Or any other, if you are up this way. I'm almost always at home, and if I'm not, Mrs. Dillaye, I am sure—"

That lady had received a sign to draw near, and she was ready at this juncture to reinforce her husband in a manner which would have been quite overwhelming to an unsophisticated young man, such as Mr. Augustus Heron, with all his good points, decidedly was not. He took his leave, but here was a report, indeed, to make to Mr. Allyn. When he made it, the next day, the man of law and subtlety sat away back in his chair and came within an ace of laughing outright.

"My dear sir," he said, "it's all plain enough now. No other business would have been handled in that way. One evening to study you, and then, 'will you walk in, Mr. Fly?' Go again, a little before the week is out. Not to be in any hurry, you know, but just the least in the world dazzled."

"I think I must look a little dazzled," remarked Augustus. "If I were only a trifle more used to the company of fashionable ladies, now!"

"That's good. Very good. You will do, my

dear sir. Upon my word you will. I am sure of it."

And, after Augustus had taken his departure,
Mr. Allyn repeated to himself his conviction that:

"Yes, he'll do. Not a bad lot, by any means, but
what an essay he could write on cheek and its uses.
I'd like to see him and Mrs. Dillaye together, without their seeing me. It would be a study for an
artist."

Mr. Augustus Heron must have managed, in
some way, to win a high place in the esteem of
Mr. Counsellor Allyn.

The days went by, however, and the young man
faithfully observed the advice of his counsel, which
was a strong sign of common sense, and timed his
next call at the Dillaye mansion just twenty-four
hours within the suggested week.

The master of the house was not at home, but
soon would be. Mrs. Dillaye—

"Please hand her my card. I will come in and
wait."

There was no other company, that evening, but
Mrs. Dillaye's greeting was all that the most rapa-
cious young gentleman caller could have demanded.

So softly, winningly cordial, and with such an
unnoticed but exquisitely rapid drift through the
friendly into the almost confidential.

How and by what masterly turn of her tongue
did she bring Augustus into a discussion of the
Browns, and at what point of it did she slip over

Fred and Mrs. Boyce and Mabel, right past Mr.
Daniel Brown himself, and his mining picnic, and
close her sudden lips upon the name of Carrie
Dillaye?

Augustus tried, more than once, afterwards, to
make out how she had done it, but, like the path
of a serpent on a rock, her windings left no tracea-
ble trail.

"My own poor, dear, unfortunate step-daughter.
How I do love that girl, Mr. Heron, and how sincerely I commiserate her.   No one knows what her
father and I have suffered on her account!"

And she never said a truer word, for nobody
knew.

Augustus could but reply with a remark which
somewhat vaguely expressed his high esteem for
the young lady in question, and there was then a
sad and motherly smile on Mrs. Dillaye's face when
she assured him that she was by no means ignorant
of his intimacy with the household of Mr. Brown.

"You must, however," she said, "be ignorant of
some things, some facts, some dreadful facts, which
even poor Caroline's nearest and dearest could not
conscientiously conceal.   That is, from any one
who, in their best judgment, had a right to know."

"Most honorable on your part, I am sure, but
nothing would induce me to pry into matters which
might be regarded as sacred by others."

"Your delicacy does you credit, my dear young

friend, but—O I hope I am not committing an error! Can I trust you, Mr. Heron?"

"Implicitly, Mrs. Dillaye."

"Then I will—I must—I feel that it is your due!"

And she did, unflinchingly. So fully, so circumstantially, so graphically, that before .she had really done full justice, in her own eyes, to the sad misfortunes of her step-daughter, she had the satisfaction, more than once, of seeing her gentleman guest change color, vividly, while the toe of his right foot beat rapidly and nervously upon the noiseless carpet. In fact, several times his mouth came open, and then shut again as if he were biting something in two, but not an audible word escaped him.

Could it be that Augustus was passing through some kind of an ordeal? Some unprecedented test of his power of self-control, and of obeying the advice of his counsel?

Very possibly, but, if so, he came out of it victoriously, for Mrs. Dillaye was herself surprised by his entire reticence.

That was when, at last, she paused, giving an opportunity for a reply, and manifestly expecting one.

None came, for a moment, and a slight flush began to arise in the cheeks of the lady, which were at all times somewhat fresh in color.

"I have tried to do my duty," she said.

"Believe me, madame, I am not insensible," slowly remarked Augustus. "The truly painful facts you have confided to me are safe in my keeping. Not a living soul shall ever hear them from my lips. Not even my brother."

"Your brother?"

"Yes, my brother Fred. He told me, once, a good deal that you have now. Some things he omitted. He may not have known them. Some other things he said that you have omitted."

"Other things? What other things?"

"Pardon me, Mrs. Dillaye, I could not be guilty of a breach of confidence with him, any more than with you. All I have learned, from either source, will be held absolutely sacred, I assure you."

He had been taking out his watch, as he spoke, and he suddenly added. "So late? Dear me, I had no idea of the time. I beg your pardon for my terribly long call. I must see Mr. Dillaye some other night."

"He will soon be in—"

"O but I have trespassed already. You are so kind, but I must not take advantage—"

He had risen now, and although Mrs. Dillaye did her best to detain him, without appearing too anxious, Augustus managed to make his escape. He did so, too, full of malicious pleasure over the assurance that he had left behind him a female mind ready to burst with curiosity concerning "those other things" which had come to him from Fred.

"It is my revenge," he muttered to himself. "I owed her that much. But wasn't it tough work, to sit and hear the old she-devil go on at that rate about Carrie? I believe the worst, now. Who'd believe a woman could have so bitter a charge of gall in her. She doesn't deserve any mercy, and she wont get any, so far as I have anything to say about it."

Nor was he innocent of a shrewd guess, repeated by Mr. Allyn when he met him, next day, at the truth, for such it was, that Mr. Stephen Dillaye had been at home that evening, and that all the "business" contemplated by his invitation to call had been quite thoroughly transacted.

Whether satisfactorily or not was one of the conundrums which remained for that gentleman and his wife to puzzle over.

CHAPTER XXXVIII.

THERE IS NO SUCH THING AS CERTAINTY IN A PAY-STREAK.

IF one being more than another seemed to have impressed his character, for the season, upon the gloriously beautiful surroundings of the wonderful mine, it was the angel of peace, if so be there is such a being, and if he is an angel, and if he has any character to impress.

At any distance from the camp the silence was oppressive, unless the ear took note of those voices of nature whose gathered and blended volume comes to us so like an essential element of genuine silence.

Up there in the rocky amphitheatre, above the narrow head of the ravine, the sound of human voices and the muffled stroke of tools on the rock or on other tools, broke through the natural charm to suggest another and stronger fascination, while out upon the prairie the feeding animals of the train, and the wild ones who came to look at them and then bound away, prevented the sense of solitude

372

from ever becoming painful. Even the adjacent cliffs were sometimes crowned with groups of " big-horned" sentinels gazing curiously down.

These latter were of interest to the hunters and the camp larder, as well as to the lady tourists, but they belonged, after all, to the prevailing atmosphere of peace which came, each day, close on the heels of the sunrise and the morning mist.

Day followed day in almost cloudless beauty, and Dr. Milyng congratulated himself and Mr. Brown that not the slightest interruption from war or weather had caused the waste of precious working time. The picks and spades had been plied with steady energy, the little "reducing mill" had been worked to its full capacity, and under the doctor's skilful direction, quite a stack of yellow ingots had already been smelted out as witnesses of the extraordinary richness of that "pay-streak." But there were clouds in the gold-mining sky, nevertheless.

"We're not doing very clean work, Mr. Brown." remarked the veteran miner one morning. "We must save all our tailings. It'll pay to work 'em over, every pound of 'em. But how the vein does improve as we go in. The boys are fairly wild about it, and they work splendidly. I have to keep a sharp lookout, or they'll get careless with their blasting. We've enlarged the tunnel, now, so we can work free, and we're ten feet further in. We shall go ahead fast, now."

"So far as I can see, doctor, the mine is all we could ask."

"We shall know more about it after we reach the first fault."

"Do you look for one?"

"Can't say. I've been up on the ledge above, and I ain't sure, but we shall know, pretty soon, where we must sink our first shaft."

"But what if the vein keeps right on into the mountain, unbroken?"

The doctor's face clouded a little, but he answered, steadily:

"That, Mr. Brown, is a good deal more than I care to promise you, to-day. We shall soon know, at all events."

"A fault. A fault," muttered the merchant, as he turned away. "I believe I know what that means. Will it be a check to all these plans and dreams of mine? The doctor does not seem to be much disturbed about it. He does not mean it shall take me by surprise if it comes. Such ore as that is. To think of the vein running out against a dead wall of rock."

And yet that is precisely the meaning of a "fault," in mining language, and sometimes it means a good deal, and sometimes not so much.

Peace and plenty, and tons on tons of rich ore, in the present, therefore, but how about the future?

That is the ever-recurring record of all the veins

in the world's history, whether their "pay-streak" involves a metal or the life of a nation. And there is always one thing which can be done, and that is to work hard while the pay-streak lasts.

So they did, and all that while the ladies found enough to do and enjoy, to keep them from wearying of their new, strange life, and Fred Heron divided his time very fairly between them and the mine.

A strange fellow he was growing to be, and Mrs. Boyce declared to Mabel Varick that he puzzled her more than ever.

"The very expression of his face has changed since we came among the mountains. There's something loftier in it, but not so much sunshine as I'd like to see. He has been through a great deal for one so young."

"And he is young," said Mabel, thoughtfully. "I half forget that."

Not old, certainly, although he felt so, at times, but he could have told his lady friends, had he chosen to do so, that his present experiences were quite equal to any he had known before. Very like a sequel to them, in some respects, with the past cropping out in the face of the present, as it is always sure to do.

"Seems to me," he said to himself, "there's a sort of a mining tunnel being bored into me. Good and deep. It hurts, too, for the picking and drilling goes on without much mercy. Wonder if anything worth while will be found at the end of it."

And then his face, for a moment, told of the hurt and the suffering, whatever may have been the cause of it.

He too had his conferences with Dr. Milyng, and perhaps he knew more than Mr. Brown of the possibilities before them. If so, he had nothing to say about it, for the work must, in any event, go on.

And the doctor himself?

Well, so far as the picnic and the lady tourists were concerned, the doctor had almost ceased to be. He was a mine, a tunnel, a pay-streak, a walking embodiment of a wonderful dream of gold, but he was very little more. The fire in his black eyes grew deeper and sometimes fiercer, day by day, and his red lips came together with a harder compression. He was polite, to the verge of extravagance, but that was only a surface indication. It was plain that he was under a pressure of excitement almost too intense for even his nerves of iron. All saw it, and Mr. Brown found himself getting moody and anxious, in spite of the apparent triumph at the close of each day's work.

"So much depends upon it," he said to Mrs. Boyce. "If all I have spent were a dead loss, I should not mind it, but if it should prove not to be a true vein—"

" How could you lose much, with such a quantity of good ore already out?"

" That would be something, to be sure. But then the future would be lost. I am not digging for gold on my own account, Mrs. Boyce."

" Indeed, I know you are not selfish in this, or in any other matter. But why do you let it worry you? Worry will not help the matter."

She was always ready to assume the attitude of a wise and gentle mentor, and she did it admirably well. All the better because her desire to be of use in that direction was unquestionably sincere.

" I'm ashamed of myself, Mrs. Boyce, but if you only knew what hopes I have built up, with that hole in the ledge for a foundation."

" Not a bad one, I hope. By the way, begging your pardon for a change of subject, have you noticed Carrie Dillaye of late?"

" No, not specially. She seems to be well, does she not?"

" Yes, well enough."

" And enjoying herself?"

" Perhaps so, but a good deal more quiet and reserved than formerly."

" Can you imagine any reason?"

" None which might not be a grave injustice to her as well as to somebody else."

" I think I understand you, Mrs. Boyce. Will

you do me the favor to advise me of anything which in your opinion calls for my attention?"

"Most assuredly I will, but I would not make a mistake in such a matter, for a good deal. And yet, you know, there have been peculiar circumstances."

"I know. I know. I am not at all foolish about such things. She might have greater misfortunes than that come to her."

"Yes, indeed she might."

That was just an hour or so after supper, one glorious evening, when the sky was all one blaze of stars, in that pure atmosphere, and Mabel Varick could have told them, if they had asked her, that Carrie Dillaye was at that very moment strolling out among the pines at the edge of the prairie, accompanied by Fred Heron.

There had been some talk, not much encouraged by Dr. Milyng, of an excursion, before long, to the ruins of the ancient city, and for some minutes the chat of the young people had leaned that way. It did so until they were safely beyond all peril of other ears, and then Fred suddenly broke away from it with:

"I have thought it all over, Carrie, and my mind is made up."

"And you think?"

"That your uncle ought to know. I have obeyed your wishes, thus far, although it has been clearer and clearer to me that I had no right to do so."

" No more have I. And yet, how can I tell him? It has been crushing me to the earth. He is so good and kind. He has done so much for me. Oh, why did I ever put myself in such a false position!"

She was sobbing, now, and Fred made no attempt to comfort her. He only said, almost coldly:

" There is but one way out of a false position. You have asked me to decide. I have waited and waited. I decided long ago—"

" But I cannot bear to do it!"

" Do you remember the hospital on the Island, Carrie, when you would not let me write to your friends, and I told you I would do so without your permission?"

" And you wrote to Mr. Brown."

" Would concealment have done any good then?"

" No, but what will he think of us?"

" Nor will it now. I cannot help what he thinks. I must do my duty. Will you tell him, or shall I? One of us must, and without any further delay."

" O if you would! I cannot. You are a man. I never was very strong. I have done weak and foolish things all my life."

" I will tell him, then, the first chance I can get. Let us walk back to the camp now."

Weak natures, erratic, unevenly-developed minds,

have one characteristic in common which is too often lost sight of. They are subject to spasms of will-power which temporarily, often hysterically, counterfeit strength.

If Fred Heron was aware of it he was expecting nothing of the kind from Carrie Dillaye, for, after he parted from her, within the circle of light from the fading camp-fire, he strode away again in the shadows. He did not see, therefore, how anxiously she looked around, or how, when she saw her uncle just parting from Mrs. Boyce at the door of her tent, she stepped rapidly and firmly forward till she could lay her hand upon his arm.

" Uncle Daniel, I have something I want to say to you."

" To me, Carrie? Well, my dear, I am ready to hear it. I like to have you come to me."

That was encouragingly and kindly said, but it reached no other ears than Carrie's, nor did her answer, nor any of the other words of a conversation, under the shadows of the lordly pines, in the course of which Mr. Daniel Brown forgot, for awhile, all about his mine and his great plans. For although he listened and said little, and although Carrie's voice was full of pleading, even of tears, it soon became plain that the wrath of the merchant was kindled within him. It is said, too, that those who are slow to wrath are sometimes more to be dreaded, more savage and unreasonable than others, when by any means their inner furnace is heated for them.

And all that time Fred Heron was strolling aimlessly around by himself, except when, at last, he found a comfortless seat on a rugged bowlder of quartz and held up his saddened, suffering face to the starlight.

CHAPTER XXXIX.

A SEASON OF VERY BRIGHT WEATHER CLOSES IN A STORM.

THE scattered ruins of the ancient city put on an air of peculiar beauty, that starlit night. In the broad glare of noon there was something commonplace about them. They were then so many piles of crumbling masonry, such as abound in the too well-known and too much described holiday-lands of Europe, and Asia, and Africa, where dates abound, and the kind of obtrusive fiction known as history robs the defenceless walls, and so forth, of half their interest.

Nobody had as yet set any lamp-posts in this western oblivion, and at night the stars had things all their own way. There was not so much as a camp-fire among the ruins, but there was a very good one a half-mile to the southward.

There was mystery enough among the relics of ancient architecture, but there was very little around that camp-fire, for even the Big Medicine was for the time being holding forth in the character of an earthly counsellor.

It was well for the excursion party from the mining-picnic that they had postponed their coming, for that particular band of Apaches had not yet held an interview with General Crump, and their council was a good deal more enterprising than pacific in the tone of its discussions.

There was force, too, in the oration of the Big Medicine.

First, he told them, a few loose miners came straggling in, and had carried nothing out, not even their scalps. Then one audacious robber had made free with his own horse and robe, not to mention the pony, and he had gone down among the buffalo bones, as was fit and proper. Then three who came to dig had been destroyed through the sagacity of his own medicine mule. So far, all was serene, but now a larger, more important party of white men, vastly better worth plundering, had ventured to make what looked like a permanent settlement. Should this be permitted, there would be no more use for Apaches in all that region. Clean work was called for, and the sooner it was done the better. What hope had they for presents from their Great Father at Washington, unless they made themselves felt and their power appreciated, from time to time?

There was no such thing as replying to such

practical eloquence as that, and the best and wariest scouts were accordingly sent out, that the chiefs and elders might not make their further plans in the absence of accurate information.

The scouts departed, the council adjourned itself, and nothing whatever remained to interfere with the peaceful character of the scenery, for an Indian village is quiet enough when even the dogs are tired and have gone to sleep after a full supper.

It is a good deal so with more civilized communities, but when the dogs are neither worked hard nor fed full the nights are apt to be noisy. Perhaps the best remedy for such difficulties is the one never thought of—not to keep any dogs.

Miles and miles away, in the mining camp, only the watchful "lookouts" were apparently stirring. Dr. Milyng was not the man to neglect that sort of precaution, under such circumstances, and he had brought with him men of whose trustworthiness he knew or could learn something.

Everybody else ought to have been sound asleep, but the thing which ought to be is rarely the thing which is.

The doctor himself lay rolled up in his blanket, under a tree, with his head on a saddle, according to his highest idea of comfort, but his eyes were not closed. They were still striving, as they had been all that day, to penetrate a few feet further into the rock his men had been drilling.

Fred Heron had gone to his tent, when he grew weary of watching the stars, but he had not thrown aside any portion of his clothing. He had stretched himself at full length on his camp-bed, but it had never before seemed so comfortless a couch and he was wide, very wide, awake.

"What right had a man like me," he muttered, "to let such a thing come in? All my other foes have crept in upon me before I knew it. I let a thing take full possession of me before I begin to fight it. Then I have to suffer the consequences of my folly. And yet, I might have been a man. I might have had a right to aspire, even to her. Seems to me I have all my life been swimming, or trying to swim, with shot in my pockets. Then I go down, down, down, every time, as a matter of course. I didn't put it all in, either. Well, who did? I don't care to accuse anybody. Gus, he's provided for. Bessie's married and happy, I hope. Her husband 'll have all the advice he can live up to, that's one certain thing. I hope he's a man of strong digestive powers. Stronger than mine. Anyhow, I must see Mr. Brown, the first thing in the morning, and get at least one load off my mind, whatever may be the consequences."

And so he lay and tossed about, and muttered, just as he had done, many another night, in the memory-crowded gloom of the hospital on the Island.

The ladies tented together, under a great spread of canvas, with all sorts of comforts and even elegancies about them. Separate couches, to be sure, and movable screens between them, but no partitions through which the sound of an ill-advised soliloquy would not have been audible.

If they were awake, therefore, they were compelled to husband at least their voices, whatever they might do with their thoughts.

Once or twice the others imagined they heard a sound resembling a suppressed and smothered sob from Carrie Dillaye's corner, but, if so, they did not tell her they had heard it.

What would Dr. Milyng have said if he had known that the thoughts of the widow were dwelling on the same subject with his own.

"A fault?" she said to herself. "I would not like to have Mr. Brown disappointed. I hope he may succeed, but not just now. Entire success or utter failure would alike be disastrous to me. Of the two I would prefer the latter. I think he would need me, then. I never intended to let myself become so deeply interested, but what a man he is. He is only ten years older than I am. He needs me, too. I wonder what sort of a woman his first wife was. Not very strong, I fancy. She and both her sisters died before they were of middle age. That's not uncommon. All married well, too. That is, what the world calls well. So did I, but the world does not always know everything. I wonder what it thinks of me. Sure to be wrong, I can answer for that, when I do not even know myself. Does anybody do that?"

As for Mabel Varick, she got to sleep at last, and Nebuchadnezzar himself would have been troubled by such dreams as came to her.

Not the first ones, of a young man and a young woman wandering away together under the pines and the starlight, although sometimes she seemed to be herself that young woman, and sometimes that young woman seemed to be somebody else.

But then the young man underwent a change, and became a mountain, a sort of human mountain, but with a terrible air of inaccessibility about it. Very grand and high, and very hard. And then she found herself mining for gold in the side of that mountain, and voices told her continually about "faults, faults, horrible faults," such as made it not worth her while to mine there, and she heard herself reply:

"But the golden heart, so rich, so wonderfully rich. I know it is in here, somewhere. I will spend all I am worth, but I will find it."

Something like that may have been running, at about the same time, through the troubled mind of Mr. Daniel Brown, but not all of his midnight perplexities came to him from the hole in the ledge.

"Betrayed," he muttered. "Insulted, deceived. Concealed it from me. I'm glad Mrs. Boyce did not know anything about it. She would have told me, I'm sure she would. She has my interests at heart. Yes, and she would respect my feelings. And yet I do not see, for my life, why I should feel it so deeply. A boy and a girl. Both fools. A good deal of worldly cunning on his part, too, I should say. But his brother. I was never so upset and disappointed about anybody. I'd have trusted—well it's no use crying over spilt milk, and the doctor tells me we shall probably get our answer from the mine to-morrow."

A curious night, all around, but it could not last forever, and people who rest badly are apt to rise early, especially if the causes of their unrest rise before them and wait for them ready dressed to say "Bad morning."

A glorious morning, too, as Mr. Brown was remarking to himself, when he looked out upon it from the border of the camp, but just then another voice came to his ears, and he turned to look into the pale and troubled face of Fred Heron.

"Mr. Brown, I have something on my mind. Something I desire to tell you."

"Ah, have you, indeed?"

The answer did not come in the merchant's usual tone or manner, but Fred went on:

"It is something I have been longing to say, and

my conscience tells me I ought to have said it be. fore. I cannot and will not keep it from you any longer."

"Spare yourself, Mr. Heron, you need not give yourself any pain. You are too late with your news. Carrie—Mrs. Heron that now is—told me the whole story, before I went to bed last night. It is a miserable affair. A most unprovoked and unworthy insult to myself. It should not have been thought of. Least of all should it have been concealed from me by those in whom I was reposing such entire confidence. Carrie is a woman. A young one. In very peculiar circumstances. I do not know that I condemn her, altogether. But a man. You—"

"You condemn me, Mr. Brown?"

"Condemn? Ask yourself, sir. How can I trust you, henceforth? What confidence can I put in a man who has once betrayed me? More than that, sir. Is not this an explanatory comment on your whole character? Does it not throw a light on your past career? What else can I think, sir?"

The old lines of suffering had been settling themselves deep and rigidly in Fred's face while the merchant was speaking. Every word and look fell like a sharp blow on an old sore, sending successive pangs through his whole being. Blows of the same sort upon a healthy organism are never felt in such a manner as that. A certain amount of education in the art of suffering is required before a man can get the full benefit of an unjust or bitter speech. Fred Heron's powers in that direction were fully developed, and Mr. Brown's angry, taunting, scornful tirade was too much for him.

He had, perhaps, expected something unpleasant, but nothing like this, for he had greatly under-estimated his own place in the merchant's esteem. The place he could now see he was losing, or had lost.

There must have been some special reason, nevertheless, why the young man turned so white, and walked suddenly away with so quick and so uncertain a step.

Mr. Brown looked after him in amazement.

" He did not answer me. What could he have said, if he had tried to? He did conceal it from me. It was not right or honorable. It was cowardly to the last degree. But how he looked. Have I said too much? Have I been unjust to him? Am I sure, now, that Carrie told me all? He came to tell me. He did not know that she had done so. Look here, now, maybe there's something about this matter that I do not understand. It is never safe for a man to lose his temper. I never saw such a face on a human being. It was mean of me to speak in that manner of his past mistakes. What do I know about them?"

Mr. Daniel Brown was a just man, and an upright,

with a righteous scorn of clandestine ways, breaches of trust, all shapes and forms of dishonor, but his very love of justice was now beginning to accuse him concerning the words he had spoken in his anger.

And Fred Heron, striding back through the camp, had passed three ladies, without knowing it, and they had all three looked in his face and read as much of it as they each knew how to read.

Carrie covered her own with her hands, exclaiming:

"O Mabel! O Mrs. Boyce! He has been talking about it to Mr. Brown, and they have quarrelled. And yet, Uncle Daniel forgave me, last night, when I told him. He said he did."

"Told him what, Carrie?" they both exclaimed, in a breath.

"O come into the tent. I must tell you, too. It is dreadful!"

And they followed her, and she told them, and Mrs. Boyce forgot, while Carrie was speaking, to so much as glance at Mabel, to see what effect the story had on her.

"Just before you left the city? Married him? And neither he nor you said a word about it to Mr. Brown? I do not wonder he is angry. If I were he, I'd never speak to Fred Heron again."

"Fred? Why is he angry with Fred?" exclaimed Carrie. "When he promised me he would forgive Augustus himself?"

"Augustus? What has he to do with it?" almost gasped Mabel.

"Do with it? Why, he is my husband. I married him—not Fred. What has Fred to do with it?

"Married Augustus?" said Mrs. Boyce, springing to her feet from the camp-stool she had been sitting on.

"Why, you've said nothing but 'Mr. Heron' and 'we,' all along. How should we know it was Augustus? Well, all I've got to say is, I'm glad it was not Fred. I should have been dreadfully disappointed."

Carrie's color was rising now, as it ought to have done, for the widow's last words were clearly not intended for a compliment to Gus.

"Fred knew nothing about it till we got here. I told him because the secret tormented me. He is my brother-in-law, now, and I had a right to ask his advice. He is not nearly so good as Augustus. He does not compare with him. But he told me he should tell Mr. Brown. I only got him to wait a few days, that's all."

She was talking pretty fast, and a little angrily, but Mabel leaned nearer and put her arm around her neck and said:

"Come, Carrie, dear, do not get so excited. . If Uncle Daniel has forgiven you and Augustus, it'll all be right. He is too good a man to be unjust to anybody."

The widow's lips were moving as if something were on them that her judgment condemned to silence, but she speedily came to Mabel's help, and Carrie was pacified concerning her husband.

They remained in the tent, however, all three of them, until it was time for them to attend to the coffee and the other last preparations for breakfast.

When they gathered at table there was nobody missing but Fred Heron, and it was odd that there were no inquiries concerning the reasons for his absence.

CHAPTER XL.

THE MOST PROMISING HOPES MAY BE WITHERED BY A SUDDEN BLAST.

MR. BROWN did not go up for a look at the mine immediately after breakfast.

Dr. Milyng went, as usual, after eating a very good allowance of bacon and broiled venison in a remarkably short space of time, but the merchant lingered long over his coffee.

After that there came a protracted private conference with Carrie, now Mrs. Augustus Heron, from which her uncle turned away with fewer clouds upon his brow than had gathered there during his morning meal. Then it was the widow's turn for a long talk, and there can be no doubt but what she gave him good advice, for when Mabel met him at the door of the tent his face wore a good deal of its accustomed benevolence.

Mabel had a number of things to say about Carrie and Augustus, but she was glad to find that no special pleading was any longer necessary.

394

He thought she had never looked sweeter in her life than when she thanked him for forgiving her cousin and her husband their silly error.

" But, Uncle Daniel," she said, at last, "is there anything wrong between you and Mr. Fred Heron?"

"Why do you ask, dear?"

" He was not at breakfast with us, and then, when I saw him, this morning, he did look so—"

" Mrs. Boyce thinks—"

He checked himself, he hardly knew why, and Mabel expressed no curiosity concerning the widow's thoughts.

"You have not quarrelled with him? Has he done anything which you cannot forgive?"

He did not seem to notice the effort it cost her to ask that question.

"Done? O Fred has not done anything wrong, at all. I misunderstood Carrie, and supposed him privy to the whole affair and concealing it from me. He has behaved most honorably, and I—"

"What have you done, Uncle Daniel?"

" Made a fool of myself, my dear, as a man is very apt to do when he is angry. I insulted him outrageously. The question is whether he will forgive me. If I'd said half as much to Dr. Milyng, he'd never forgive me to all time."

" But Dr. Milyng is not Mr. Heron."

" No, and the worst of it is I hardly know how to get at it. I must make haste, though. He's just the man to take himself out of camp and away, with such a driving."

"Away, Uncle Daniel?"

"Yes, and if he did we would never see him again, I think. I must be going, Mabel, before any mischief comes of it."

Wise man! As if enough of mischief had not come of it already. But he strode away in the direction of the mine.

Mrs. Boyce came out of the tent, just then, with a very serious look on her face.

"Well, Mabel," she said, "is it not too bad?"

"Why, Mrs. Boyce, if they really love one another. They've been wrong and foolish, but then—"

"Yes, Mabel, and she and Augustus are well enough suited to one another. But poor Fred— how he must feel! His own brother, too. It sounds like some doleful old romance, I declare it does. Poor Fred."

Mabel was looking in the direction taken by her uncle, and she did but silently echo the widow, in a sort of dreamy way, for she only murmured:

"Poor Fred—Mr. Heron, I mean."

And the young man himself, the object of so much sympathy, really deserved a good deal, for his quarrel with Mr. Brown had cost him his breakfast, and one's appetite is apt to be somewhat keen in the bracing air of the mountains.

He had gone to the mine, instead of the breakfast

table, and the excited miners were not long behind him. When the doctor arrived he found them all at work, with an energy born of something more than their five dollars a day and rations. The ore they were taking out, indeed, was quite enough to stir a fever in the blood of veteran " prospectors" such as they were. Never before had they seen anything approaching it, among all the gold-bearing Sierras, and they were ready to believe, with the doctor, that the " heart of it all" had been found, at last.

That is, if that vein held out.

The doctor could do very little more than stand and look on, although there would be work for him at the mill, before long, and Fred had a good opportunity to tell him the interesting story of his brother's clandestine marriage.

At any other time the doctor would have entered into the spirit of the thing as fully as anybody, but now, with that hole in the ledge before him, and the muffled sound of the mining tools in his ears, he heard as one who heard not, only putting in a word of comment, here and there, until Fred came to the details of his interview with Mr. Brown, that very morning. Then indeed the doctor withdrew his gaze from the mouth of the tunnel, and listened with all his ears.

" Did he say that, Fred ?"

" Every word, and more."

"And without any just cause or provocation? It seems almost impossible. What did you say?"

"Nothing. I had nothing to say. I turned in my tracks and left him. I have come to see you before leaving camp, partly because I owe you that much, to say the least, and partly because I'm a trifle green on the plains, and want a few directions as to the trail I had better follow."

"Trail? Leave camp? You?" exclaimed the doctor. "'Well, now, I reckon not. Not quite so bad as that. You hold on till we've made this blast and I'll talk to you about it. There they come."

"They" were the gang of miners who had been at work in the tunnel, preparing for a blast of more than usual size and of great anticipated effect, at its inner terminus.

The drilling and charging were done, and now the fuses were lighted and it was time for everybody to get out of range of that hole in the ledge, for there was no telling how far some odd fragment of quartz might be projected.

A moment or so passed in impatient waiting, and the doctor hardly seemed to breathe. Then there came a dull and thunderous detonation, a strong puff of smoke and dust and bits of ore from the mouth of the tunnel.

"Hold on, boys," exclaimed the doctor, "the whole charge may not have gone off. There it comes."

A second detonation, fainter than the first, and Dr. Milyng sprang forward, followed by Fred. He carried in his hand a powerful reflecting lantern, and it was needed, even near the mouth, for the smoke of the gunpowder lingered in the long and slightly irregular gallery. There were broken masses of quartz lying here and there, but there was no need to stumble over them, and the doctor and his young friend were quickly at the end of the tunnel.

"See that, Fred?" said the doctor, as he passed his hand over a surface of remarkable smoothness, before them. "The blast has peeled the fault as clean as a pane of glass."

"But the vein, where is that?"

"Where? Why, down below, somewhere. The rock has an incline of about fifteen degrees, I should say. That points us away to the left, but we can strike it, as sure as shooting, if the fault keeps on down as perfect as this. The vein-bearing rock, the matrix, broke off and settled in cooling, that's all."

"But how far down is it? How can you find it?"

"Sink a shaft, run galleries out from it to the distance indicated by the cleavage. Perhaps further. We haven't begun to mine yet. That's the sort of thing that eats up the money. The machinery for it is on the way. Everything we need."

"You are not discouraged, then?"

"What, with a rock like that before me, that

seems as plain as print? If you'd worked in as many drifts and galleries as I have, you'd know what it means to strike a strange rock in a place like this. Cleavage wrong. Signs of chaos and general confusion in all that lies beyond."

"We would be all at sea in such a case?"

"Certainly. Nothing to guide us, or to calculate by. It's one of those things it's hard to make plain to an outsider. Even experienced miners, that are used to working in other kinds of rock, can't make head or tail of a fault in this old quartz, sometimes. It's the only rock such a vein as ours could be in, anyhow. Let's walk out and get a breath of fresh air."

Very coolly he talked, for, now the result was obtained for the time being, the enthusiast's excitement fell to its every-day level very rapidly. The other miners, who had followed, remained to examine and discuss and their interest and curiosity appeared to be as great as ever.

Just as Fred and the doctor stepped out into the sunlight, they found themselves face to face with Mr. Brown, and very benign he was looking, as he held out his hand, but Dr. Milyng did not keep the secret of the mine for an instant.

"We've found it, Mr. Brown. We've uncovered the fault. It's there."

"There? The fault? I was just going to speak about it—"

"Well the blast left it bare, and it's plain enough. We must begin a shaft at once. I've got all my plans clear in my head, and I haven't a shadow of doubt as to the result."

Mr. Brown's thoughts concentrated themselves on the mine, while the doctor was speaking, and Fred Heron was temporarily put aside. Not a word had been said to him, directly, and there was no reason why he should remain, and run the risk, as he imagined, of a repetition before witnesses of the unpleasant affair of the early morning. Before, therefore, the two older gentlemen took any note of his movements, he was striding rapidly away, already too near the mouth of the ravine to be recalled. In a moment more he had disappeared.

"He will not run away?" exclaimed Mr. Brown.

"Yes, he will," replied the doctor, "but not without seeing me. I wouldn't stay in your camp if I were he. Not over night. Reckon he's gone to get his traps together."

"He must not go, doctor. You must stop him. It is all a mistake—I owe him an apology."

"O you do. Well, that's another sort of an affair. I'd hardly take one, myself, but he may. I'll go after him, in a little while, if you'll explain it to me. According to his story, he's been as straight as a string."

"So he has. But I did not get it right, at first, and so I lost my temper. He told you all about it?

About his brother's marriage with my niece?"

"Yes, he told me of that."

"Then let's finish our talk about the mine, and you go and see if you cannot arrange the matter. I feel very badly about it."

"That's right," said the doctor, bluntly, "so you ought. But he's worth a wagon-load of his brother. There ain't many men I'd tie to in preference to Fred Heron. He isn't perfect, but then!"

"I know. I know. Don't let's say any more, just now."

And in good truth they had other matters of importance, quite sufficient to absorb them, and Mr. Brown's next business was to enter the hole in the ledge and inspect it for himself, aided by the doctor's lucid and very hopeful exposition of the costly and difficult engineering operations rendered necessary by the "fault."

Meantime, ignorant of any favorable change in the tide of his affairs, Fred Heron became more and more keenly conscious, as he walked swiftly down the ravine, not only of his wrongs, but of his hungry condition of body.

It was a most unromantic but a very positive fact that he had eaten nothing since supper the evening before, and it was now nearly noon. He made his way into the camp from the forest side, through the corral. The horses and mules were being herded on the prairie, just outside, but Fred managed to reach the camp kitchen, as he thought, unobserved, and at once began a furious attack upon a saddle of cold roast antelope which he was fortunate enough to unearth.

He worked away, diligently, for a quarter of an hour, and had paused for a rest before taking hold again, when he was aware of a light footstep behind him.

"Mr. Heron."

"Miss Varick."

"I am glad you have not lost your appetite as well as your breakfast."

There was a manifest effort at friendly cheerfulness in the young lady's voice and manner. Too plainly manifest, altogether, for it was a direct suggestion that something had gone wrong, and that she knew it.

Fred's hunger disappeared in the twinkling of an eye, and his heart bounded so, for a moment, that he could make no reply, while his face took on a set, drawn, pallid look.

"Can he be so angry?" thought Mabel. "Or is Mrs. Boyce right?"

But she added, aloud:

"Carrie has told us all about her marriage with your brother. So wrong of them to conceal it from Uncle Daniel! But he has forgiven both her and Augustus, and she is quite happy again."

"I hope she may continue to be so, Miss Varick.

I love my brother very much, and I rejoice heartily over his good fortune."

He spoke sincerely, heartily, but there was a strange tremor of pain in his voice, which seemed to go through Mabel's ears, down, down, till she, too, was conscious of a tremor.

"O Mr. Heron, I am truly sorry there should be anything unkind between you and Uncle Daniel. But he is such a good and just man—"

"I know it, Miss Varick," said Fred calmly, as he rose to his feet. "I am not good, but I can try to be just, even to myself. I do not blame your uncle. You may tell him so, if you will do me so great a favor. I should blame myself, however, if I did not now make my escape. Now and forever. Please tell Dr. Milyng to meet me at the further lookout, after dark, and bring my horse. He will know what else to bring. God bless you, Mabel Varick. If I stay another minute I shall either die or say that which I ought not. Believe me, I have never been—I am not now—I never shall be, so bad as you have thought!"

Terrible words, for they sounded like cries wrung from a brave and strong man in the last extreme of a great agony, and, before Mabel Varick could find breath to answer him, he was gone. She saw him dash into his tent for his weapons and ammunition, and she wanted to call him back, but the name she strove to utter died faintly on her lips.

Perhaps she might have called to him, but there had been one brief, electric, flashing moment, when the young man's burning eyes had poured a flood of intense meaning deep into her own, and she was trembling all over. with the thrill of her struggle against the meaning of that look. Such pain came with it!

But had he gone? Would he never come back? —Why did she let him go!

Ought she not to have even followed him, as, rifle in hand, he had walked so swiftly away through the forest?

Follow?—When she was trembling so from head to foot, and when all her face was crimson with the answer which had risen from some hiding-place in her soul to meet that last look of his?

He had not seen it, but Mabel was only half-sure of that.

She did not, could not know how, at that moment, the faults of Fred Heron's past life were rising before his agonized sight as a more terrible barrier between him and hope than the smooth face of quartz at the end of Dr. Milyng's tunnel was to the further search for the Golden Heart.

No, she could neither call him back nor follow him, but she could hide herself, for awhile, in the seclusion of her tent.

CHAPTER XLI.

FRED AND OLIVER ENGINEER A SURPRISE PARTY.

IT was a good two hours after Fred Heron's visit to the camp that the doctor and Mr. Brown returned from the mine. They came with cheerful and pleasant faces, although they brought and announced the news of the fault in the vein.

Mrs. Boyce drew a long breath when she heard of it, but she held out her hand to Mr. Brown, with a smile that was brimful of sympathy and encouragement, as she said:

"And how bravely you take it. Dr. Milyng, too. I am proud of you both."

It was an excellent thing to say, and she said it from her very heart, and Mr. Brown felt, as he had never felt before, that there was hardly anything more desirable, more helpful, than the support and admiration of such a woman as the widow. He had known her for years and years, but she had never at any time seemed to have so much in her as she did just then.

406

She heard Dr. Milyng ask, at that moment:

"Has anybody seen Fred Heron? Has he been in the camp?" and she turned to reply:

"I saw him go to his tent for his rifle, about noon. Then he walked away into the prairie."

"Did he get anything to eat? Did he leave any word."

The doctor's voice was keenly anxious.

"Yes," said Mabel Varick, "I think he ate quite a hearty lunch, and he told me to ask you to meet him at the further lookout, just after dark."

It was odd, for a young woman like Mabel Varick, but it did seem as if it cost her a great effort to say those few words. Not only that, but she turned away her head as she spoke.

"He said you would know what else to bring him, besides his horse."

She added that as she walked away towards her tent.

"It's all right, then, Mr. Brown, I can fix him," said the doctor, but the merchant was following his niece.

"Was that all he said, Mabel?" he asked, as he slipped through the canvas door, behind her.

"No, not all, Uncle Daniel."

"Anything about me?"

"He said he did not blame you. He wanted you to know that. He is suffering a great deal, I am sure. I do not think I ought to tell all he said. He may not have meant to say it."

"I think I understand you, Mabel, my dear. You have a perfect right to your own decision in such a matter. But, Mabel, you need not have sent Fred Heron away on my account. I never saw a young man—"

"O uncle, you do both him and me a terrible injustice," exclaimed Mabel, with the tears beginning to start down over her burning cheeks. "He did not say anything of the kind to me—nor did I send him away."

"Talk of honor!" exclaimed Mr. Brown. "I believe that young man is too honorable for his own good. Tramp or no tramp, Island or no Island, I hope he will come back again."

"O I am afraid he never will!"

"The doctor must take care of that, I think. I shall go with him, myself, to meet Mr. Heron. Now, Mabel."

"What is it, uncle?"

"Smooth your face a bit, and let us go out as if nothing particular had happened. You must play the hypocrite a little, I think."

Trust a young lady for something like perfection in an art-effort of that kind where her pride is concerned. When Mabel came out of the tent, not the eyes of Mrs. Boyce herself were able to detect the trace of a cause for her sudden disappearance.

Still, it was just as well that they all had plenty

to talk about, and were even eager to talk
about it.

And, all that time, Fred Heron was thinking
about his friends quite as much as they were thinking about him. He thought so much, so intensely,
that he hardly noticed what was going on around
him, and failed, therefore, to avail himself of two
or three fair chances at various game. Could he
have hit anything, with his mind in such a condition as it was, that afternoon? Perhaps, or perhaps
not, but he had walked on till he had hit a clump
of trees and bushes. A " towhead" of the usual
pattern, but there was nobody there to tell Fred
Heron of the shelter it had given that wise mule,
Oliver, during the first hours of his short-lived and
anxious freedom.

It offered shade from the sun, however, and a
capital place to lie down and think in, and that
was just the thing for what was left of that afternoon.

Fred took no note of time, but he became aware
that the sun was well down towards the horizon at
the same moment that the sound of a horse's feet
on the sod near by warned him of the approach of
somebody. He had "served," and a quick return
of his old campaigning instincts bade him lie still
till he knew more than the pad of the hoofs could
tell him.

"What? An Indian?"

He crept closer in among the bushes, for the red horseman was all alone, and he was plainly making for that very towhead.

"He may be an enemy, and he may not, but I think the doctor would tell me to get ready for him. In fact, I hardly know if that is all he would do. Glad there is only one of him."

Now, if that towhead was a good place for Fred to lie and think, it was also a good cover for an Apache warrior to wait in until the arrival of dusk and more Apaches. He could have no suspicion of any other presence, and as he rode in he sprang from his pony, and secured him to a tree, well out of sight of any one passing on the prairie. Then he would not have been an Indian if he had not proceeded, lance in hand, to a close inspection of his surroundings.

"No help for it," thought Fred, as he sprang to his feet. "He will find me."

He stepped forward, holding out his hand in token of amity, but that was not the errand on which that Indian had come, and the reply was a thrust of the lance, so quick and so savage that only a practised swordsman could have parried it. Fred did so, however, with a forward spring and a blow of his fist, "straight from the shoulder," that sent his cowardly assailant sprawling on the grass. He was up with a bound, but the carbine was extended now, in place of the open hand. A flash and a report, and Fred Heron was again alone in the towhead.

No, there was the mustang, a good one, with a saddle and other equipments which betokened a brave of some rank for his master.

"Sorry to have to kill anybody," said Fred, "but there was no help for it. To think of boxing with an Indian warrior. He'd have boxed me, soon enough, but for my rifle. I'm mounted, now, at all events. Yes, and there's one thing more. I can't leave the expedition if it's in any danger of this kind. I must warn the doctor. Who knows but I can get a chance to die with some credit. They've one enemy the less, already. Even such a man as I am can shoot Apaches. Mr. Brown himself cannot deny that. I'll lie right here till the sun is down. That is, unless I see some reason for getting out of it."

He lay there, therefore, among the sumach bushes, but now and then he crept out and crawled to the top of a neighboring knoll, from which he could see more of the plain beyond and what was passing on it.

"This is my last," he remarked, as the sun was setting and he lifted his head above the grass. "I'll mount now, and—hullo, there they are! They've got by me! One, two, three, a round dozen of 'em. What'll I do now? They will be between me and the camp. I must let them get well ahead and then I must take my chances. No such squad as that will venture an attack."

No, indeed, but there were other just such squads on the plains beyond, whom he could not see, and a much larger one was even then creeping slowly up at the edge of the forest, under cover of the trees. They were none of them in a hurry, for their scouts had reported all things in good and promising condition for a most complete and overwhelming surprise.

Waiting was hard discipline, under such circumstances, but the night falls quickly on the plains, after the sun is down, and the trial was not so prolonged as it was severe.

"They shall not be surprised if I can help it," said Fred, hoarsely, as he sprang to the saddle and urged his prize to a swift gallop in the direction of the camp. "I think, now, I ought to have ridden in at once. And so I would, but for one thing."

There was a sting in the fact that he had not done so, nevertheless, and it made him somewhat reckless in his movements, which was just as well for all concerned.

He did not draw rein until he not only saw before him the dim twinkle of a campfire, through the trees, but within a short distance of him, right ahead, a score or so of dark forms on horseback.

"I must break through them at all hazards," he said to himself. "They won't be looking for an attack in the rear. I may succeed, and anyhow I'll make noise enough to alarm the camp. Hullo, what's that? I never heard a warwhoop in my life, but that sounds more like ten mules braying at once. What a horrible noise."

It was followed by a sudden commotion in the line of dark horsemen, and Fred saw that his time to strike had come.

Not around them, to meet other and unseen enemies, but right through the middle of the group as they clustered, for some reason, more closely together, and plying his revolver right and left as he did so. A splendid charge, carrying with it the security which so often rewards utter audacity, for the fleet mustang bore him safely on, while more than one red warrior pitched sickly from his pony into the grass.

The shout Fred himself gave was nothing at all to the savage yells which followed him, but he had broken up that surprise party.

That had been a busier day in the mining camp than Fred Heron was at all aware of. Before his adventure with the Apache in the towhead, Dr. Milyng had returned from a visit to the reducing mill with something more than a report of the day's work. He beckoned Mr. Brown one side and said to him:

"I reckon we won't have the ladies camp down here, to-night."

"Not here! Why?"

" Well, Broadus, the scout, tells me he isn't sure
but he saw Indians, this afternoon. I don't mean
there's any danger, but there's no use in taking
risks."

"Of course there is not."

" I had all the heavy wagons hauled up beyond
the mine, when we came, with just that notion. Now,
it won't take half an hour; after supper, to move up
the camp fixings. I'll have the horses and mules
drove up, when they come in. The tents can come
down now, and be all ready. Only, we needn't alarm
the ladies."

" They'll miss the shade of the trees. But then
their picnic is about over, now we've reached the
fault."

"Yes, there's no telling how long it'll take to sink
the shaft."

And so, while Fred Heron had been brooding
over his troubles, in the towhead, things at the
camp had undergone a change. There had been
room for criticism, indeed, of Dr. Milyng's prudence
in ever pitching it in so exposed a position. But it
had been so exceedingly pleasant, with ladies to
care for, and the citadel above the ravine had been
so near a refuge.

The latter would hardly have been sought in time,
however, if it had not been for the keen eyes of
Broadus the scout and the prompt action of the
doctor. As it was, although little now remained

besides the trees and the dying camp-fire, and the men were for the greater part busy getting things to rights in the new location, there were reasons why the rest of the party lingered on the deserted spot as if loth to leave it.

There could be no secret made of the expected conference between the doctor and Fred Heron, and the general interest in the result was by no means diminishing as the hours went by.

"I'll go with you, doctor," Mr. Brown had said. "I must be the bearer of my own apology."

"So much the better. There's plenty of wild blood in Fred, but I reckon we can make him come down."

Mabel Varick had given her uncle a very grateful look, but the one thought which insisted on returning to her, was:

"Could I not have kept him?"

It was a thought with a sting in it, now, for she had heard Mrs. Boyce say to Mr. Brown:

"O dear me! If there is really any danger coming, Mr. Heron must have walked right into it."

And the merchant's face had worn a graver and more anxious look from that very moment.

"It'll be a lesson to me as long as I live," he said to Mrs. Boyce, but Mabel had not a soul to whom she could say anything, and it was but a doubtful comfort to have Carrie put her arms around her and murmur:

"O Mabel, dear, I'm so glad it isn't Augustus! What should I do if he were out there alone!"

But the time passed, and, as the sun went down and the shadows faded into the one great shadow of the coming darkness, Dr. Milyng and the merchant, rifle in hand, but leading no horse for Fred, strolled thoughtfully out towards the spot where it had been customary, ever since their arrival, to station a night sentinel, a "lookout." It was a lonely sort of place, but there, chatting and peering restlessly out upon the prairie, they waited the return of the wanderer.

Very naturally, their talk turned upon Indian tactics and doings, and the doctor had full store of subjects for such talk as that. He told, among other things, how, just a little while after he discovered that mine, he had gone out for game, further than usual, and had descried what seemed a small party of white men, in the distance. And how, almost at the same time, a band of Apaches made their appearance. He could only guess what became of the strangers, but he himself had ridden for his life, back towards the mine. Ridden so long and so hard that he had used up his mule.

"But what if they had followed you to the mine?"

"I'd have given 'em a good time in that narrow part of the ravine and then I'd have taken to the rocks. No Indian ever followed me far over the mountains, on foot. They won't go any great distance without a horse, and they're no kind of climbers. But don't I wish I had that mule, Oliver, now? Why, I used to turn him loose, at night, and in the morning I'd give a finger-whistle, and he'd hear it, ever so far, and he'd come in, a-kiting. So."

And the doctor suited the action to the word, putting his fingers to his mouth and giving a whistle so shrill and piercing that almost any listener would have wanted to know the meaning of it. Even a mule.

And the whistle was answered!

"I declare," exclaimed the doctor, "that's Oliver. No other mule on earth can pitch a bray like that. Here he comes! See him?"

It was most extraordinary. And, before Mr. Brown could find words to express his astonishment, a very large and long-eared quadruped came trotting swiftly in, whimpering as he came, and Dr. Milyng actually dropped his rifle and threw his arms around the neck of that mule.

He snatched up his weapon quickly enough, however, for his next words were:

"Saddled and bridled? The red-skins are here, Mr. Brown. Hark, do you hear that? What can all that mean?"

Rapid pistol shots, a shout, fierce whoops and yells, and then a single horseman dashing in upon them with:

"Doctor! Dr. Milyng! Apaches!"

"Fred, my boy, is that you? Did you pepper any of 'em?"

"Two or three, besides the one I got my horse of. Ah! Mr. Brown! No time to talk now, sir. It's life and death. It's more than that. Where are the ladies?"

All three of them moved rapidly onward, as the breathless sentences sprang from Fred's lips, but the doctor was as cool as Oliver himself. He briefly stated what had already been done for safety.

"Now," he said, "we must lose no time. They're checked for a moment. We'll take the ladies—no, Mr. Brown, you and Fred take the ladies to the ravine under cover of the trees. There's two of the scouts handy to help you. I'll keep along outside and see what's going on."

"That'll do," began Mr. Brown, hastily striding forward, but Fred Heron firmly responded:

"No, doctor, Mr. Brown and the scouts are enough for that. I'll stay with you," and he sprang from his captured mustang as he spoke.

"Good for you, Fred. I may need help. They're riding in closer. Do your best walking, Mr. Brown."

A moment later, in response to his hurried, but not panicky explanation, Mrs. Boyce exclaimed: "And Fred has been fighting them already? All alone? The brave fellow!"

And Mabel Varick added, in a lower, more anxious tone:

"O Uncle Daniel, where is he? Is he hurt?"

"Not a bit. He's out there with Dr. Milyng, holding the rascals in check while we run for the ravine."

And neither Mabel nor Carrie made any further remark just then, for each one was saying to herself, "If it had not been for me."

And they were both wrong about it, each in her own way.

CHAPTER XLII.

THE SUCCESS OF THE EXPEDITION AND THE FINDING
OF THE HEART.

THE Big Medicine had looked remarkably well on the big medicine mule, as he rode forward among his clansmen, that afternoon, and all things had worked to his entire satisfaction, so far as he or they knew, until, as they halted in the gloaming, within sight of the camp-fire which was so soon, they thought, to light them to all sorts of plunder and murder and glory, that mysterious whistle came shrieking across the grass. Some of them had seen a locomotive, and wondered at its power of voice, but no branch of the Pacific Railway had ever wandered in among those solitudes. They were sure of that.

The Big Medicine dropped his bridle to listen, but Oliver's ears came forward with a jerk, and all his being seemed to melt in sound as he stretched his neck towards the forest and the camp-fire.

It was not altogether the mere force of that bray

420

which sent the Big Medicine so suddenly out of the saddle, for Oliver had other resources, but he used them remorselessly on a rider taken unawares.

And all the rest of the squad were also taken unawares, for Oliver sprang away like a quarter-horse, and no hand was put out to stay him. Was he not a medicine mule, and was not his medicine master in the grass? Their first duty was to their dismounted conjurer, but before he could more than rise to explain, another surprise came, charging among and through them, sending lead and death on either hand. One horseman attacking twenty, and escaping their hasty shots and thrusts unharmed.

"A great brave," they said, but their vengeful wrath boiled high within them as they picked up their fallen.

There was an empty saddle ready, now, for the Big Medicine. A "vacancy" provided in the nick of time, as happens curiously often for those who are ready to spring into the empty saddles of the men who fall.

Squad after squad of wild riders came dashing fiercely up, but the minutes they were consuming in determining what to do next were of more importance than they had any idea of. More would have been lost, but for an order from their great "war-chief," now with his men on the edge of the forest, to dash on to the mouth of the ravine and cut off the flight of the white men he was about to drive out of that camp.

Good strategy, for the Indian leaders sometimes exhibit remarkable evidence of the absence of political influence in the matter of their appointment to office.

Wisdom is none the less wisdom because it is a trifle late in its operation, and history is a long succession of lost guesses as to whether some Blucher or Grouchy will get to the right spot first. In every case the man that guesses wrong loses his bet.

Forward dashed the redskins, but O how earnestly Mr. Brown and his now thoroughly frightened lady friends did thank God for every minute of that brief delay.

This was a picnic, indeed!

And out there on the edge of the camp, the doctor and Fred Heron kept slowly on, so as to be between the hawks of the prairie and their trembling prey.

"We'll make it," said the doctor. "They don't know we've quit the camp. You've done a big thing to-night, Fred. There—forward! They're flanking us. Let 'em have it. One's down. Keep under cover. Forward!"

Well that the distance was short, for the merchant had hardly urged his panting charge inside the rocky mouth, perilous refuge as it was, before the great chorus of yells which had been swelling behind him was suddenly doubled, and he understood two facts at the same moment.

The rush of the war-chief and his braves into the camp had been made, and that section of the whooping was chargeable to the "disappointment account," say to profit and loss.

The other and, alas, the nearer, meant an immediate and close pursuit.

"O Uncle Daniel, where is Fred?" exclaimed Mabel Varick.

"And the doctor?" said Mrs. Boyce.

"Hear the rifle shots, right down there? Here they come!" shouted Broadus the scout. "Run, ladies, run for your lives. Tell the other boys to hurry down if they want to save our skelps and their'n too."

Run, it was, although their trembling limbs would hardly have carried them, but for the help and encouragement of Mr. Brown. Mrs. Boyce looked at the merchant's pale face a hundred times, in admiration of his calm and steady courage. He had never been in a fight before, but it was plain that the stuff for one was in him.

The two scouts, Broadus and the other, were thoroughbred plainsmen, and they faced about, but they could hardly have told whether Fred and the doctor or the foremost Apaches were upon them first.

Steady, now. Four dead-shots, armed with repeating carbines, make an awful fence to ride up to, even at night, in a rocky pass less than fifty feet wide and narrowing. Shoulder to shoulder stood the white men, retreating as they fired, and firing as they retreated. Had that first rush of Apaches been all, that would have been the end of it, for too many of them were going down and the narrowest part of the pass, the mere "gate," was close at hand. But other swarms were coming. So many of them, so full of yelling and whooping and murder and all evil!

"Are you hit, Fred?"

"I can stand it, doctor. If I go down, tell them I did my best for them."

"Good for somebody," exclaimed Broadus. "Hear them wheels."

Who would have expected war wisdom from a Beaver Street merchant!

Nobody, and very correctly, for it was Mrs. Boyce who suggested that the big wagon standing near the head of the pass, should be rolled into it, and Mr. Brown did but give the order.

"Under the wagon, doctor. Under the wagon, boys. Creep through. We're ready for 'em."

Even the Apaches gave back, for a moment, as they heard the shouts.

"Pick him up," exclaimed the doctor. "They shan't get his hair while I'm alive."

But Broadus was just then lifting the body of

his comrade, and straining all his remaining strength
to thrust him under the wagon, and D: Milyng
stood alone in front of his prostrate friend.

"The mine is safe, anyhow," he muttered. "Old
Brown won't fail to work it. Take that, will you.
How they do crowd in. I'm glad Old Brown and
the ladies ain't hurt."

"So am I," exclaimed a cheery voice at his side.
"Get him in, boys. We'll keep them back for a
moment, doctor."

It was the merchant himself who was plying his
carbine so coolly, amid that tempest of yells and
shots and hissing arrows, and beside him were half
a dozen brawny forms that had followed him under
the wagon.

"Now, doctor. Now, boys."

Even in that crowded ravine, the savages had
been slow to dismount, for their centaur instincts
almost forbade them to fight on foot. Otherwise
no man of that brave squad could have made the
retreat he did.

Once on the other side of the barrier, frail as it
was, the riflemen were at a most manifest advantage,
which they were increasing with every fragment of
rock and with every box or barrel they could add
to their rampart.

"The Indians don't live that can force that against
a dozen repeaters," remarked the doctor, and a similar conviction expressed itself in the fierce yells of

disappointment which arose from the other side.

The rifles were at work, however, without cessation, and it was safer to ride back, down the ravine, than to stay there and make night hideous.

Dr. Milyng had so sternly attended to his first duty, of beating off the Apaches, that he had missed one or two little incidents.

The body of Fred Heron had been closely followed under the wagon by that of Mr. Daniel Brown, but hardly had the latter resumed an erect posture before a white hand was on his shoulder.

"O Mr. Brown, it was splendid! You are a hero! But are you hurt?"

"Not a scratch, Mrs. Boyce."

"I'm so thankful!"

And the widow covered her face with her hands and burst into tears.

"She was thinking of me, then, and not of herself," muttered the merchant, with a queer feeling in his throat, but he said to her, in a tone that surprised him very much and gave her no pain whatever:

"My dear Mrs. Boyce, you must not stay here, among these flying arrows. Where are the girls? They will need you."

But "the girls" had a care of their own, just then. Carrie was sitting on a bowlder, a hundred yards further on, and sobbing.

"O I'm so sorry. How shall I ever tell Augustus. He was so kind. So brave. So true. I owed him everything."

But Mabel Varick was neither crying nor talking. She was sitting on the ground, with the head of a prostrate man in her lap. The face, never a very handsome one, was pale now, with streaks of blood and of gunpowder on it, here and there, to make it less so, but, for all that, it wore an expression of placid manliness which was worth any good woman's while to look upon.

"Oh, if I could do something for him," she said, at last. "His pulse is beating yet. He is not dead."

It must have taken some courage for her to have found that out, and, in a minute or so more, another form dropped on its knees beside her.

"Arrow through his leg. Mustn't pull it out, just yet. No, not poisoned. It's a hunting arrow. Lance cut in the side. Rib turned it. Bled a good deal but missed the vitals. Awful rap on his head. Redskin threw his club. Wonder it didn't break the skull, but it didn't. He'll do, Miss Varick, but you must give him to me and Broadus, for awhile."

"He's not killed, then, doctor?" exclaimed the voice of Mr. Brown.

"Not a bit. My word for that. But he told me, in case he was killed, to tell you all he did his best for you."

Something like a big sob came from the breast of Mr. Brown.

The doctor and Broadus were promptly lifting the wounded man, to carry him to a safer and softer couch than that patch of flinty gravel, but Mabel Varick did not rise to her feet at once. Mrs. Boyce was close behind the merchant, and Mabel may not have cared to look the widow too directly in the eye at that particular juncture. Her uncle's hand was reaching out to her, now, and she seemed to cling to it nervously, as he lifted her. Such a strong, kindly, comforting sort of hand.

"The doctor says they will not attack us again, to-night. He thinks they have had enough for once."

"Was anybody else hurt?"

"One of the scouts is killed, and several more have arrow wounds. The doctor himself is cut in several places, but he doesn't seem to mind it. No more gold for me, if I've got to give blood for it."

Time had sped faster than they thought, and they were astonished to find how late it was. The running and fighting seemed to them now to have lasted but a few minutes. But there was little enough of sleeping done, except by the hardy scouts and miners, during the remaining hours of that anxious night.

Just as the dawning day lit up the open tent where Fred Heron was lying, his feverish rest was broken by the entrance of a soft, light step.

"How is he now, doctor?"

"Doing very well, Miss Varick. All he wants is care—"

"He must have it—"

"Will you be so kind as to sit here a minute? I want to take a look at the other fellows."

"I shall be so glad to."

But the doctor vanished as she sat down near the sufferer's head, and she was left alone.

Could Fred Heron have been aware of her presence?

Perhaps, in the vague and misty consciousness that belongs to half-awakened men, feverish from wounds and loss of blood. He did not speak to her, but his tongue was busy. He murmured, with queer pauses between the words, here and there:

"The doctor says so. I can get away in a few days. They're safe, now. So is the mine. She can't say I told her. No; I kept my secret. That was pretty well, for a tramp. A fellow from the Island. A disgraced man. Would she feel degraded if she knew I had dared?—" and as he said that his head turned on his hard camp-pillow, and was lifted a little.

"Miss Varick? You here? What is that? There is blood on your dress? You are not hurt?"

"Hurt? No. O Fred, it is your own blood. Yours—"

"Mine? I do not remember—the doctor did not tell me—"

"O Fred, you will get well? For my sake. Won't you, Fred?"

Could it be a dream? A consequence of having stopped that Apache war-club with his head?

Or was it a reality, and the haughty and beautiful niece of Mr. Daniel Brown was kneeling beside the wounded tramp? The poor fellow who had suffered so much and fought so well?

He had not told her how much of his suffering and fighting had been done for her, but in some mysterious way, the knowledge had come to her.

And Fred, on his part, dimly understood what must have happened to transfer so much blood from his broken head to that beautiful white robe there, that seemed to have a glory shining round it. He could not lift a hand without pain, but both were raised and clasped, in spite of that, and his eyes closed for a moment.

"I do not understand," he said, in a faint whisper. "I am not worthy of it. Can I have found what Dr. Milyng has missed?"

"The heart?" she said. "The Golden Heart? No, Fred, I think I have found that."

"But the fault?" he murmured, dreamily.

"Faults? Yours cannot be greater than mine. I have never been tried as you have been. O Fred—"

Just then there came the sound of another footstep behind her, and she turned her head.

"O Uncle Daniel, is that you? He is better, now. I am sure he will live. It was Uncle Daniel, Fred, that helped Dr. Milyng keep back the Indians and bring you in. He risked his life for you—"

"Glad I had a chance! Glad I had a chance! I owed him some kind of reparation."

"Mr. Brown, if you only knew," began poor Fred, but he was interrupted by another voice, that of Carrie:

"I found them for you. I knew there was a box of them left, somewhere in the store-wagon. Most of them were spoiled, but these are good."

"Lemons?" said Mabel.

"He gave me all he had, once. I'm so glad. I know they'll do him good. I'd give him anything—"

"I never thought of lemons," said Mabel, with a half-jealous tremor in her voice, "but I've given him all I could!"

"Have you?" exclaimed Mr. Brown, excitedly. "Have you, Mabel?"

"O Uncle Daniel, I don't care if Carrie is here! He is my Fred, now, Uncle Daniel! Mine! Nobody else has any right—"

"Glad of it, my dear. From the bottom of my heart. But what's that? Music?"

Only the sweetness of a cavalry bugle, borne up from the ravine by the glad-winged breeze of the prairie.

"Hurrah, girls! Hurrah, Fred, my boy! No more Apaches. That's from some of Crump's men."

He and Carrie sprang away, and it was Mabel Varick's hand, after all, that pressed the cooling drops of juice upon the feverish lips of the wounded man. Who shall say what else was dropped upon them, then and there, with more of help and life— for love is help and life—than could have come to him in any other way?

But the bugle sounded again, so sweetly, telling of Crump's men.

They had come, a full company of them, to break up the mining-picnic, and escort it back to safety. It brought word, moreover, that, in view of the threatening attitude of the red men, all mining operations in that region must be suspended until more quiet times.

"You see," said the gruff general to Mr. Brown, when he met him, some few weeks later, "the army is so enormously large that it interferes too much with the liberties of our red-skinned fellow-citizens, and so Congress cuts it down. Otherwise I could protect you. As it is, I thought I'd send and save your scalp while I could. One of these days, perhaps, you can try it on again."

The machinery and the rest of the mining outfit had been detained, as a matter of course, and the cavalry had made forced marches.

It was some days after their arrival, however, be-

fore the wounded men could safely be moved, and
Dr. Milyng employed every hour he could in grinding and smelting.

It was a terrible thing to leave all that ore lying
there in the sun, and that hole in the ledge leading
to the very spot from which a shaft could be sunk
to the treasury of the world. Still, there was no
doubt but what the company would get a perfect
title to that mine, however long the Apaches might
keep them from working it. There would be no
"jumping." Trust the red men for that, especially
as the loss of his mule had prevented the Big
Medicine from any other loss, or even exposure,
during the careless shooting which had taken place
already.

Fred Heron's hurts healed more rapidly than
those of the other men, and he was soon able to
discuss almost any subject with Mr. Brown. He
had no further reason to complain of anything said
to him by the merchant, but he was justly astonished by the enthusiasm of Mrs. Boyce's congratulations. It was as if she had set her heart on his
winning Mabel Varick, and had now little left to
ask for.

Dr. Milyng had to be sought for at the reducing
mill, by those who would commune with him, but
he knew what was going on, nevertheless.

"Doctor," said Fred to him, one day, "life has
a centre, whether the mining region has one or not.

I've struck a fresh vein, leading straight to it, without a fault in the way."

The doctor took off his sombrero with a reverent look, as if he were saluting something.

" Don't say any more, my boy. I believe that. I rode one mule, from the Dalles of the Columbia, clean down through the Sierras, hunting for the Golden Heart, and you've found a better mine without half the trouble."

" Half the trouble?" echoed Fred. " I think I know something about trouble. Is that Oliver, yonder ?"

" The very mule that carried me."

"Well, the mules I used to ride didn't have so much sense as he has. A good deal of the time they turned about and rode me."

" Well," drawled the doctor, " see that you don't let your ears grow again, that's all."

The Apaches came not again, being doubtless aware of the arrival of the men in blue, but a day dawned, at last, on a deserted mine and a wagon train in motion. The doctor and Mr. Brown and their friends lingered till the last.

" I'm so glad about Fred and Mabel," said Mrs. Boyce to the merchant, as they rode through the ravine, side-by-side. " You will have them live with you, will you not ?"

" If they wish, perhaps I will. But her property is ample, and he is very energetic and independent.

I think they will prefer to set up for themselves."

"And leave you all alone?"

Her face was turned half from him as she said that, which was unlike Mrs. Boyce.

"Alone, Mrs. Boyce? Would you do that? Would you, now—could you leave me all alone? I had almost hoped I could persuade you, if Mabel went away, and I had nobody to take care of me— I'm an old sort of a fellow, Mrs. Boyce—"

"Mr. Brown! I fear I do not understand you. I wish—I'm afraid—I know more than I did once. Only a very good woman, a great deal better than I am, is fit, is worthy, has any business whatever— my dear friend, you must not say any more to me, just now—"

"I do not want to say any more, Mrs. Boyce. I've all the answer I need. Mabel, dear, please ride this way?"

And Mabel came.

"You may tell Fred and Carrie and the doctor, too, if you like, that there will be more than one wedding when we get home. Is it not so, Mrs. Boyce?"

"O Mr. Brown! Mabel, dear, I am so happy. Lean over here and kiss me."

"That's for me," said Mr. Brown.

The only gloomy man of that returning picnic party was Dr. Milyng. He insisted on riding Oliver,

and on having that worthy animal shipped eastward as far as St. Louis. There he, the doctor,
parted from his other friends, and when Mr. Brown
renewed, for the hundredth time, his assurances
that work on the mine should be resumed as soon
as it could be without risk to human life, he responded :

"I don't think anything could kill me, with that
to wait for. I'm right down glad you're going back
so happy, considering how much the trip has cost.
You and Fred have struck good veins by it, anyhow. I shall rest awhile, and then I shall try the
mountains again."

"They cannot have two hearts?" suggested Mrs.
Boyce.

"No," he said, "but when one has found a heart,
he wants to live as near it as he can."

"Poor doctor," exclaimed Mrs. Boyce, after the
farewells were completed. "But there was a good
deal of truth in one thing he said."

On their arrival in the great city it was easy
enough for Mr. Brown to adjust his relations with
Mr. Augustus Heron, as the husband of Carrie and
as the brother of Fred, but that was probably as
much as Augustus expected, under the circumstances.

Mr. Counsellor Allyn had a very complete and
business-like report to make. Mr. Dillaye had successfully "postponed" until, as a last resort, he was

informed of his daughter's marriage. Even his wife advised him to settle at once when she heard that news.

Fred wrote to Bessie that the mining enterprise was temporarily a failure, but that he was about to get married, and he received in return a most admirable epistle.

"You should have told me something about it before," she said, among other things, " but I fear it may be too late, now. How do I know that your choice has been a wise one? You do not even give me her address. No one can talk to her about you as I can. No one knows you as I do. I shall write to her at the first opportunity. Have you told her all? It is only right that she should know. Otherwise she cannot be the help to you that she ought. If indeed you are to be married, and I see no way of preventing it. After the failure of your ridiculous mining affair, too. When will you learn to avoid speculators? I do hope you will redeem yourself. Imitate Augustus. He writes me that he has married a lovely woman. An heiress, too, but her parents are still living. And you are to marry an orphan. But you never would be guided by me."

There was a good deal more of that letter, and it was all very good and wise and sisterly, as Bessie's letters and conduct had always been. Fred did not read it to Mabel. He offered to, but she took the

paper from him and then threw it on the carpet
before she had finished a page.

" Augustus, indeed ! What can she be made of !—
Well, I suppose Carrie is satisfied, but Fred—
Fred—"

" What is it, dear?"

" I have found more than she has, or Bessie, or
Dr. Milyng, either. None of them know what a
heart is—a golden heart—"

" But, Mabel, the fault ?"

" We're away beyond that, Fred."

Mr. Daniel Brown's business friends understood,
in a vague and general sort of way, that his western
trip had been a tremendous success. So habitually
close-mouthed a man was not expected to say much
about it, and he did not offer any shares for sale.
He evidently intended to be sole proprietor of his
mine.

The approaching marriages were duly announced,
although they were to be strictly private. As to
that, so perfectly was the privacy secured that
"society" never afterwards got it clearly through
its curious and gossipping head whether or no the
marriage of Carrie and Augustus took place at the
same time with the other two. All three of them
were " published" together.

THE END.